Praise for *Worth the Risk*

"A bold blend of science, story, humor, and wisdom that helps us reimagine fear and embody courage, creativity, and positive contribution. A must read for anyone wanting to shine brighter without burning out."

SCOTT BARRY KAUFMAN, PHD
author of *Transcend* and host of *The Psychology Podcast*

"With great candor, spirit, and expertise, Kristen Lee shows us that small acts of courage aren't small at all. A must read for anyone willing to get more comfortable with the uncomfortable and live with the aliveness the world needs to be better and brighter."

AGAPI STASSINOPOULOS
author of *Wake Up to the Joy of You*

"What's scarce in the world isn't smart people or people with good ideas, but brave people willing to show up and do the work of cocreating a better world. This wonderful, entertaining, and ridiculously practical book shows how becoming more brave can be a fun, imminently doable adventure, not a road to terror or burnout. Read it, microdose bravery, and start finishing the bridge to your 'what is' life."

CHARLIE GILKEY
author of *Start Finishing: How to Go From Idea to Done*

"Every chapter is a therapy session that teaches in elegant but easily understandable language several logical but pragmatic strategies to increase your resilience. And once you start reading the book, you can't put it down."

DILIP V. JESTE, MD
author of *Wiser* and senior associate dean for Healthy Aging and Senior Care, University of California, San Diego

"A brilliant fusion of science and story that reminds us we are never alone, that courage is always within reach."

ALISON MALMON
founder and director of Active Minds

"*Worth the Risk* stands out from the pack. Dr. Lee's writing distinguishes itself, sparkling with originality. And her own courage and sense of urgency are certain to inspire, comfort, and motivate."

DAVID VAN NUYS, PHD
host of the *Shrink Rap Radio* podcast

"This book is the gateway drug to building your courage. Dr. Kris cuts through the BS of self-help with a detailed how-to list of creating a courageous life filled with thrilling creative risk-taking. From looking in to speaking out, she shows us that we can microdose courage in an effort to make a beeline toward a life of (possibly messy but meaningful) energy, passion, and purpose."

KATIE GOODMAN
award-winning comedian and author of *Improvisation for the Spirit*

"Witty, honest, and grounded in science without a whiff of pretentiousness."

CAROL PELLETIER RADFORD
bestselling author of *Teaching with Light*

Kris(ten) Lee
EdD, LICSW

Worth
the
Risk

How to Microdose Bravery to Grow
Resilience, Connect More, and Offer
Yourself to the World

sounds true
BOULDER, COLORADO

Sounds True
Boulder, CO 80306

Published 2022

Cover design by Mia Cupidro
Book design by Linsey Dodaro

The wood used to produce this book is from Forest Stewardship Council (FSC) certified forests, recycled materials, or controlled wood.

Printed in Canada

BK06285

Library of Congress Cataloging-in-Publication Data
Names: Lee, Kristen, author.
Title: Worth the risk : how to microdose bravery to grow resilience, connect more, and offer yourself to the world / Kris(ten) Lee, EdD, LICSW.
Description: Boulder, CO : Sounds True, 2022. | Includes index.
Identifiers: LCCN 2021059257 (print) | LCCN 2021059258 (ebook) | ISBN 9781683648505 (hardback) | ISBN 9781683648512 (ebook)
Subjects: LCSH: Resilience (Personality trait) | Self-actualization (Psychology)
Classification: LCC BF698.35.R47 L44 2022 (print) | LCC BF698.35.R47 (ebook) | DDC 158.1--dc23/eng/20211217
LC record available at https://lccn.loc.gov/2021059257
LC ebook record available at https://lccn.loc.gov/2021059258

10 9 8 7 6 5 4 3 2 1

For Georgia Klamon-Miller, the mintiest
of mints and definition of brave.

And Auntie Pat, the ultimate character.

I've been absolutely terrified every moment of my life—
and I've never let it keep me from doing
a single thing I wanted to do . . .
GEORGIA O'KEEFFE

CONTENTS

NOTE TO READER

You Are Not Here to Live a *What If* Life

Brave is not something you should wait to feel.
Brave is a decision . . .
GLENNON DOYLE

There are times when it becomes clear that certain risks are worth taking. For me, it happened at 9:01 pm on a Thursday. Within .02 seconds, Ms. Pat has total command over the sold-out audience at Laugh Boston Comedy Club. Rips into a young couple in the front. Cracks jokes about being too old for blowjobs.

I am there with my comedian friend J. Smitty: he's hoping to get Ms. Pat to headline his show the next night. The ice has melted in our drinks. We are laughing too much for even a quick sip. He hadn't said much about her—just that she was funny and that "all the shit she talks about is true."

Patricia Williams, whose stage name is Ms. Pat, has overcome *serious odds*. As in *being shot in the nipple, run down by a truck, raped, pregnant at fourteen, facing racism/sexism/classism, serving jail time kind-of-odds*. It's hard to believe the whole room is gasping for air, not out of shock, but side-splitting laughter while she drops one trauma truth bomb after another. But that is Ms. Pat's brilliance.

At the end of the performance, her tone changes. It is the first time of the night when the neon-blue room with the word **LAUGH** spelled out in globe lights comes to a hush. She tells us to be brave, to tell our stories. No matter the cost. She tells us this is *what we must do*. That courage can pay off, even when it first seems like too big a risk. She is living proof that our own healing can inspire collective healing. We cheer wildly. Ms. Pat tells us to meet her at the merchandise table. She's holding up a T-shirt that says, "It's never too late to tell your truth." The laughs vanish—she's no longer joking.

When the lights come up, we jump off our metal swivel stools and wait in line alongside eager fans whose stomachs hurt from queso fries and uncontrollable laughter. I buy her memoir and thank her for her bravery. I awkwardly tell her that I too am a writer and speaker; that I've told my story publicly. Her polite smile is generous—the only guns I saw in my white, rural small town were for hunting, there was always food on the table, and the only time I'd been in a prison was while working in a minimum-security unit during my early clinical training. Not exactly comparative to her experiences as a Black woman on the streets of Atlanta. Ms. Pat signs my book and J. Smitty convinces her to do his show. We are both smiling as we duck through the Boston rain and smush into our Uber that smells like wet dog with a hint of Vanillaroma.

By the next afternoon, I'd already read every word of *Rabbit: The Autobiography of Ms. Pat*. It's a page turner.[1] Sadly, it is not unique. Her story is all too familiar for far too many Black women and BIPOCs (Black, Indigenous, Persons of Color).

In all my years as a therapist, social justice activist, and resilience researcher, this is the *very first time* I've seen someone tell their story of heartbreaking intergenerational poverty and trauma in a way that makes you laugh and cry at the same time.

By the end of the weekend, I'd seen Ms. Pat twice, read her memoir *without even getting up to go to the bathroom or checking my phone*, and binged on her expansive collection of podcasts and comedy specials. I couldn't help but see the connections between her story and what I've seen ring true in my clinical work and research on human resilience. That we are wired to digest small risks, and that over time microdosing bravery leads to the kind of resilience that not only positively impacts our own lives but has a collective contagion effect.

When a social worker saw Ms. Pat's talent for humor and storytelling and suggested she go into comedy, she originally hesitated. She'd been in plenty of risky situations before, but laying out your life in front of strangers takes mad courage. She eventually took to the stage at open mics, building comfort in telling pieces of her story, generating momentum that's led to big impact for Ms. Pat.

This is more than just a feel-good story of a comedian with sold-out shows. Ms. Pat extricated herself from intergenerational cycles of poverty and became not only an influencer, but a *liberator*: one who has set herself and others free. She's one of many liberators throughout this book illustrating ways we can strategically decide what risks are worth taking to allow us to grow beyond our insecurities, labels, trauma, and what the world heaps on us, and choose a *what is* life over a *what if* life.

When fear rules, we miss out. We may think we're doing ourselves a favor when we "play it safe" or give in to anxiety, but instead we give up the many treasures life can deliver when we take strategic risks.

I've seen the consequences of misguided relationships to risk repeatedly in my professional and personal experiences. On one end of the caution continuum, there's the daredevil who takes wild chances for the sake of adrenaline and ends up repeatedly hurt. On the other, the dreamer who yearns to try something new for their whole life, but winds up stewing in regret and what ifs because they never pursued the ventures of their heart. Then there's the perfectionist who's consumed with what people think, hustling to please everyone else while stewing miserably inwardly. The person who stays in a toxic relationship, much to the detriment of their well-being. The creative who foregoes their spirit and sticks to society's script of success, leading to stagnation and emptiness. The irate citizen who salivates for social change, but is afraid to stick their neck out, remaining hopeless and horrified by the state of the world.

I've also seen the elation of those who've nourished their courage through small, intentional doses of risk that prove well worth it. Those who have engaged with risk strategically, opening doors for joy, adventure, and healing. Who are not held hostage by fear of embarrassment, scrutiny, and loss, but instead realize that playing it safe comes at the cost of being able to develop the stamina, momentum, and resilience that helps us grow and give. Who have discovered that bravery is a process worth engaging with, but are wise in how they calculate and maneuver risk.

Nourishing courage comes in many forms and circumstances, and often involves the beginning step of speaking up even when our instincts first tell us to hide. Take Sage, a patient of mine who has had an extraordinary legacy of impact, working at a high velocity through her career as leader in education, moving freely before the 2020 pandemic. In all her circles, she was seen as the model of courage, but as the world began opening up after the end of the initial COVID lockdowns, Sage found herself struggling to integrate back into society. She was in a state of overstimulation and anxiety, filled with fears, and unsure whether she could carry out her duties. Mostly, she was afraid to tell anyone what she was experiencing: that she felt the most anxiety-ridden and least resilient she'd ever felt in her entire life.

As a high achiever, Sage's pride in her grittiness made it almost impossible to become vulnerable enough to name what was going on. She was used to giving help, not receiving it. She considered resigning so no one would ever find out, but knew full well that an early retirement would have detrimental effects. Eventually, Sage bravely shared her situation with a close colleague who suggested she negotiate a hybrid work arrangement to balance her desire to break through her fear without totally overwhelming herself. This initial step helped her build the courage to come to me to therapy, where we focused on how safe exposure to what we're afraid of can help us to work through fear and build resilience. Sage began strategically using the tools of distress tolerance to nourish her courage rather than giving into fear.

The biggest lie anxiety whispers at us is that we're the only ones, that it's some sort of moral failing when we need help. Don't trade the short-term comfort avoidance gives for the long-term relief that comes with working through what's uncomfortable . . .

While I watched Ms. Pat at LAUGH Boston, I realized that she had taken countless steps to nourish her courage. Her ways of being brave are right in step with the discoveries of modern brain science, human behavior, and social consciousness that can help us grow our resilience and identify the *risks worth taking*. Her story, and the principles of *Worth the Risk,* are not exact templates for microdosing bravery, but reminders of what is available to all of us when we venture beyond our fears and hesitancy to take risks:

Small doses of risk can lead to big impact. A microdosing approach to bravery simply means we take on small doses regularly to experience the beneficial therapeutic effects of risk taking: resilience, greater connection, and being able to offer ourselves to the world. Microdosing allows us to digest and integrate experiences, rather than becoming oversaturated. Courage is not always found in grand and dramatic gestures or jaw dropping feats. It is the grassrootsy, unassuming brand of bravery that should not be underestimated. Microdoses add up.

We must take risks. Life is full of them; risk is unavoidable. We are hardwired to take them. Playing it "safe" doesn't necessarily make life less dangerous. Many risks are worth taking. Risks can be highly nourishing, allowing for important growth to happen as we become more comfortable with the uncomfortable. We can leverage this feature of our brain to experience a bold, adventurous, colorful life.

We are wired for resilience. The human spirit is indomitable. We are not our trauma, our labels, fears, or raw emotions. We are adaptable as a species, capable of significant growth, healing, and momentum. Even when we have faced atrocities and what seems insurmountable, resilience can be cultivated.

We must hold one another in reverence. Moving from *me* to *we* is *the only way forward.* We must evolve from territory protection and "selective neighboring"—caring for those we look like, love like, and affiliate with—to a place of solidarity and holding one another in *highest regard.* For those holding dominant identities that carry privilege, it's essential to stay accountable and seek ways to forge change, standing fervently with and for those who have been marginalized, oppressed, or discriminated against because of race, class, gender, sexual orientation, age, ability, country of origin, or other social identity categorizations. Resilience is activated in contexts that have moved from mere tolerance or acceptance to *human reverence.*

We are liberators. We are here to liberate ourselves and one another from shame, what ifs, fear, isms, oppression, and violence. To stop cowering in the face of ridiculous societal impositions. To reject so-called "leadership" that uses power over to destroy. Liberation happens through solidarity, consciousness, community, and creativity. It is the ultimate offering we can give to ourselves, and one another.

We are inexplicable, creative sages. The world doesn't need our airbrushed stories or curated, scripted, boring, conforming selves. It needs our truths, messiness, weirdness, creative energy, and resistance. Our authentic identities are art. We can express ourselves in many forms and mediums: stories, painting, music, dance, poetry, writing, and performance. Creative flow is contagious. Expressing our *true stories* and *essence* and *seeing one another* is *The Great Gift* we bestow on each other.

We are here to live a **what is** *life.* As the architects of our experience, we are here to design and live a *what is* life, not a *what if* life. Bravery is a choice, an active process of taking *psychological agency*—ownership of our path. We must identify what is within our locus of control.[2] This allows us to consciously choose risks that help us innovate, influence, lead, liberate, actively contribute to the world, and create a life of incredible experiences and impact, rather than living in regret, ruminating over what could've been. We can focus on *what is* possible, and work toward it so that we can offer ourselves fully to the world.

> Greatness and madness are next door neighbors, and they often borrow each other's sugar.
>
> JOE ROGAN

Risks can nourish us when we engage in small, strategic, values-aligned ways, allowing us to grow and give more, leading to deeper purpose and impact. By expanding the ways we offer ourselves, we deepen our capacity as active contributors in the world. Offering ourselves to the world doesn't mean we neglect our own needs, rather it allows us to nourish from an intentional place so that we can effectively and authentically contribute to the greater good.

Risk tolerance is different for all of us. Strategic microdosing can help us during times when we are grappling with loneliness, depression, anxiety, existential crisis, identity confusion, relationship distress, break-ups, adjustments, and opening our hearts to love and be loved—even after being hurt.

> Incremental change is better than ambitious failure . . . Success feeds on itself.
>
> TAL BEN-SHAHAR

Risk doesn't always have to be serious. It can pay off in fun ways. Take Jembi, who loved horseback riding as a kid but was extremely nervous to try again as an adult. He didn't want to let fear stop him from enjoying moments, especially when his career and personal stress was so high, and there were rare chances to cut loose. At first, Jembi was afraid he might get hurt, but once he mounted up, his fear quickly shifted to

6

deep, childlike joy. Jembi went on to make this a monthly ritual that turned out to be a powerful offset to the stress of his high-demand life.

Microdosing bravery can also help us while we're trying to learn new things, like leading teams, teaching students, parenting children, and caring for family members. Small acts of courage over time can help us build the resilience we need to navigate interpersonal and systemic traumas including global pandemics, conflict, climate change, economic crises, hatred, polarization, violence, illness, death, and combating racism, classism, sexism, heterosexism, ageism, ableism, and xenophobia.

The idea of being a risk taker and liberator might seem intimidating when there's so much at hand. Being brave doesn't mean you need to be a Nelson Mandela incarnate or Ms. Pat copycat. The prerequisites to bravery are not fancy titles or formal positions. You don't have to be a public figure with punchy one-liners or thousands of followers.

"Risk-taking behavior" tends to have a bad rap, carrying with it a strong negative connotation that conjures images of disastrous consequence. We can reclaim and allow it to take on a new meaning in our lives when we open ourselves to the healthy disruption it can bring. Many of us are sold limiting ideas about risk that perpetuate aversion to it, preventing us from seeing the many benefits of microdosing it. Risk is pictured as something of a self-destructive, impulsive, high-stakes nature. When we go through trauma and pain, risk aversion can interfere with our imagination's ability to envision, and subsequently, our ability to then take chances that can lead to healing. When we microdose bravery strategically and intentionally, we can experience the therapeutic benefits: fun, growth, freedom, and the connection that makes discomfort worthwhile, enjoying *what is*.

> The 'what should be' never did exist, but people keep trying to live up to it. There is no 'what should be,' there is only what is.
> LENNY BRUCE

Architect a *What Is* Life

Know the difference between a *what is* vs. *what if* life

What is life:

- Refuses to base identity and sense of worth on socially constructed ideals about what is cool, acceptable, or desirable. Is led by values, not comparison to false and harmful standards of so-called "success" and "worthiness."

- Demonstrates investment in identifying what's within and beyond our locus of control. Carefully evaluates and radically accepts what can't change and focuses attention on what can. Adopts a strengths-based approach: appreciating what is and practicing gratitude for it.[3]

- Acknowledges difficulties as an inherent part of the human condition. Understands the realities of impermanence: that nothing stays the same; works to relish in positive moments and cope with challenging ones.

- Asserts psychological agency to architect a life marked by intentionality, authentic identity, presence, creativity, joy, and awe.

- Willing to take strategic microdoses of bravery, tolerate discomfort, integrate the discoveries, and forge ahead. Acknowledges difficult emotions and sensations but refuses to let them interfere with actions that lead to growth. Remains curious and open to evolving learning processes.

- Leverages strengths, resources, and possibilities through incremental, strategic risk-taking within a supportive, conscious community.

- Seeks opportunities to add positively to the collective, given the realities of systemic injustice. Even when circumstances are complex, works imaginatively towards active contribution in the world.

The *what if* life:

- Fixates on past regrets, stays stuck in a state of unsettledness and hindsight bias, embodying the fallacy that "If only I'd done this or that, or if that awful thing didn't happen to me things would've turned out better," or "When this or that passes or happens, or some kind of Golden Ticket arrives, things will be fine."

> Every act of creation is first of all an act of destruction.
>
> PABLO PICASSO

- Fantasizes about a better future without tangible plans or actions to advance goals. Engages in magical thinking without putting in the work to bring about progress.

- Engages in social comparison, experiencing someone else's success as threatening, while remaining blind to one's own potential. Has contingent self-esteem and fixates on what people think rather than ways we can co-inspire, motivate, help, and learn from one another.

- Hesitates to take chances, and stews in a state of analysis paralysis. Has difficulty seeing the law of averages in taking chances. Does constant mental gymnastics over which approach is "right" or "wrong," remaining in a state of rigidity.

- Holds back on trying new things and putting oneself out there while wondering what the experiences and outcomes would've been. Is mistake averse and often terrified of failure.

- Passively bystands, wishing things would be different, but struggles to operationalize plans, act, and contribute in impactful ways.

- Haphazardly engages with maladaptive, risky behavior that contradicts personal values and ethos. Feasts off dopamine rushes that temporarily numb discomfort but fuel a deeper state of discontent and demoralization. Fails to recognize consequences of actions on individual and collective well-being.

Shri, a student of mine, inspired me with his efforts to move from a *what if* to a *what is* life. While painfully shy, he craved social interactions after moving abroad to study. Though nervous to initiate social conversations, his loneliness was getting to him, and he knew he couldn't stay stuck any longer. Shri finally took a chance and introduced himself to someone new, which evolved into one of his closest friendships. He was beyond glad that he shifted his thinking and behavior. It doesn't mean his introversion was magically cured; it's still hard for him, but he's more compassionate towards himself and knows that he's building a stronger stomach for risk, rather than letting fear immobilize him.

This isn't to say that all risks have a happy ending. Sometimes disclosures of vulnerability exacerbate vulnerability, pursuits don't go as planned, and we get bucked off horses, figuratively and literally. It's why we need the right support, so that we enact a strategy that helps mitigate anxiety, rather than ramping it up. When risks align with who we are and what we hold most central to our lives, the law of averages can pay off, and we wouldn't be able to imagine our life if we hadn't been willing to go beyond discomfort.

> One of the most calming and powerful actions you can do to intervene in a stormy world is to stand up and show your soul.
>
> CLARISSA PINKOLA ESTÉS

There is no doubt that the painful rites of passage across our lifetime can cause us to clam up in the face of ongoing risks and decision making. As a psychotherapist and human resilience researcher, I worry that the myths surrounding risk prevent people from taking important steps to grow. It's easy to go all or nothing in the face of pain and trauma. Getting back on the horse is tough. But I've seen many times when avoiding risks creates more pain than good. Fear has a way of disillusioning us to stay "safe," even though engaging with risk can turn out to be the best decision we make.

Assess Your Relationship to Risk

Engagement with risk can help grow resilience, but it takes reflection to ensure we aren't falling into trappings of avoidance. Monitoring your relationship to risk can help you determine if you're missing opportunities for healthy disruption. If you're not sure where you fall on the spectrum of risk affinity and aversion, ask yourself how (un)comfortable you are with the following:

- **Acknowledging my true thoughts and feelings:** Am I willing to advocate for my needs to be met?

- **Living true:** Do I own my strengths and go after what I really want, pursuing dreams with fervor and not needing to explain myself to naysayers with other ideas on what should fulfill me.

- **Leveraging my resources:** In what ways do I demonstrate that I'm enjoying what I have (without overspending and overindulgence), be it through enjoying moments, sharing what I have, making investments, or seeking new ventures?

- **Speaking out:** How inclined am I to use my voice for causes I care about? When something is unjust and unfair, am I willing to speak out and advocate for change?

- **Adventure:** What types of new foods, travel, experiences, and interests am I willing to try?

- **Creative expression:** In what ways am I allowing my artistic, zany, and "weird" juices to flow and be seen?

- **Non-conformity:** How does my life reflect ways that I've broken out of the cages of convention, tradition, and the "way things have always been done," and not going along to get along?

As you undertake this book you don't necessarily have to start with the most provocative question, but understanding your baseline relationship to risk can help you work through your fear rather than let it control you. By strategically calculating risks wisely and intentionally, you can build bravery and grow resilience.

> Fear is the main source of superstition, and one of the main sources of cruelty. To conquer fear is the beginning of wisdom.
>
> BERTRAND RUSSELL

Worth the Risk is your invitation to clarify your values to live a *what is* not a *what if* life. To microdose bravery according to your own unique identity and variables, whether that means telling your story as a means to heal; asking for help; getting up on the literal or figurative horse and discovering childlike joy; forging a path towards growth and discovery despite insecurities; or examining your relationships and ensuring they are aligned even if it means self-advocating, setting boundaries, or ultimately walking away. Even when it's awkward, you might just find that putting yourself out there will help you know that you are not alone and to find your thousand year soul friends and fellow risk-takers.

This is not to say that all risks are a Golden Ticket. There are times when they don't yield the results we hope for. Still, microdosing bravery is the risk we must take, the choice we must make. This is clear within our shared stories, within the most cutting-edge developments in brain science, and amongst the ancient spiritual traditions. They all show us this: that small steps of courage can lead to growth.

Healing from trauma is amongst the bravest acts humans are capable of. Given how trauma can become one of the biggest impediments to risk, *Worth the Risk* devotes an entire session to building courage safely through a trauma-informed lens. Given the enormity of impact that trauma can have on our lives, additional resources will be suggested since this book's primary aim isn't to address the many facets of trauma's influence on our lives.

Worth the Risk provides an opportunity for you to learn to engage with risk in new ways, building resilience for deeper growth and positive impact. Chapters are called "sessions," inspired by the ways I've always strived to run my therapy room and classroom, to encourage you to move from "knowing" to "doing." Each session provides a blend of stories, composite sketches, science, ancient wisdom, behavioral science, and practical exercises to help you strategically work toward taking small steps of courage. The sessions are organized to help you examine what might be getting in the way, and to inspire you to pinpoint the small doses of bravery that will help you grow, connect, and contribute. While not essential, using a journal can help maximize your engagement with the concepts. Similarly, working through the material with a friend, partner, or small group can help you discover risks worth taking and grow as you go.

> Although the connections are not always obvious, personal change is inseparable from social and political change.
> HARRIET LERNER

It's not what we're born into, or the grand gestures and wild chances that we take that fuel resilience, but how we learn to microdose bravery in a way that helps us to gain momentum to be able to grow in ways where we can liberate ourselves and one another—the very reason we are all here.

—kris(ten) lee, June 2022

You Are Not Your Fear

If you risk nothing, then you risk everything.
GEENA DAVIS

Choose Agency Over Complacency

It's been since scrunchies and round wire glasses were last in style that we've seen each other. We're locked into such an intense conversation that the waitress apologizes profusely every time she approaches the table in a reluctant whisper to ask whether we need more coffee or there's room for dessert, even though *it's rare, but not completely unheard of,* for anyone who polishes off the entire plate of veggie tempura to do so.

I'm sitting at the coveted window corner table at Trident Booksellers on Newbury Street in Boston, watching my long-lost friend Tracy, who ran circles around all of us intellectually in high school, sip around the edges of the foamy heart with crooked leaves adorning her cacao-infused turmeric latte. It is nothing short of a miracle we are even sitting face to face: it took the last five years of promising we'd find a time and at least thirty-seven text messages until the Scheduling Gods allowed for this highly anticipated reunion. Tracy is polite as I pepper her with questions; I'm making no secret that I want to know every detail of the courageous life moves she's made.

Tracy and I were mostly in-school friends, except for Thursday afternoons when we were allowed to leave early and drive ourselves to the local university for "Project Spotlight," an enrichment program that looked like a scene from *The Big Bang Theory* meets *Revenge of the Nerds*. Every week we'd inevitably get lost and show up late, because we could never remember *whether the exit number was 12A or 12B*, leading to growing speculation amongst our enrichment peers (who were always early and never broke rules) that we might actually be up to something fun and not just severely directionally challenged.

The only other time Tracy and I were permitted to hang outside of school was an overnight speech competition, and that ONE.TIME! Tracy's mother let her meet us for breakfast to "work on a school project." Tracy won the strictest parents award: she wasn't even allowed to celebrate common holidays within the Jehovah Witness religion she was raised in. Associate in non-proselytizing ways with people outside her faith community? *Fuhgeddaboudit.*

Before our meet up, I tried to stalk Tracy on Facebook to see what she'd been up to, but it was refreshingly void of today's usual *we really needed to know you mismatched your socks today, opinions on Jill Biden's dissertation, that your kid is not taking well to the potty training, ALL! the places you've checked into, full analysis of what Lady Gaga was wearing, that your fourteen-modifications Frappuccino wasn't precisely the way you liked it, or seeing you hooked up to those tubes and machines because of that unfortunate event with the beehive.* All I could really glean was that Tracy had become a nurse practitioner and it seemed like she was having fun in her life, something that made me smile, and a strong clue that she'd probably managed to break away from the rigid rules of her childhood. Now that she's fully caffeinated, she's not going to keep me in suspense any longer. Tracy fast forwards to the moment she's sitting in front of the Jehovah Witness elders: telling them she's leaving the faith, with them telling her what she knew already: she'd be excommunicated from her entire family (she'd already suffered the death of her mother) and community of origin after the three-day waiting period they allowed her to "think things over."

Despite the enormity of the decision, Tracy tells me that she knew immediately when she got home that night that she was never going back, this was it. The elders weren't bluffing: from that moment on, she was erased by her father, brothers, and entire community. Even years later at her brother's deathbed she remained invisible to them.

Even though we haven't seen each other since our jet-black hair was filled with Aqua Net and one step away from being an official mullet, Tracy immediately recognizes the *my Himalayan-salted, Brussel sprouts-filled stomach is doing serious vicarious trauma gymnastics at the thought of all this psychological abuse that's been inflicted in the name of love* look on my face.

She sips the last foamy drop of her latte and thank God she now has the precise turmeric-to-black pepper ratio in her so she can remind me that the moral of the story isn't that she's a fearless courage-bot who eats nails for breakfast. It took over a decade for her to calculate the risks and benefits of staying or leaving and to build the stomach for her eventual big stand against her family and community of origin.

I needed to know how. It's one thing to aggravate your family, and another to face being cut off in such a harsh way. Many people go along to get along throughout their entire lifetime to avoid such turmoil and trauma. Tracy keeps repeating that it took nearly ten years to finally break out, that her courage isn't to be romanticized. She emphasizes that microdosing fear, morsel by morsel, was key. Small steps she took, like making new friends outside of her religion, led to bigger acts of courage. As she digested the discomfort, she found herself building a greater tolerance, becoming bold enough to let go of the ideology she'd been fed. Tracy set needed boundaries with her family and continued strengthening her bonds with people outside the oppressive community, allowing her to do the emotional work of detaching from what was unhealthy while building a safety net. It was no surprise to me that Tracy cited a close friend, Andrea (who was also raised a Jehovah Witness and was similarly breaking out at the same time), as instrumental in growing her courage. They became valuable resources to each other given the parallels in their stories. This, along with her new relationships, proved to have a big pay off when she faced the ultimate moment of truth. Unlearning the harmful ideology she'd been force-fed wasn't a flip of switch for Tracy. The gradual, small-dose ways she engaged with risk eventually gave her the gumption to build a life of impact, meaning, and fun that she'd only dreamt of, without being held hostage by the oppressive and abusive ways of her primary attachments.

I am *blownnnn* away by Tracy's courage and reminded of the value of taking small steps to liberate ourselves. Ultimately, Tracy should have never been put in this position, but she bravely met it by asserting *psychological agency*—taking ownership of the parts of her life she could control. Psychological agency allows us to take initiative, self-advocate; to take matters into our own hands for positive change. It helps us set boundaries, clarify values, own our identity, refuse to go along to get along, and choose courage over complacency.

> It is not fear that stops you from doing the brave and true thing in your daily life. Rather, the problem is avoidance. You want to feel comfortable so you avoid doing or saying the thing that will evoke fear and other difficult emotions. Avoidance will make you feel less vulnerable in the short run but, it will never make you less afraid.
>
> HARRIET LERNER

Despite exorbitant pain, Tracy maintains that microdosing bravery through agency led to enormous growth, joy, and liberation. She looks me in the eye and tells me, "It was worth the risk, . . . I wouldn't trade my life for anything." Our waitress reads the room well and manages to somehow slip us the check. Tracy and I promise to stay in touch— she tells me she's writing her story for therapeutic purposes and would consider sharing it to help others. She winks; her hint isn't lost on me. Tracy knows I'm writing a book on risk taking, courage, and resilience and it hits us both at the same time: there's a reason the Scheduling Gods had granted us our highly anticipated meeting.

Tracy's courageous example illustrates the human capacity to microdose bravery to make a change in our lives and move toward a place of healing. This doesn't happen in the wave of a wand: it took years of consistent microdosing to expand her capacity for bravery. Tracy went on to see how her sustained choices over time helped prepare her to speak truth to power, not only having a dramatic positive effect on her own life, but now her story inspires us to take psychological agency within our own variations of imprisonment.

Design Your Own Blueprint

Being brave requires us to take *psychological agency*—taking accountability for the parts of our lives we can control.[1] Sometimes we are so shut down, we don't realize the options we have in designing a meaningful, growth-focused, connective life. We can become so used to being told what to do, how to feel, and what's important or acceptable that we miss the chance to take agency and make needed shifts. Noticing starts with reflection. Consider the following:

- Who/what are my primary influences in my life?

- How often am I willing to elicit feedback from people I know and trust?

- How open am I to going against the grain when there's pressure to conform?

- In what ways am I inviting novelty and variety into my life?

- What areas of my life suggest I'm on autopilot?

- What aspects of my life show that I work regularly to challenge myself and expand?

When we reflect on our relationship to agency, it allows us to work toward becoming *architects of our experiences*, ones whose blueprints are stamped with our very own signature in the corner, along with our biggest, truest, fullest, muddiest fingerprints all over them that prove we have taken initiative and ownership. Microdosing bravery in this way gives us the strength to reject downloading someone else's template for living: we know it's not an option if we want to live truly and fully.

Microdosing bravery through agency can be a lot to stomach, but the risk of complacency is greater. While Tracy's circumstances are amongst the most harsh and abusive a person can go through, her story resembles so many of the patients and students I've worked with for the past two decades. Like Tracy, agency starts out bumpy for all of us. As we come of age, we are encouraged to obediently follow the designs of our original blueprints crafted by our Family of Origin (FOO). While some FOO's offer flexible blueprints, others are cemented in stone. Tracy reminds me of a patient I served in therapy, Norah, whose blueprint may as well have been written in red Sharpie. Raised in a strict, conservative tradition, her FOO was adamant their design was best for her, even though it was the very underwhelming, uninspired, borrowed *Good Girl/Nice Woman template* that everyone around town was using:

FOO:

Stay within these lines and boxes and you will be safe and successful (rough translation: find a man who will protect you and provide for you. Keep him happy even if that means sacrificing your own happiness). Think, look, and be a precise way. Do not deviate or engage with risk. Follow the good girl rules. Be pretty, but not too sexy. Be smart, but not a know-it-all. Be perfect, but not arrogant. Be complacent, unless directed otherwise. Whatever you do, don't make waves.

NORAH:

Hmm. This blueprint doesn't match Real Me and it's very gendered/ sexist/heteronormative/dominant centric/limiting. There's no room in this plan for me to be my own architect. This conflicts with my values and creative vision for my life. I need to speak up.
(Periods of silence.)
(Periods of intense fighting.)
(Periods of extreme discomfort.)

NORAH:

Sigh. I'll go along to get along. It'll probably be a lot of work to draft my own blueprint anyway.

FOO:

Good job. Keep following: this is how you will be accepted, worthy of love, and find "happiness."

NORAH:

Happy is a thing? This feels miserable.

FOO:

Stop this foolishness. We don't believe you. You've changed. Turned
your back on us. You're to blame. It's you, not us. But because
we're *good people*, we *still* love you. We love you *unconditionally*.

NORAH:

Is that supposed to be comforting? *Still? Unconditional love?*
Seriously? I need to be the architect of my experience.
(*Periods of silence, internal fighting, and turmoil.*)
(*Periods of intense fighting, unflinching gaslighting and scapegoating.*)
(*Periods of extreme discomfort.*)

NORAH:

I love being my own architect. Joy is returning and I'm having a blast
with the redesign. I've found fellow brave travelers. My values are
aligned. I am becoming brave. Practice is paying off. I'm glad I didn't
choose complacency over agency. It's been worth the risk.

Everyone has their own version of misaligned FOO blueprints. And as predictable as these tensions are for everyone, they can be EXCRUCIATING. We don't inherit templates from well-intended kin because there weren't 15,600 parenting books to choose from in their day, or because they are bad people, it's simply the way FOO stuff works. I've yet to meet someone who has been handed a perfectly crafted template that requires no revisions. FOOs have their own histories, ideals, organizing frameworks, narratives, traditions, suspicions, and superstitions to uphold. Cycles are hard to break. FOOs give us the best blueprint they can, but it is up to us to take agency as the lead architect.

Norah's story is much like the stories of the thousands of patients and students I've served in my therapy room and classroom. It's not just Good Girl/Nice Woman templates being handed out that are problematic. The Strong Boy/Tough Guy toxic masculinity blueprints being distributed do

> It is debilitating to be any woman in a society where women are warned if they do not behave like angels, they must be monsters. ... Patriarchal socialization literally makes women sick, both physically and mentally.
>
> SANDRA M. GILBERT AND SUSAN GUBAR

a number, too: don't cry, be tough, man up, be a provider. Gendered templates, like racialized, heteronormative, caste-based ones, hurt us all.

Stirring the FOO pot is a huge risk. I've never met a family where there wasn't high drama involving some variation of guilt, shame, and anger when blueprints are confronted. It's a sensitive topic to initiate with people we love, who have raised us, tried their best. They are our primary attachments. Many psychotherapists would argue taking this risk is THE PLACE to start, *lest we see our mommy and daddy issues go on foreverrrrrrr.*

> Imbalanced systems, whether internal or external, will tend to polarize.
> RICHARD C. SCHWARTZ

The Internal Family Systems (IFS) Model is a helpful framework in navigating FOO issues. It emphasizes the mind's multidimensional nature and that everyone has a Self, which can and should lead one's internal system. It allows us to recategorize the various parts of ourselves and in doing so be able to renegotiate our relationship to the outside systems we're a part of.[2]

> A self is not something static, tied up in a pretty parcel and handed to the child, finished and complete. A self is always becoming.
> MADELEINE L'ENGLE

Taking accountability for our various Selves to assert agency within family structures and dynamics is arguably the hardest place to override fear, but can be done in small, consistent doses. Handing back templates and starting our own requires enormous finesse, strength, and courage. This building block microdose is essential: realizing we are the architects of our experience who take steps to set the right boundaries toward building and living a life that is ours. If we can be brave enough to take agency in FOO, we can be brave everywhere. You are not your fear. You are brave.

Design Your Own Blueprint

Courage is not the absence of fear but fear walking.
SUSAN DAVID

Become the Architect of Your Experience

Confronting Family of Origin (FOO) dynamics is a risk worth taking, even though it's arguably one of the most fear-provoking steps towards resilience. Asserting psychological agency—taking ownership of the parts of life we can control—helps us to set boundaries, clarify values, own our authentic identity, refuse to go along to get along, and choose courage over complacency. Doing so can lead to vital renegotiation, growth, joy, connection, and liberation.

Psychological Agency Check: Reflect

In what ways have I already asserted psychological agency?

What FOO messages have been helpful? Harmful?

What types of templates have I inherited? How do they affect me?

Which areas of my life require more attention and practice?

What gets in the way?

Who or what will help me microdose bravery to make steady progress?

In what ways am I demonstrating that I am the lead architect of my experience?

Action Steps: Finesse Your Fear

Fear doesn't have to keep its grip on us. Taking psychological agency is a critical step toward becoming the architect of our own experience. Consider the following to help maneuver through fear and pressure:

1. **Clarify your values.** Review the blueprint you inherited and determine which aspects you wish to carry over and which you do not. Write down your values and chart out your unique needs for psychological safety, well-being, and contribution in the world. Prioritize and protect your values: decide what should be in pencil or in Sharpie marker. Revisit the drawing board frequently to continue to allow it to evolve as you grow and gather data on what helps you thrive and offer yourself to the world.

2. **Don't go along to get along.** Set boundaries. It might not be clear to those around you that you need them to respect your values and thresholds. Consider writing out your thoughts and sharing them to set ground rules for conversation. Resist any forms of scapegoating, gaslighting, gender stereotyping, and any form of identity oppression. Enlist the support of someone you trust to help you strategize your communication points. Use statements like "It would mean a lot to me if you would . . ." or "Our relationship is important to me, so let's try to find a way for us be creative on how we can try some new ways of interacting that account for both our feelings and needs . . ."

3. **Seek a healthy surrogate community.** Therapists can be great supports in navigating family dynamics, trauma, and working to rebuild relationships within and outside the family. Internal Family Systems work is focused on healing our various Selves. When FOOs are not able to accept our revised blueprints, we can benefit from expanding our network and definition of family to ensure we have support, especially when things become contentious. Surrogates can provide healthy mirroring to us and serve as sources of nurturing and nourishment when we are grappling with the gamut of family dynamics, from slightly tense

to severely toxic levels. Consider reaching out to someone that you admire to try and build connections that nurture you.

4. **Operate from an empathic, not a blaming lens.** FOO conflict can elicit strong emotions. As Ram Dass said, "If you think you are enlightened, go and spend a week with your family." When we employ an empathy lens, we work to see that everyone is doing the best they can, and that family dynamics are inherently challenging. This calls us to see how we can generate empathy rather than stay in a finger-pointing stance, unaware of how someone else feels. Ask yourself, "In what ways is the person who's frustrating me acting in a way that reflects what they were taught?"

5. **Keep your sense of humor.** The tragicomedy and predictable drama that surges in families can be entertaining and relatable. Humor is an essential skill for navigating family dynamics: if we can't laugh, we will surely cry. We're not the only ones to endure family tensions. As David Sedaris puts it: "My family isn't really all that different from anyone else's. Well, maybe they're a bit more entertaining." What dynamics in your family could be their own skit? In what ways does humor help you cope with family drama?

> If you want to have a life that is worth living, a life that expresses your deepest feelings and emotions and cares and dreams, you have to fight for it.
> ALICE WALKER

6. **Seek inspiration and support.** Who are the Tracy's and Norahs in your life? Ask them to describe their own process of taking agency. Consider how their experiences might inform your own strategic microdoses of bravery. Try working with a therapist for tailored suggestions on how to navigate FOO complexity and identifying risks worth taking to help you grow resilience.

Session Two

You Are Not Your Keg Stands

The more we practice, the more we are gentle with our fear
and are able to embrace it, the more the fear goes away.
THICH NHAT HANH

Choose Progress Over Posturing

Before we can learn to identify risks worth taking, we need to question our grandstanding #BossUp #Badass #Slayallday *never let anyone see you sweat unless it's to show off your hot yoga class* world that hypes us DO.EVERYTHING.BIG! . . . lest we seem weak, uncool, or basic. There's posturing at every turn. Grandiosity has become sport, and dopamine, our Gatorade. It's like we're in a scene from an *Avengers* meets *Fear Factor* meets *Animal House* mash-up, being egged on to *chug-chug-chug* away with full velocity.

Bingeing random risks for the sake of showing off or alleged quick relief is a *big fat triple U: unwise, unhealthy, and unsustainable.* Yet, we are egged on to keg stand our way through life, trying to win big at every turn as quickly as possible to beat out everyone around us. The Keg Standing Method of Risk is an easy sell: it promises fast relief, big payoff, and lots of applause if we guzzle heartily. It promises a full reset all in one sitting: a quick escape route from the pain and doldrums of life.

This method of risk tells us that to be tough and cool, we need to take it like a champ and show off, even when our stomachs are crying uncle, and the aftermath isn't pretty. This keg standing formula cheapens the actual benefits of risks worth taking that can nourish, helping us create a life of meaning, fun, and impact. If we want to grow resilience and truly live a life that's not contrived or potentially destructive, we need to detoxify from the glamorous illusions we're force fed, which leave little imagination for actions that lead to real growth and progress that matters.

> Progress, not perfection, is what we should be asking of ourselves.
>
> JULIA CAMERON

Don't Keg Stand Risk

Eric is a prime example of someone who fell hard for the Keg Standing Method of Risk. He came to me in his thirties for therapy in the aftermath of his wolf-it-down macrodosing approach to life, with enough stories for his very own Netflix special that would inevitably lead to an appearance on Joe Rogan. Eric is the ultimate risk chugger, taking on everything with full fervor and little restraint. He's made and lost a lot of money, gone on endless expeditions across the world, and seems without any inhibitions. It took only a few sessions with Eric to see the cycle of despair he was entangled with. When the dopamine wore off, he had nothing to show for it. While his spirited ways of operating seemed daring and admirable, he was simply creating an illusion of courage, all while foregoing opportunities for real risk that nourishes.

Real risk isn't always grandiose. The act of swallowing bravery is often so miniscule, it goes completely unrecognized by the outside world. In due time our psyches and souls are primed to adapt, integrate, and digest even the rustiest, clankiest, most bitterly jarring parts of life; to become more comfortable with the uncomfortable so much so that it becomes lifeforce. Microdoses help us build the fortitude to absorb, integrate, expand, co-contribute, and construct the new matrix of presence and inter-beingness. The cumulative effect of such actions cannot be overstated. Consistent microdoses of bravery have powerful, palpable effects. Vitality emerges through the nourishment of real droplets of risk, sustained over time; not impulsive grand gestures and binges disguised as noble and big.

Eric began to see that thrills weren't demonstrative of valiance, they were him deflecting opportunities to take small, meaningful risks connected to his deeper strengths, values, and dreams. Pumping himself with big thrill placebos was only leaving him on the hunt for more rush moments, and the crashes weren't pretty. Knowing this was unsustainable and self-destructive, he began rethinking risk, directing his energy in ways that were truly courageous rather than staying entrapped by vices and maladaptive behavior disguised as bravery.

The trappings of the Keg Standing Method of Risk are hard to avoid. Thrills are thrilling. But they leave us at risk for maladaptive patterns, with little room to digest substantive risk that nourishes, like filling up on cake before a healthy main course. While a lack of inhibition can have its place in life, it can also be a form of avoidance. Numbing behaviors involving alcohol, food, shopping, sex, overwork, or binge-watching/scrolling can indicate avoidance of real risks that could advance personal values and dreams. When we keg stand risk, it seems like we are living a spontaneous, spirited life, when in reality we are dodging opportunities to microdose the kind of meaningful bravery that helps us be well and do well.

> I believe that one of life's greatest risks is never daring to risk.
> OPRAH WINFREY

Rethink Bravery

To avoid miscalculating which risks are worth taking, we must challenge the ways bravery has been sold. Before we lose our first tooth, we are entrained to believe that being brave means big, as in *Malala-Mother-Theresa-T'Challa-Nelson-Mandela* big. Bravery is pitched as follows:

The Invincible enters the scene. They fearlessly swoop in and save the day like it's *no big deal*. They valiantly perform heroic acts at full velocity without blinking. This is the standard we're supposed to emulate, like we're freakin' *Avengers* characters.

The perfectionistic prototypes being propagated never seem to run short on courage, energy, and sheer willpower. They woke up like this. They are the ultimate keg standers who always go big and never stay home. The Herculean risks they take always seem to pay off. *Being brave,* we're taught, equals powerful, endearing, indispensable. This is a lot to live up to when we're trying to make our way and bring impact in the world but even on good days we feel more like Cowardly Lions than Mufasas.

As if it weren't already enough to figure out what risks are worth taking, society talks out of both sides of its mouth when it comes to risk. On one hand we're egged on to be brave, to face life fully, not to be soppy snowflakes; all while being told to avoid risk like it's the plague, *as if* it can actually be avoided. There are endless cautionary tales about risk:

- The afraid-to-fly passenger whose plane crashes

- The employee who speaks truth to power and loses their job

- The artist who takes a creative risk and is critiqued or undermined

- The entrepreneur who takes a business risk and loses their shirt

- The romantic who puts their heart on the line and is rejected

- The strong-willed renegade who speaks their mind and loses friends and family

There are epithets galore about risk. "A bird in the hand is worth more than two in the bush." "Play it safe." "The grass isn't greener on the other side of the fence." "Stick with the program." "We've always done it this way." "Curiosity killed the cat." "Risk is synonymous with instability." "Risk equals jeopardy."

Bravery has been explicitly and tacitly pitched to us in strange ways. It's no wonder heads spin. What does it mean to be brave? Should we go big or stay home? Keg stand or fast? What kinds of risks are worth taking? How can we calculate risk for the greatest good? What about our values— how do we make sure they don't go missing in the mix of overachievement and cancel culture? And there's so much bravery needed to overcome society's inequities—where do we begin?

There are risks and benefits to everything: all choices to be made have trade-offs. Contrary to popular belief, being a risk taker doesn't mean you have to be a manic skydiver jumping unabashedly out of a plane, or the one who bets it all at the Bellagio or invests your entire life savings in Bitcoin. In our winner-take-all, go-big-or-stay-home world, we often miss seeing opportunities to calculate and microdose risks that nourish, and come with substantial long-term benefits. Consistent tiny droplets of risk add up, rather than occasional, erratic keg standing that ends up leaving us in greater turmoil.

> Everyone has a 'risk muscle.' You keep it in shape by trying new things. If you don't, it atrophies. Make a point of using it at least once a day.
> ROGER VON OECH

Every day, we are forced to calculate the value of risk in our lives. The very act of stepping out our door is a risk; so is staying home. Our stomach for risk can waver in the face of living in a world where change is the only constant and fear appears at every turn. This can cause us to play it safe, even though avoiding risk has its own consequences.

When we step on a treadmill, we run the risk of injury, but when we don't, we risk atrophy and other health issues associated with not exercising. When we choose not to date out of fear we'll be hurt again, we inherit other difficult circumstances like loneliness and bitterness. When we fight to keep things the way they've always been, we risk not identifying novel solutions and innovations to longstanding problems. When we try a new food, we risk foregoing the sure bet of enjoying what we know we like, but if we stay with our usual order we miss broadening our palate, remaining with a limited repertoire.

The same limited repertoire principle holds true for new interests (leisure, love, learning, creative endeavors, hobbies). It may seem "safe" to avoid risk, to stay in our routines and nests, but we are really just inviting unwanted consequences like stagnation. We're also missing the chance to build adaptability that will inevitably be needed in other

> Risk is, for some people, the fear of failure. If they take no risks, they have no failure. But failure, as like risks, can be a great teacher. Don't let fear stop you from taking a risk to achieve your dreams.
> CATHERINE PULSIFER

areas. Risk is a staple that we must learn to incorporate in our daily lives for maximum benefit in strategic ways, rather than pulling a keg stand and dealing with the hangover that macrodoses can leave behind.

Maybe you used to live less inhibited, but as time passes, you've become more risk averse and find yourself taking fewer chances. Anxiety and superstition have a way of blocking us from going after what we really want. Or like Eric, your risk taking is disproportionate and misdirected. It's a lot to sort through and find your sweet-spot dosing. Our relationship with risk and bravery is complicated. It can help to pinpoint the sources of your fear to overcome them. A consistent theme across my patients and students is that they hold themselves back because they're afraid to risk:

- **Overload.** Concern on going beyond reasonable limits with risk; not being able to take in risk in healthy doses, even though risk is often nourishing and builds our thresholds for coping with change and disruption.

- **Failure.** Worry that outcomes won't turn out as hoped and planned, even though this is how we learn and grow.

- **Judgment.** Fear that saying what I really feel and being my true self will lead to rejection, humiliation, or being outed, even though this is how we find authentic connection and community.

- **Trying new things.** This new choice won't compare to what I'm used to, even though change is inevitable, and novelty and variety are vital nourishment for the mind, body, and soul.

- **Attachment.** Holding back because of concern that something good will end; not letting myself get attached, even though this blocks me from fun, pleasure, and savoring moments.

- **Getting hurt.** Avoiding any scenario when emotional or physical risk is in the realm of possibility, even though pain isn't entirely preventable and avoiding it can create its own set of negative consequences.

- **Wasted investment.** Disappointment over putting so much into one goal or vision without the return being what I wished for, all while missing the other positive outcomes and opportunities at hand.

- **Being wrong.** Not wanting to admit skill and knowledge gaps, mistakes, misperceptions, and biases, even though it's part of being human: doing so can serve as a catalyst for needed change and growth. Apologizing and asking for a second chance is amongst the hardest pills to swallow, but one that can lead to bonding and deeper connection.

> Life shrinks or expands in proportion to one's courage.
>
> ANAÏS NIN

- **Sense of safety.** Fearing danger to the point of total avoidance, even though exposure to fear can help us mitigate anxiety, improve distress tolerance, and build resilience.

In all these themes, the through line is fear of loss, something that's unavoidable. Ironically, we can be just as afraid to win big as we are to lose big. When we really follow our dreams with full velocity, and experience grand success, the fear of losing it can become all consuming. The more we have, the more we have to lose. We finally experience joy, then worry it's going to get ripped away. When we decide not to pursue dreams based on such fears, we're still losing. This can cause us to engage in misdirected keg stands to try and compensate and numb disappointment. We're not finding the courage to go after what we want in a measured, strategic way.

Skirting risk isn't an option, but this doesn't mean we have to ignore our overloaded, oversaturated thresholds and keg stand it to show off our moxie. Just as life's stressors have a cumulative effect, so do the small steps of bravery that help us grow resilience.

> Perhaps the biggest tragedy of our lives is that freedom is possible, yet we can pass our years trapped in the same old patterns. . . . We may want to love other people without holding back, to feel authentic, to breathe in the beauty around us, to dance and sing. Yet each day we listen to inner voices that keep our life small.
>
> TARA BRACH

See Brave in Context

Bravery must also be contextualized for us to get our teeth around it. We must see *why we need to be brave* in the first place. We are so inclined to romanticize brave and see it as a solo act or one of sheer will and courage that we often skip over the systemic issues in societies that create the need to be courageous to begin with; the kind that require strategic, consistent effort to overcome.

> The strongest are those who renounce their own times and become a living part of those yet to come. The strongest and the rarest.
>
> MILOVAN DJILAS

Being brave requires us to face the suffering that we've inherited. Race, ethnicity, gender, social class, sexual orientation, religion, able-bodiedness, appearance, place of birth, and dwelling are the forces that determine who will live or die, be seen or invisible, be welcome or cast out, feel safe or violated, have rights or not, have access or not.[1]

These are realities that cannot be overstated. As Isabel Wilkerson explains in *Caste: The Origins of Our Discontents,* "Society is built on a fixed, embedded ranking of human value that sets the presumed supremacy of one group against the presumed inferiority of other groups." While Wilkerson was studying the caste system in India, she realized that the United States consists of a social order that feels like "the natural order of things" but really has to do with a longstanding tradition of dominant groups abusing their power and privilege.[2]

Within the presumed supremacy group, privilege may be so automated, it goes unrecognized. This can be a hard sell for those who know how to pronounce "charcuterie" or "Buttigieg" with great precision, but who don't know how (or even try) to say "Kamala" correctly. Or a white person who has a lot of "Black friends" but doesn't believe in systemic racism. Or a man that declares sexism and misogyny as "bad" simply because they "wouldn't want their daughter, mom, or sister to experience them."

Contextualizing bravery begins by realizing that we do not live in a vacuum. If societies weren't built on bias, discrimination, greed, and power over, we wouldn't need so much courage. Brave is a requirement of living within contexts of human suffering. To do nothing about this is to risk complacency and become a bystander to racism, classism, sexism, heterosexism, ableism, and xenophobia. There is also the risk of seeing further violence and deterioration within society, rather than becoming an *active contributor* toward making it better. When we are brave, we know that inaction isn't an option. We know that complacency bears grave consequences, and we work to direct our energy toward progress rather than ignoring our roles and relationships to social inequities and change.

Microdose Bravery: Make Bravery a Practice

We don't develop a stronger stomach by slugging down massive heaps of risk. First, we need to expand our risk palate, to grow in our willingness to try something that feels like a step outside our comfort zone. This is hard in a world where fear is being served up 24-7, leaving little room to digest and integrate vital nourishment for the mind, body, and soul.

Microdosing bravery is a *deliberate practice* that allows us to engage with risk strategically, so our decisions on *what we risk* are framed by *why we do so*. The *why* is critical. For Tracy in Session One, she could no longer participate in coerced behavior she found damaging and oppressive. Her desire to live freely in the world and create a life of meaning led by her own values allowed her to finally take a stand. For Eric in this session, his insight that his big risks were obstructing, not advancing, his values helped him make needed shifts. This discovery helped him renegotiate his relationship to risk so he could still live with zest but also focus his energies in a values-directed way. Ultimately, each of us need to define bravery for ourselves, rather than succumbing to outside pressures. We cannot fall for the fallacy that keg standing will provide fast relief, some sort of big payoff, or lots of applause. Even if people are cheering us on, we will be underwhelmed if we're not aligned with our why.

Fear can create blind spots in seeing the benefits of risk, making us want to purse our lips instead of opening ourselves. While we may perceive this as playing it safe, avoidance is its own risk. Strategic risk helps us

> The owner of an old house knows that whatever you are ignoring will never go away. Whatever is lurking will fester whether you choose to look or not. Ignorance is no protection from the consequences of inaction. Whatever you are wishing away will gnaw at you until you gather the courage to face what you would rather not see.
>
> ISABEL WILKERSON

grow, learn, discover, have fun, and become more resilient in the long run. Especially when it's for the sake of our values and collective progress, not just personal gain or for a good story.

The doors to the world of the wild Self are few but precious. If you have a deep scar, that is a door, if you have an old, old story, that is a door. If you love the sky and the water so much you almost cannot bear it, that is a door. If you yearn for a deeper life, a full life, a sane life, that is a door . . . All the 'not readies,' all the 'I need time,' are understandable, but only for a short while. The truth is that there is never a 'completely ready,' there is never a really 'right time.' As with any descent to the unconscious, there comes a time when one simply hopes for the best, pinches one's nose, and jumps into the abyss. If this were not so, we would not have needed to create the words heroine, hero, or courage.

CLARISSA PINKOLA ESTÉS

Reframe Your Definition of Bravery

Bravery comes in multiple forms, allowing us to be creative on how we define it. Even unusual acts of courage can be nourishing and help us live our why without being keg stand-y. It is worth examining how you've come to define brave and ways you can expand your definition. What one sees as an act of bravery ranges widely from person to person, such as:

Asking for help even though it first feels awkward and embarrassing

Embracing your quirks even though you may risk being judged

Chatting with a stranger even though you consider yourself shy

Phoning someone you've been out of touch with even though they may be upset

Trying a new food even though it might be easier to default to your usual

Getting on a plane even though you have flight anxiety

Singing in public even though you're no Lady Gaga

Drawing a picture even though you don't consider yourself artsy

Initiating intimacy even though you're unsure how your partner will respond

Starting a business venture even though there's no guarantee how it will go

Leaving a dysfunctional relationship even though it's all you've known

Engaging with risk isn't all rainbows and butterflies. We all have scars from risks gone wrong. The law of averages is a thing: some risks work out much better than others. Risk must be handled with care and consciousness: strategic ingestion is paramount. There is no one-size-fits-all formula magic dose of risk. Risk needs to be carefully calibrated based on our own bandwidth and life variables so we can digest properly and increase immunity from fear paralysis. Proper microdosing builds the fortitude we need to protect, nourish, and sustain us. We must avoid the Keg Stand Method of Risk that creates the illusion we are big risk takers, when really we are avoiding taking small, meaningful ones that add up and bring lasting impact.

There are trade-offs in every scenario in which we choose one risk over another. Some choices will bring about the outcomes we hope for; others won't. Microdosing bravery as a practice helps us to remain agile and resilient. It relies on our willingness to get comfortable with uncomfortable and stand up to power structures—even when they "mean well." Embracing risk doesn't mean we aren't filled with fear. But we refuse to let risk choose us—instead we take small strategic steps based on our values, so we do not risk foregoing what matters most to us at great cost.

You are not a hot mess or hopeless cause just because you're scared or out of sorts. We cannot hang up on the call for courage that speed dials us every day. If facing the simultaneous brokenness and possibility of living were easy, we wouldn't need therapists, besties, teachers, scientists, coaches, healers, artists, and comedians nudging us to critically think, take agency, be more self-compassionate, see our shared humanity, and to stop taking ourselves and our so-called "failures" so seriously. "Failure" is how we learn and grow. Community and solidarity are how we heal.

Risk is part of life. We must renegotiate our attachment to "safe" outcomes—that is how we'll stay exactly where we are. Trying to skirt risk is how we squeeze out all the fun and stunt the most wondrous gift: imagination. Once we recognize and face this, so begins the messy, necessary process of *really living*—knowing full well that there are no guaranteed pathways to safety or "success." This doesn't mean we have to keg stand risk, but we can't go on risk fasts and expect to grow. Practice won't make perfect, but we will keep expanding in our risk affinity and capacity to imagine every moment as a clean slate. We will lose, we will fall down, we will upset people, we will be laughed at and talked about. We will bite our nails and kick ourselves, but we will have quite a collection of stories and have built up plenty of nerve in the meantime. Chances are, when we embody bravery in our daily practice, we'll have inspired some needed positive collective dissent too. Progress, not posturing, is how we move forward together.

You are not your keg stands. You are your microdoses.

There are so many ways to be brave in this world. Sometimes bravery involves laying down your life for something bigger than yourself, or for someone else. Sometimes it involves giving up everything you have ever known, or everyone you have ever loved, for the sake of something greater. But sometimes it doesn't. Sometimes it is nothing more than gritting your teeth through pain, and the work of every day, the slow walk toward a better life. That is the sort of bravery I must have now.

VERONICA ROTH

SESSION TWO WORKSHEET

Microdose Bravery

Don't ask what the world needs. Ask what makes you come alive and go do it. Because what the world needs is people who have come alive.
HOWARD THURMAN

Change Your Relationship to Risk

Keg standing risk for alleged quick relief is unwise, unhealthy, and unsustainable.

Macrodosing bravery in grandiose form can create an illusion that we are courageous, all while preventing us from digesting substantive risk that nourishes and helps us grow. To rethink bravery and our relationship to risk, we must reject perfectionistic and avoidance propaganda to find our sweet spot and maximize the benefits of meaningful risk. Holding ourselves back due to fear of failure, judgment, change, attachment, getting hurt, wasted investment, being wrong, and loss of sense of safety can cause us unintended consequences. Brave needs to be contextualized so we can clarify our roles and relationship to social inequity and change. Progress, not posturing, is how we move forward together.

Dosing Check: Reflect

Where do I fall on the spectrum of macrodosing and microdosing bravery?

What kinds of risks have I taken that have led to positive outcomes?

In what ways are maladaptive and adaptive behaviors impacting my life?

What messages have I received about risk?

How does perfectionism show up in my life?

Of the fears discussed in this session, which are most influential and or erosive to me?

How do the inequities of the world impact me?

What does my current microdosing bravery practice consist of?

How might I build increasing tolerance for risks worth taking?

Action Steps: Microdose Bravery

Microdosing bravery as a deliberate practice helps us frame the why behind our decisions and consistently make substantial progress. Even though risk can go wrong, we can stay agile and resilient when we become more comfortable with the uncomfortable and open our imaginations. As we build the stomach for it, we come alive as the nourished active contributors, liberators, and creators we were born to be.

1. **Evaluate your relationship with risk.** Ask yourself whether you tend to keg stand risk or refuse to engage with it. In what ways and pacing are you swallowing bravery? Is it nourishing? What types of substantive risk would you benefit from? Identify ways that past experiences have shaped your current behavior. Remember that you are not a cautionary tale if past risks have led to distress. All choices have tradeoffs.

2. **Identify your fears.** Review the common fear traps that create risk aversion: failure, judgment, change, attachment, getting hurt, wasted investment, being wrong, and loss of sense of safety. Of these, which tend to hold you back? Select one that you can start microdosing bravely with. What steps might you take to begin confronting what's at hand?

3. **Seek inspiration from everyday heroes.** Who around you embodies healthy microdosing practices, consistently walking in their values towards progress without having to posture? Ask them what contributed to their capacity for this. What did you learn? How might you apply this to your own life?

4. **Examine the context of fear.** Society calls us to be courageous with its longstanding travesties in human rights, inequity, oppression, and violence. Seeing bravery in this context helps us to stay accountable and become active contributors. What might you do to demonstrate accountability if you hold any forms of privilege?

    > Where your fear is, there is your task.
    > CARL JUNG

5. **Use light to dispel darkness.** Don't take your opportunities for meaningful risk that leads to social change lightly. Humor is a powerful path to calling out social issues. It can help diffuse and teach, exposing the insidious nature of social institutions and the human condition.

Session Three

You Are Not Your Automations

We have memorized a select set of behaviors, attitudes, beliefs, emotional reactions, habits, skills, associative memories, conditioned responses, and perceptions that are now subconsciously programmed within us. . . . About ninety-five percent of who we are by midlife is a series of subconscious programs that have become automatic—driving a car, brushing our teeth, overeating when we're stressed, worrying about our future, judging our friends, complaining about our lives, blaming our parents, not believing in ourselves, and insisting on being chronically unhappy, just to name a few.

JOE DISPENZA

Choose Regulation Over Automation

All eyes are on the clock. After five full days of continental breakfasts with unripe melon, Werther's Originals, lectures, and awkward networking rituals with proverbial exchanging of business cards and Twitter handles, only to never speak again, everyone is READY for the conference to be done. I'm there with a distinguished group of psychology professors from around the world, and while we love talking shop about brain science and human behavior, we ALSO. LOVE. that we are a stone's throw from Stanley Park in Vancouver,

British Columbia. It finally adjourns: we say goodbyes, promise follow-up emails that will inevitably go to spam, and depart ways.

The second I step outside, my phone alerts me that I've received seventeen text messages from my overzealous cousins, whom I actually call "The Cousins," who are hosting me for the weekend with an itinerary that implies they were definitely tour guides in a past life—and also if Leslie Knope were a real person, she'd be very proud and a little jealous.

Their enthusiasm is infectious UNTIL we arrive at Whistler Mountain and they casually announce to me—*the one who is both low sugar and has clinically significant anxiety with a moderate fear of heights*—that after lunch we HAVVVVE.TO.DO. the 360 peak-to-peak gondola ride. As in the world's *highest lift of its kind, 1,427 feet above the valley floor, ALL.GLASS. so you NEVER.HAVE.TO. miss a minute of how high up you are* ride.

I smile politely, then immediately suggest we grab gelato and walk around instead. After all, I don't want The Cousins to "feel obligated when they've already done so much," and "ohhh, look, salted caramel and hazelnut!" My hints aren't working. It isn't until we've waited forty minutes in line that I finally blurt out my fear of heights. The Cousins quickly retort with a Judge Judy meets Marianne Williamson tough love tone, leaving me the "opportunity" to work through my fear.

The clinical part of my brain knows this was exactly what I need. Exposure to fear is the gold standard way of overcoming anxiety and intrusive thoughts. I know that my fear is based on brain pattern recognition and that if I can get it together, the ride could even turn out to be fun. I love adventure, the last thing I want is to chicken out.

My Worst-Case Scenario Brain (WCS), however, wants nothing to do with this little exercise in desensitization and emotional regulation. Worst-Case Scenario Brain is already five steps ahead, envisioning being airlifted after the dreadful cable snap that witnesses later describe as "jarring and horrific"; then flashing to my funeral, where I'm greeted by the overpowering smell of lilies as my daughter plays "On Eagle's Wings" on an out of tune piano, while she courageously fights through her grief and seasonal allergies with no one even giving a second thought to slipping her a Zyrtec—or at least a squirt of Flonase—so she can make it through the song. The best they can come up with is a crumpled tissue and THE. BRAVE. GIRL. STILL.DOESN'T. MISS. A. NOTE.

The incense causes my aunt to sneeze and toot at the same time, which causes my nephews to erupt into laughter they insist I would have found hilarious. By now, my colleagues have already read the "Sad News" email my dean sends about a "tragic accident," mentioning my "teaching impact" and that free counseling would be available to anyone who needed it. My Facebook feed already has 743 comments from people who probably couldn't stand me but now I am a patron saint who never did ONE. THING! wrong and NO.ONE. will ever be able to look at a gondola without completely losing it from this day forward.

The Cousins have already shuffled me to the entrance and despite my urge to bolt, the anxiety of letting them down wins. I visualize the salted caramel gelato in the chocolate-dipped, hazelnut-laced cones awaiting, and enact everything I've learned about yoga breathing on YouTube. I'm relieved when I see that we are the only ones in the gondola, lest anyone see my ~~coping skills~~ hyperventilation antics. When the door is about to close, a family of four squeezes in. The parents have the telltale *who the eff's idea was it to travel with two tweenagers* look; the daughter has bangs in her eyes that scream indifference, while the son's expression reads all he wanted was Oreos and Cream, that he wasn't exactly a stan for heights, and certainly NOT family vacations.

We take off, and at the precise moment of my deepest Vinyasa breathing, Oreos lets air out too, but not from his mouth. It sounds like a super-sized whoopie cushion and smells like cilantro-infused five-day-old egg salad. The whole family turns beet red, scolding Oreos with yells poorly disguised as whispers.

This was not exactly the 4D sensory experience I was hoping for on a hot summer day, but sometimes paradoxical interventions work. Despite it being THE.WORST. dose of aromatherapy I've ever encountered, somehow this breaks the tension: the gondola begins shaking with uncontrollable laughter: first by me, next *The Cousins*, then the entire family, *including Indifferent Sister,* and somehow I'm not ONE.BIT. scared anymore.

This isn't an advertisement for weird aromatherapy. Maybe you're thinking it seems like the moral of the story is that my rational brain came from behind to take the win over my Worst-Case Scenario Brain. That we can overcome fear when there's enough positive pressure and tough love to do so, and that all risks have happy endings. But modern brain science has a different, more accurate story to tell.

Neuroscientist Lisa Feldman Barrett, who is amongst the top one percent most-cited scientists in the world, is leading the way in dispelling outdated theories of human emotion that have been widely taught even by Carl Sagan, *Harvard Business Review, National Geographic*, and nearly every psychology textbook written. My fears in Vancouver are a prime example of how emotions can have the power to paralyze us if we're not careful.

Barrett is overturning two thousand years of "common sense" to help us give up our "cherished beliefs" that suggest we have a "triune brain," with three different parts for thinking, feeling, and survival.[1] Her research shows that we are not at the mercy of how well these alleged sides of the brain are firing on a given day. Emotions are not fixed circuits that get triggered. Rather, emotions are part of the brain's predictive system, guessing on the fly, based on what it thinks it's supposed to experience unless we reorient ourselves to work through discomfort and cultivate positive emotions. When I saw the height of the gondola, my brain quickly assessed threat and came up with the conclusion of danger, based on past sensations of heights. The risk of crashing was much lower than my brain wanted to lead me to believe, and luckily I was able to override my instincts to bolt and take a risk that turned out to be fun, funny, and one that helped me see I could manage anxiety, even if the initial flooding made it seem wayyyy out of reach.

> Nothing in life is to be feared, it is only to be understood. Now is the time to understand more, so that we may fear less.
>
> MARIE CURIE

Barrett explains: "You have the capacity to turn down the dial on emotional suffering and its consequences for your life by learning how to construct your experiences differently."[2] We don't have to stay stuck with Norah Jones' "Feelin' the Same Way" on repeat throughout our lifetime. Feldman is presenting us with an opportunity to retrain our brains and make shifts in our lives.

Identify Your Automations

Unwanted automations don't vanish into thin air because we want them to. It can be helpful to identify the types of automations we are most likely to fall into so that we become better equipped to regulate our emotions. Consider the following mind patterns that commonly arise:

- **Automations of prior experiences.** Feeling the same way you felt in a past situation, without accounting for current resources, coping skills, and experience. Emotions become mashed up and conflated, disrupting capacity to separate what's provoking you now vs. what's provoked you previously. This can cause fear in venturing out again given past cycles of anxiety, hurt, humiliation, disappointment, and loss. Take Janine, who began online dating after heartbreak but was instantly on the defensive with new partners because of prior disasters, leading to serious projection and frustration.

- **Automations of bias.** Believing negative stereotypes about a particular social identity group, being fearful of "other" and not seeing beyond what has been conditioned and indoctrinated. Take Archie, who's had little exposure to diversity and diversity of thought, grouping people into broad categories without getting to know them.

- **Automations of deficit.** Taking things personal, internalizing negative views of ourselves and one another, believing that issues are unresolvable and fixed. Take Wendell, who's so hard on himself that he thought anything that went wrong was his fault, oblivious to his strengths, gifts, and opportunities that equip him to navigate challenges.

- **Automations of social comparison.** Measuring our worth up against someone else's presentation of their lives. Afraid to admit vulnerability and risk being seen as less than. Social comparison can elicit feelings of jealousy and fan the flames of insecurity. Take Molly, who spends endless hours scrolling on social media, obsessing about how she measures up to what everyone else is posting.

- **Automations of self-protection.** Wanting to be right and convince everyone else of our positions. Struggles to accept varied viewpoints and that perceptions and beliefs run a wide gamut.

Invests time embroiled in conflict, evangelizing to others, rather than listening with curiosity, and searching for common ground. Take Darryl, who constantly pushes his beliefs, always agitated, and doubling down on his positions without seeing any nuances or being able to empathize with varied perspectives.

- **Automations of trauma.** Reliving trauma repeatedly, seeing recovery as insurmountable. Reluctant to face what's transpired. Take Duke, who spends endless time ruminating over horrific events, reluctant to reach out and seek proper support.

- **Automations of loneliness.** Struggling to feel seen and understood. Hesitant to risk vulnerability and put self out there. Take Bretta, who feels she can't be herself and that it's impossible to live her authentic identity and forge substantive relationships.

- **Automations of another time and place.** Romanticizing or regretting the past (hindsight bias: I should have done this or that differently) and fantasizing or anticipating the future, while having trouble being present in the now. Struggling to let go of what was and embrace what is now. Embodies a 'what if' life vs. 'what is' life. Take Kendi, who beats himself up for past decisions, stays stuck in regret, and believes it's "too late" for a new start, forgetting all he's learned could be leveraged in new situations for better outcomes.

- **Automations of overwork.** Operating in hyper-performance mode. Hooks into belief that what you do is who you are. Afraid to risk being seen as lazy, a weak link in the chain, or not demonstrating success. Take Maribel, who prides herself on her work ethic to the point that she stigmatizes herself when she's not in high octane mode day and night, basing her identity unhealthily around metrics of performance.

- **Automations of stagnation.** Staying stuck in a so-called "safe" place through maintaining outdated traditions or rigid routines. Risk averse and uninclined to gravitate towards novelty, variety, and growth. Take Mel, who has nearly the same daily routine and refuses to be flexible enough to shift beliefs, habits, and routines that could provide his brain with risks that nourish through novelty and variety.

- **Automations of labels.** Internalizing labels that have been assigned as part of identity. Subject to stereotype threat: living according to the erroneous projections upon social identity groups (i.e. a woman not being good at math, viewing a person of color as apt to be better at athletics vs. academics, stigmatizing a person with bipolar as hopelessly flawed). Take Ronnie, who struggled with school due to undiagnosed and misunderstood learning differences, still seeing himself in the negative light many of his early teachers did, despite overcoming incredible odds.

- **Automations of Family of Origin (FOO).** Imprisoned by forced ideology and ways of thinking. Strugglling to maintain healthy interdependence and let own views of the world guide behavior. Afraid to risk being left out, punished, or shunned. Take Gurt, who was gaslighted for years by her family and forced to go along to get along, often defaulting to feelings of guilt, unworthiness, and fear of being in trouble.

Untended automations make it hard for us to microdose bravery, and if left unfaced, we will expend endless unproductive energy instead of acting toward growth and taking risks that nourish. Fortunately, when we confront automations, it helps ensure they don't become permanent fixtures in our lives. We can regulate our emotions, thoughts, and behaviors so that we can free up energy to focus strategically on choosing risks worth taking, rather than repeating cycles of automation. As we work to regulate ourselves, we become better equipped to put up our *talk to the hand* signal when our automations get carried away and begin taking small steps towards mitigating their harmful hold on us.

Architect Your Sweet Spot Between
Worst- and Best-Case Scenario Brain

Worst-Case Scenario Brain is the lovechild of Eeyore and Tigger, governed by Murphy's Law and holding advanced certificates in Worst Imaginable Outcomes, Impending Doom, and Total Catastrophe. Its signature moves include marinating in intensive anxiety, spending excessive time locked in what-if mode, and imagining dreaded outcomes. On a good day, WCS helps us avoid toxic positivity and forced optimism, to provide the necessary counterbalance of caution, realism, and skepticism in our diet so we can calculate risk wisely and brace for challenges. When Worst-Case gets carried away, it becomes paralytic: the stew of anticipatory anxiety and unproductive thoughts can sabotage our chances for growth and fun. Remember that WCS Brain isn't literal, it's brought on by a depleted body budget, and our brain's predictive system of what we're "supposed to feel." Same is true for Best-Case, hunting for its instant dopamine rush by putting all its eggs into anticipating glorious future outcomes.

Best-Case Scenario Brain is the Great Expectations, ALL.HYPE! mind played by Will Farrell and *definitely an Enneagram 7* who owns nothing but rose-colored 3D glasses. Best-Case's signature move is romanticizing life with the excessive optimism of a *The Price is Right* contestant that moment they're told to come on downnnn. This mode of operation leaves us apt to become disappointed when big expectations fall flat. Think anticipation over a vacation that ends up being underwhelming, or a date where you expected magic that devolves into a scene from *Curb Your Enthusiasm*, or realizing that the profession you thought would make you the happiest of happy somehow shrank in the dryer of life and is now actually the wrong fit with itchy tags. Best-Case Scenario Brain excels in generating needed doses of enthusiasm and optimism, but has trouble modulating expectations, leading to constant disappointment and chasing.

Best-Case Scenario Brain is always on the hunt for more, with lofty expectations that create peril. In *The Molecule of More,* Daniel Z. Lieberman and Michael E. Long explain that we are conditioned to yearn for big breakthroughs and dopamine rushes, setting us up for massive letdowns. When our expectations in life are disproportionately high, we can come crashing. They say: "From dopamine's point of view, having things is uninteresting. It's only getting things that matters. If you live under a bridge, dopamine makes you want a tent. If you live in a tent, dopamine makes you want a house. If you live in the most expensive mansion in the world, dopamine makes you want a castle on the moon. Dopamine has no standard for good and seeks no finish line. The dopamine circuits in the brain can be stimulated only by the possibility of whatever is shiny and new, never mind how perfect things are at the moment. The dopamine motto is 'More.'"

> The only way to discover the limits of the possible is to go beyond them into the impossible.
> ARTHUR C. CLARKE

Finding our sweet spot between the Worst- and Best-Case Scenario Brain requires finesse. Imagining scenarios in such a binary, all-or-nothing way can disrupt progress towards greater regulation. We can renegotiate our relationship with such extremes by catching ourselves in the act when our wild imaginations are taking over, and work to change our automated responses. When we strive to be in a place of measuredness, we become more apt to be pleasantly surprised when things turn out better than expected and to avoid being wildly disappointed when they don't. It can help us find the balance between Murphy's Law— "Anything that can go wrong will go wrong"—and Gene's Law— "If anything can go well, it will." Working toward this sweet spot requires devotion to tending to our body budget, which can be difficult in the modern world where most of us are walking around sleep deprived, jacked up on coffee, and spending way more time on screens than in nature. Living a life where we can do well and be well hinges on our attention to this. We cannot let our automated, unchecked emotions dictate our life. Our brains' predictive system can be outmaneuvered, but not without microdosing bravery and confronting what's at hand.

Move From Automation to Regulation

We don't have to stay stuck in the extremes of automations. Consider the following concepts from leading scientists and thought leaders who are showing us how to shift toward regulation:

Craft new behavioral patterns. Daniel Kahneman warns against the human tendency to associate new information with existing patterns or thoughts, rather than creating new patterns for each new experience. Together with his late colleague Amos Tversky, Kahneman's Nobel Prize-winning work includes a model of heuristic thinking to help us recognize the limitations of perceptions.

Heuristics are strategies we use based on previous experiences to solve in the moment. Science reveals that this can lead to incorrect inferences and decision making. For example, a teacher limited to heuristic thinking who has a student with a behavior issue might be reminded of a past student with similar challenges without considering the unique circumstances of the present student.[3]

Build emotional agility. Susan David cautions against buying into thoughts and treating them like facts. An award-winning founder of the Institute of Coaching at McLean Hospital of Harvard Medical School and faculty at Harvard Medical School, David pioneered the concept of "emotional agility" and is recognized as one of the world's leading management thinkers. She asserts that we "pay too much attention to internal chatter and allow it to sap vital cognitive resources that could be put to better use."

David's research reveals that emotions are "data," and we do not have to take them on as directives that drive behavior. She emphasizes the importance of avoiding rigid and repetitive thinking. We can wield emotional agility to avoid getting tangled in the mire of reactivity.[4]

Leverage your capacity to rewire. Norman Doidge emphasizes that our brain is capable of changing itself. A psychiatrist, psychoanalyst, and researcher, Doidge's internationally recognized work highlights one of the most important breakthroughs in neuroscience: neuroplasticity. The brain is a living organ that changes its very own structure.

Doidge emphasizes that our thoughts can switch genes on and off, altering the anatomy of our brain. Rather than believing that we are set in our ways, that generational patterns can't be stopped, or that when trauma or difficulty occurs, there is irreversible damage, Doidge reminds us of our incredible capacity for resilience and rewiring.[5]

We can work toward emotional regulation to influence emotions in ourselves or others.[6] Barrett, Kahneman, Tversky, David, and Doidge all offer us important lessons. Rather than believing we are under the tyrannical rule of automations, we can learn to regulate. Emotional regulation relies on active monitoring and use of strategies to shift perspective and reframe situations.

> Our feelings, thoughts, and memories are all very complicated, but behaviors are very concrete. They are the 'control panel' for the rest of it.
>
> ANDREW HUBERMAN

Leverage Science to Make Room for Risk and Resilience

Emotional regulation can help us become savvier in choosing risks that nourish and build resilience. Confronting our unruly brains can help us move from automation to regulation. Here are some ways you can apply these groundbreaking discoveries:

Question your unhelpful automations. When unhelpful automations arise, resist the urge to engage in an in-depth analysis of your life. Start with the simple: Am I thirsty, hangry, overtired, or overworked? Am I basing my current reality on old memories? Am I operating out of a place of fear? Am I catastrophizing—putting things into the worst possible extreme disaster categories? (i.e. I did poorly on the test, next I'm going to fail out of school, never find a job, and end up an epic failure).

Practice self-compassion: Instead of defaulting to self-criticism, recognize your need for self-nurturing. Kristin Neff, a leader in the field of self-compassion, underscores how essential it is that we give ourselves the same measure of kindness and care that we'd give to a good friend.[7]

Step up your name game. When you are undergoing unpleasant sensations that manifest as dark emotions, work to name what is happening using a non-judgmental stance, one that avoids assigning blame and holds a neutral position. Barrett suggests we are capable of activating a process known as "emotional granularity."[8] This means that the more we can precisely name what's going on, the better equipped we are to recategorize our emotions and not let them own us.

Work to regulate. Recognize that you have the capacity to self-regulate. You are not at the mercy of automated sensations and emotions. Thoughts are data, not facts. You can reframe your initial responses that initially produce unwanted, unhelpful automations.

Invest in your bodily resources. Regulation is less likely when we are overtired, overworked, dehydrated, undernourished, or glued to the screen constantly. *Lifestyle medicine* involves active investment in well-being through proper sleep, nutrition, exercise, and healthy living.[9] When we make deposits toward our body budget, we are equipping ourselves to better overturn automations and find solutions in a positive direction.

Find the sweet spot between your Worst- and Best-Case Scenario Brain. Prior experiences do not dictate your now. You are not hardwired for certain responses. It is within your capacity to recategorize and regulate automated unhelpful responses with a new approach that allows you to avoid going into the same cycles of reactivity, anxiety, and distress.

We are not Pavlovian rats, subject to constant triggers and reactivity. We do not need to spend endless energy engaged in futile mental gymnastics. We can break cycles that consume us and prevent us from bravely facing challenges. We do not have to resign ourselves to unhelpful automations. It is within our power to disrupt these patterns. The new science reveals we are capable of making this shift. That we can move away from subscribing to outdated theories of emotions that emphasize hardwiring, triggering, and permanent injury to a place of learning to regulate our experiences and engagement with life.

Moving away from negative automations and choosing regulation can help us avoid flying by the seat of our emotional pants. Instead, we become equipped to reprogram our emotional responses in ways that allow us to take perspective and cope with what's at hand. When we focus on doing and being well, we can leverage the discoveries of modern brain science to avoid unwanted repeated emotional patterns. We can microdose bravery and optimize our skeptical and optimistic sides to initiate new ways of living.

You are not your automations. You are the regulator.

Regulate Your Emotions

Until you make the unconscious conscious, it will direct your life and you will call it fate.
CARL JUNG

Seek Regulation Over Automation

Strive for Emotional Regulation

Modern science reveals that we are not at the mercy of our primitive emotions—
that we can tend to our body budget and avoid automations that keep us from
doing and being well. There are a host of automations that require courage
to stand up against, including those of bias, deficit, prior experiences, social
comparison, self-protection, trauma, loneliness, another time and place,
overwork, stagnation, labels, and trends of families and communities of origin.
Luckily, automations are not fixed, and we can leverage our knowledge of
heuristics, emotional agility, and neuroplasticity to regulate our minds. We
can learn to question automations, practice self-compassion, draw upon
emotional granularity, and reframe them to prevent constant triggering and
reactivity.

Automations Check: Reflect

What types of anxiety-provoking moments have I been able to
work through?

In what areas of life am I most subject to unhelpful emotions and
automations?

What kinds of deposits am I making towards my body budget
through lifestyle medicine?

What types of adjustments in my routines might lead to greater resilience?

In what ways am I demonstrating emotional agility and granularity (avoiding rigid, reactive thinking)?

What helps or prevents me from staying in the now?

In what ways is self-compassion showing up as part of my practice?

Action Steps: Move from Automation to Regulation

You are not at the mercy of your emotions. Brain science shows us that we do not have to resign to unhelpful automations. Work to identify patterns and trends to help you make needed investments in your body budget. Focus your energy on not letting common automations dictate your well-being. Instead, work to regulate your mind, body, and soul through a variety of mindsets, skills, behaviors, and habits.

> **Identify automation traps.** Reflect—which automations come up for me most regularly? (Bias, deficit, social comparison, past experience, self-protection, trauma, loneliness, another place, overwork, stagnation, labels, or FOO.) What steps I could take to start catching myself doing this and choosing something different?

> **Work on emotional granularity.** Keep building language to describe your emotional experiences and work to pivot away from internalizing automations as hard data. Know that the framings you come up with have a dramatic impact on your capacity to regulate and move toward allostasis. Write out a challenging experience using vivid language to describe your emotions. What did you discover? Is there a safe person in your life you can share this with?

> **Become a generous, consistent investor in your body reserves.** Prioritize making regular deposits to bolster your body budget and stay calibrated through intentional lifestyle medicine practices. Tracing your health habits, including walks, sleep,

nutrition, hydration, and screen time is shown to help behavioral change stick. What system helps you stay organized with this? Is there a person in your life you can enlist for help?

Stay in the now. Resist yearnings for the past or engaging in hindsight bias—that you could have/should have controlled past outcomes. Identify what resources, assets, and tools you have at this moment that help you stay regulated such as gratitude, awe, and presence. Consider writing out the "what is" things you're thankful for.

> Between stimulus and response there is a space. In that space is our power to choose our response. In our response lies our growth and our freedom.
> VIKTOR E. FRANKL

Give yourself room to grow. Automations are powerful forces that do not disappear magically. Allow yourself time to strategize and implement new habits and keep track of how they are influencing you. Refinement and so-called "mess-ups" are part of the process of moving towards regulation. Be self-compassionate. Microdosing bravery is a practice that gains momentum over time. Write a note from your past self to your current self that reminds you how much progress you've made.

Session Four

You Are Not a Snowflake

There is a vast difference between positive thinking and existential courage.
BARBARA EHRENREICH

Choose Resilience Over Resignation

L egend has it that anyone born after 1990 is a snowflake, and the younger you are, the more likely you are to melt during the firestorms of life. I think about this when I look at the picture of my late Grandma Jennie atop my desk, the one that always gets the same "OMG! You are her carbon copy" reaction.

This is true. Same mischievous smile, chocolate eyes, wavy dark hair, and crooked pinky finger. Both terrible drivers. Obsessed with oysters, word games, and poetry.

I take it as a compliment when people notice our similarities. She was a generous, quick-witted, beautiful Italian woman, the definition of resilience. Jennie was nine when her father died in the Spanish flu pandemic of 1918. She and her siblings were forced to leave school, go to work, and live off pickled vegetables they had personally grown and canned themselves. *In mason jars.* The ones we now tout with smoothies and cocktails on Instagram and Pinterest. Jennie and her sibs would probably find the mason jar trend suspect, and that there's such a thing as "foodies" who pay big money for fermented foods downright annoying.

In March 2020, When COVID-19 first hit Boston, Massachusetts, I had a hard time coming to terms with working virtually from my Pottery Barn desk in my high-rise apartment. I worried whether I'd stockpiled enough acai packets, kimchi, and kombucha from Trader Joe's. And how long Whole Foods delivery might take.

I wasn't sure whether two MacBooks, a desktop, iPhone, large screen TV, Alexa, and Siri would be enough to keep me company and some version of occupied/connected/entertained/sane. I figured I could make it through the estimated two weeks we figured the pandemic would last. My busy travel season was approaching, and there's few things I hate more than cancelled plans.* At first, My Google searches looked something like this:

How late does Whole Foods deliver?

Pause Rent the Runway subscription?

Fun things to do in Seattle . . .

Tickets for *Hamilton* NY May 2020 . . .

Distance between Dublin and Netherlands . . .

Glennon Doyle new book release . . .

Soon after, my searches turned to:

How deadly is Coronavirus?

Can you get COVID twice?

Who is considered non-essential?

---

* Actual journal entry, January 1, 2020: Resolve to NOT "make/break plans this year . . ." Life has a strange sense of humor, yes?

What are the rules of shelter-in-place?

Is it safe to take a walk with a friend?

What are the best foods to keep you alive for long periods of time?

Can the curve be flattened?

How long do vaccines take to develop?

#Everythingscancelled starts trending on Twitter. We're instructed to shelter in place. States of emergency are declared. How are we supposed to "socially distance" without losing our minds? Didn't the Universe know how lonely and tethered to technology we already were?

The sobering reality sets in. Lockdowns. Rapid spread. People are dying. Not enough ventilators. Vaccines take time. Economies are crashing. Violence erupts. No promises of any of this madness ending soon. Things look and feel bleak.

I try to summon my grandmother's strength. I think about her mom, Eliza Prendini, who immigrated by herself from Bologna, a city in Northern Italy, to the United States when she was sixteen. The chest Eliza used to carry her belongings to America sits next to my desk, where I'm madly scrolling through my iPhone trying to figure out if the world will ever be okay again.

I stare at Jennie's picture. We resemble each other in looks and personality, but our life circumstances are dramatically different. I was able to earn a terminal degree and publish. Jennie had a third-grade education but could complete the *New York Times* crossword puzzle and answer all the questions on Jeopardy! without Google, something I cannot do. I've had my ACL repaired by the doctor of the Boston Celtics. When Jennie broke her knee after a near-death car crash, it was up to her to work to straighten her leg, there was no surgery or physical therapy in sight. A heavy pocketbook and a few shots of ginger brandy did the trick.

I rub Jennie's picture for luck, like it's the Buddha's belly. I want to invoke the hardy spirits of my family line. The shock of COVID is setting in. It feels like nothing will ever be the same.

Pictures ofscary red amoeba blotches and people wearing masks flood our feeds. Everything shuts down. The museums. Live shows. Sporting events. Yoga studios. Restaurants. Businesses. Many of them never reopen. There is carnage everywhere, and comfort is hard to find in the polarized, fear mongering, animosity-driven brouhaha. The sickness goes far beyond COVID.

How did Jennie's generation cope?

They weathered the Spanish flu, the Great Depression, and World War II without therapy. There weren't any mindfulness apps to help them breathe. No streamed yoga classes, Fitbits reminding them to get up and walk, crisis hotlines, or books on resilience. No podcasts. There was no TikTok, Houseparty, or Zoom cocktail parties. No Netflix binging, Facebook feeds, virtual book clubs, online karaoke, or Candy Crush. Maybe the "lack" of modern escapes gave them an advantage, allowing for less noise, clearer thinking, and tapping into the creative process. Perhaps this allowed for greater resourcefulness, presence, and capacity to maneuver the realities at hand without any quick escape doors. Maybe not being tethered to screens gave them an edge. They knew people were dying but they didn't have to relive it and be blasted with the blowtorch of anticipatory anxiety every waking minute; they were pre-doom scrolling and knowing every last political position of every friend you've ever known.

According to snowflake folklore, if we lived 100 years ago under this kind of heat without our phones, we would've pulled a hard Frosty the Snowman without any hopes for coming back to life. Allegedly we Crocs and Doc Martens-wearing folk don't even know what bootstraps are, never mind being able to pull ourselves up by them (did you know that some clever, smartass Z figured out that it is physically impossible to pull oneself up by the bootstraps?!) How will we ever compare to the strength and fortitude of generations past who walked miles uphill in the snow, surviving off Moxie soda, scraps of bread, and chicken liver, living barebones before minimalism ever became a thing? They grew their own organic food and would be horrified that anyone would pay nine dollars for a four ounce container of microgreens at Whole Foods. Would the quintessential advice of their generation be relevant or even a stitch helpful? We've heard the mantras repeated at every family gathering since we were toddlers:

- **Suck it up.** Don't let anyone see you sweat. Bite your lip. Don't be such a wimp.

- **Tough it out.** Stop complaining. Just be happy. It could be a lot worse. You don't know how bad we had it.

- **Stop being such a snowflake.** Get over it. You're going to melt if you don't grow a thicker skin.

These old adages are of little comfort given the differences in our times. Unfortunately, when negative depictions of resilience bombard us continually, we run the risk of internalizing them. When we feel like we're not resilient, we start believing we're not, and stop taking actions that help us grow it. If we listen to the snowflake theories about how soft and coddled we are, we would think that there is NO WAY ON THIS EARTH that we can make it through any kind of crisis—whether the COVID-19 pandemic or the many other forms of trauma and strife we face across our lifetime.

> Not everything that is faced can be changed, but nothing can be changed until it is faced.
>
> JAMES BALDWIN

Contextualize Your Resilience

"Special snowflake" and "OK boomer" tensions often turn nasty. Everyone bickers over which generation is tougher and who has it worse. Comparing such starkly different contexts with unique pressures and variables is futile. Each generation has different things to escape from and different means of escaping. Every advantage one generation experiences is a trade-off for the other:

- Pandemic with limited ability to know global effects and less advances in science and technology vs. pandemic with infodemic: incessant news and social media cycles lambasting distressing messages 24-7, stirring up distrust of evidence and severe polarization over merits of science and proper course of action.

- Global humanitarian crises are less known with less advanced solutions available vs. global humanitarian crises are known with more evidence-based solutions available but with a lack of consensus, leadership, and collective will to effectively implement.

- More affordable living, proportionate living wage, and equitable wealth, less commercialism (no Amazon), family businesses mainstays within communities vs. billionaire dominance, mass consumerism, consumption, and corporate greed.

- Avoidance of discussion of politics, religion, and sex vs. knowing the play-by-play of what everyone is up to, day and night.

- Limited access to college vs. pressure to hyper-perform at top-tier institutions to be viable in today's market, with crushing levels of student debt.

- Overt bullying in school and peer pressure within the confines of school and local realm vs. non-stop social media bullying, FOMO, and pressure to promote one's own brand from a young age with the entire internet.

- Keeping up with the neighbors, no mani/pedis and designer wardrobes vs. having to keep up with celebs, ready to jump on the set of Justin Bieber video at a moment's notice.

- Not allowed to talk about feelings, limited access and understanding of mental health vs. analysis paralysis, tyranny of pop psychology, and overmedicalization of normal within a decontextualized view of resilience.

- Limited entertainment and enrichment options vs. overscheduling and endless options for pacification, distraction, and indulgence.

- Prescriptive (and potentially oppressive) religious constructs vs. fluid spirituality and humanistic values and consciousness.

- People connected to their neighbors and extended family vs. loneliness is "the new smoking" as modern health risk, globalism, individualism, and hyper-performance impacts isolation and access to community with shared values.

There are plenty of tradeoffs for each generation. Life has always been hard, and it always will be, in different ways. The battle over which generation is most resilient will likely continue to be hastily fought. The fight is marked by resistance to the changes the new generations are proposing that feel threatening to those who built, inherited, and endured those very systems and institutions. Evolution is as inevitable as the resulting tensions. But allowing such tensions to govern can prevent us from harnessing the lessons we have to teach one another. Resilience isn't exclusively yesteryear, it is also now . . .

Across time and space, regardless of what we are enduring, we're a species wired for adaptation.[1] This is clear within times that we have the scientific literacy to precisely name it, and it was true when we didn't. One of the prevailing myths is that we are either born resilient, or not. We now know that resilience is something that we can cultivate. Rather than it being a fixed state, research is proving that resilience is a process over time, one which we all have the power to influence through deliberate action.[2]

It is now understood that our mindsets, habits, and behaviors can help us grow resilience. Every one of us have what are known as "protective factors" in our lives.[3] There are dozens of protective factors that have been identified through rigorous research.[4] These mechanisms can move us from feeling like we're about to melt to knowing how to withstand and not resign as snowflakes who can't survive tumultuous conditions. Some of the most protective elements include authentic relationships, conscious contribution, adaptability, creative zest, spiritual practices, humor, a sense of purpose, and self-compassion.[5] When we mobilize and engage with these factors, they can help shield and sustain us through challenges. This starts with paying attention to what's right in front of us.

Pay Attention to Grow Your Resilience

The Invisible Gorilla Experiment conducted at Harvard University is well-known in psychology for its lessons about human tendency to miss the obvious.[6] Research subjects were asked to view a video of people—three in white shirts and three in black passing basketballs around. Their instructions were to silently count the number of passes made by the people wearing white shirts. A person in a gorilla suit enters the middle of the circle for nine full seconds. Only half of the participants noticed the gorilla. The experiment reveals that we are inclined to miss things that are right in front of us.

When it comes to resilience, Invisible Gorillas are the protective factors that surround us, but we're often too busy glaring at the basketball passes—the problems swirling—to see them. When our attention is diverted to solely raw emotions, turmoil, and fear, we miss seeing *what is* working well. Here are some types of Invisible Gorillas we can stay on the lookout for in our daily lives to help us take risks that nourish and build our resilience:

People in our lives who care about us and are willing to help. Many of us are much more willing to give help than receive it, and thus overlook people right in front of us who want to support us.

Resources we can tap into. In our modern world, there's an abundance of excellent information and programming that can help us be well and do well.

Prior experience. As life goes on, we grow in wisdom, perspective, and experience. We can sometimes suffer from the "curse of knowledge" where we minimize the value of our knowledge set, thinking everyone knows what we know, and miss chances to transfer certain skills and understanding to a wide range of situations.

Strengths and assets. Society emphasizes deficits and problems so heavily that it can cause us to completely overlook the strengths in ourselves and one another that help us take strategic risks and build resilience.

To maximize the Invisible Gorillas in your life, it can help to reflect on your comfort level with the following:

- Saying what you really want/think/feel.

- Being an accountable ally for BIPOC/LGBTQ communities.

- Leaning into discomfort—rather than escaping.

- Setting boundaries.

- Pursuing things you've always wanted to try.

- Having fun, even when hard things are going on.

- Working to break through traumas/intergenerational cycles.

- Disclosing personal details within safe and trusted company to build solidarity and support to aid healing and recovery processes.

The Invisible Gorilla Experiment is the ultimate cautionary tale and metaphor for our lives. The IGs are always showing up, flailing their hands, nudging us to look beyond what we are conditioned to see. We cannot be unsuspecting participants in the experiment of life, attending only to what we're told to attend to, all while missing important cues to see beyond. When we only focus on what's erosive, what's not working well, and the swarming problems that infest our lives, we increase the risk of resigning. When we fall prey to confirmation bias, our brain's tendency to only pay attention to what we believe is true, we ignore contrary data that could help us see a bigger picture.[7] We will be more likely to give up and miss the chance to microdose bravery and fully adopt a *resilient identity.*

Own Your Own Indomitable Spirit

Identity is defined as the fact of being who or what you are. A resilient identity embodies an *indomitable spirit.* The Latin translation of indomitable is "unable to be tamed." Originally, when it was first used in the 1600s, it was synonymous with "wild," but this connotation shifted from problematic to virtuous. By the 1800s, the term was used for people whose bravery and persistence helped them succeed in hard circumstances.

Each of us can build a resilient identity. This starts with rejecting antagonistic snowflake folklore. That when it's hot, it's okay to say it's hot, and to join forces with those who are willing to do the same. And that we don't need to keep our eye on the ball everyone tells us to watch, but to see the whole picture in front of us and capitalize on opportunities for small, strategic acts of bravery. Doing so allows us to avoid resignation to our raw emotions and worries, and instead harness energy that spurs on courage.

We all have the opportunity to consistently take agency to redefine resilience and determine the kinds of nourishing risks available to us each day. We need to remember that keg standing risk is not what makes us strong. Sensitivity has a bad rap, but showing vulnerability is one of the bravest acts, despite popular snowflake opinions that we must follow a certain method to be truly brave.

Microdosing bravery is a way to keep nourishing your indomitable spirit. You hold your values as central and refuse to be tamed by society's pressures for grand gestures of resilience. It's the small risks within our relationships and ways of showing up in the world that help us grow resilience. You become willing to embrace feeling unsettled, rather than risk settling for a meat-and-potatoes, business-as-usual life. This path is harder, but worth taking. You pay attention to cues from Invisible Gorillas that flag you down and encourage you to:

1. **Put yourself out there.** Because you value connection, you keep an open heart and mind. You risk being hurt over risking being lonely or isolated.

2. **Tell the truth.** Because you value honesty, you tell your truths. You risk popularity over risking inauthenticity.

3. **Own your strengths.** Because you value active contribution, you know you cannot operate from a deficit lens. You risk going after what you most care about rather than stewing in fear you're not enough.

4. **Be accountable.** Because you value being an anti-racist, anti-sexist, anti-classist, anti-homophobic, and anti-dominant group centric individual, you work tirelessly to unlearn bias and fight for justice. You risk looking bad and forego personal comfort so you can see and do better.

5. **Take psychological agency.** Because you value growth, you stay agile in your learning/unlearning/relearning process. You risk feeling unsettled and having to change original perceptions and positions over clinging to rigid, cliche, conditioned automations of thought and behavior.

6. **Claim your indomitable spirit.** Because you value creativity, you take psychological agency to live with full fervor. You risk being critiqued or alienated instead of taming yourself and accepting someone else's template.

7. **Ask for help.** Because you value progress, you find support even when it's hard. You don't pretend to be normal when life is far from it. You don't internalize snowflake stigma just because you need help. You risk vulnerability over suffering and martyrdom.

8. **Ignite freedom.** Because you value liberation, you work to break free. You risk penalty over passivity. You stand up for what's right and stay on the side of dismantling social ills and bringing positive and productive influence.

Across generations, there has always been pressure to put up a front, rather than take the risk to share our truths and ask for help. But this is a signature risk of resilience. People who build spaces of trust where they let others see their sweaty meltdowns are more likely to be resilient than those who think they have to show up as hardened ice sculptures who never show emotion and keep to themselves.

Resilience is generated when we move from "me" to "we." Hiding only erodes resilience and weakens our bonds with one another, the very thing that can cement our indomitable spirit and keep us from total ruin. Pretending we are "fine" is not an act of courage, nor will it truly protect us from the gnawing pangs of thinking that we're the only ones. The biggest lie our minds can tell is that we are the only ones when the only way to break free is to tell our truths.

We have advanced our understanding of resilience significantly since previous generations. This doesn't mean that their examples don't have something to teach us. In addition, we can transition away from paradigms that encourage silence and resignation when we don't "feel strong" and instead point us to looking for what we can harness within community, to cultivate resilience. When we stay on the lookout for Invisible Gorillas, we will be less likely to buckle under the weight of circumstances, even when they're dire and grim. We will know we are not alone and will microdose bravery consistently to strengthen our indomitable spirit.

You are not a snowflake. You are resilient.

To be hopeful in bad times is not just foolishly romantic. It is based on the fact that human history is a history not only of cruelty, but also of compassion, sacrifice, courage, kindness. What we choose to emphasize in this complex history will determine our lives. If we see only the worst, it destroys our capacity to do something. If we remember those times and places—and there are so many—where people have behaved magnificently, this gives us the energy to act, and at least the possibility of sending this spinning top of a world in a different direction. And if we do act, in however small a way, we don't have to wait for some grand utopian future. The future is an infinite succession of presents, and to live now as we think human beings should live, in defiance of all that is bad around us, is itself a marvelous victory.

HOWARD ZINN

SESSION FOUR WORKSHEET

Rethink Resilience

I can be changed by what happens to me. But I refuse to be reduced by it.
MAYA ANGELOU

Seek Resilience Over Resignation

Focus on Strengths and Context, Not Antiquated Folklore

Generational comparisons can lead to tensions and inhibit us from proper evaluation of social context and ways we can cultivate resilience. Despite prevailing snowflake theories, we as a species have always been wired for adaptation even in the most trying of times. Antiquated ideals about what it means to look resilient can detract our attention away from what we need to do to build it. Sucking it up, toughing it out, or growing a thicker skin focuses attention on individual levels of resilience rather than contextualized, collective levels. Today's times require us to consciously evaluate the impact of the culture we are raised in on our resilience. When we start to pay close attention to ways we can build resilience, we can take the risk of microdosing bravery—taking small steps to growing, giving, and living our deeply held values. This helps us channel an indomitable spirit that allows us to put ourselves out there after loss and heartbreak, tell our truths, own our strengths, be accountable, take psychological agency, claim our resilient identity, ask for help, and ignite freedom.

Snowflake Check: Reflect

What messages have I received about my capacity to withstand heat?

What types of Invisible Gorillas, i.e., protective factors, strengths, resources, and opportunities to practice microdosing bravery are available to me?

What causes me to feel like resigning?

How is adaptability showing up in my life?

Am I willing to ask for help when I need it?

What beliefs support or inhibit my indomitable identity?

Action Steps: Move from Resignation to Resilience

You are not a special snowflake when you are reacting to the heat around you. You can harness your indomitable spirit and take on a resilient identity through deliberate microdoses of bravery.

1. **Don't compare with prior generations.** Perhaps you have experienced shaming from prior generations or even FOO members telling you to be stronger and braver without accounting for today's context. Take some time to write out some rebuttals to these unhelpful messages and consider what lessons from the past can be beneficial to you.

2. **Take your eye off the ball.** Stop hyper-focusing on passes around you that distract you from seeing your capacity to cultivate your resilient identity. Keep track of what is pulling you away from feeling strong and taking risks that lead to nourishing your growth and contribution. Stay on the lookout for distractions and notice what helps you overcome them.

3. **Find your Invisible Gorillas.** Pay attention to the strengths, resources, and assets you have and use them as fuel to enact microbraveries. Keep your IG's well nourished so you can sustain yourself during tumultuous times. Identify specific activities that keep you from wanting to give up.

4. **Seek community.** Resilience happens in community, not isolation. Identify two to three people in your life who can encourage you to claim your indomitable identity. Share your goals and ask for accountability support.

5. **Use humor to gain perspective.** Watch Leslie Jones's *Time Machine* and Sarah Silverman's *A Speck of Dust*. What points resonate? What would your past self say to your current self? Future self?

> You can choose courage, or you can choose comfort, but you cannot choose both.
>
> BRENÉ BROWN

6. **Immerse yourself in well-being resources.** See "Recommendations for Identifying Risks Worth Taking and Growing Resilience" at the end of the book.

Session Five

You Are Not Your Trauma

Beneath the surface of the protective parts of trauma survivors there exists an undamaged essence, a Self that is confident, curious, and calm, a Self that has been sheltered from destruction by the various protectors that have emerged in their efforts to ensure survival. Once those protectors trust that it is safe to separate, the Self will spontaneously emerge, and the parts can be enlisted in the healing process.

BESSEL A. VAN DER KOLK

Choose Truth Over Hiding

Jeremy is sitting in my office clutching onto Tara Westover's *Educated* book like it is holy text, reciting passages with equal parts relief and horror. His voice signals he's made a breakthrough. Jeremy tells me that while, unlike Westover, he didn't grow up enduring repeated trauma in a junkyard in Idaho, he relates to the powerful emotions in her story.

Westover's *New York Times* bestselling book seemed to have similar effects worldwide. Raised in a survivalist home with abusive and neglectful parents, Westover found the courage to take the risks that nourished her and eventually led her to break free and become a prestigious scholar.[1] She was named one of *Time*'s 100 most influential people of 2019.[2]

Finding her way through this was no small feat, nor was it glamorous. Beyond the magazine covers, prestigious awards, speaking invitations across the world, and rave endorsements from Barack Obama and Oprah Winfrey, Westover's courage to take the risks to stand up to her family came at a price. Still, she knew that the risks of not speaking out were greater.

Jeremy told me that he related to this. He'd faced both a chaotic home environment and violation by the one adult he'd trusted, a coach whom everyone adored, leaving him without the sense of safety he felt he needed to disclose the abuse. He couldn't risk telling and not being believed, or worse, blamed. Jeremy told me that besides the serious flooding symptoms he experienced, including flashbacks, panic attacks, and nightmares, one of the worst consequences of the trauma was his risk aversion.

Playing it "safe" became a way of life for Jeremy, given how out of control his early years were. He realized that he wasn't living fully, with only a few superficial friendships where he kept his guard up due to the shame that piled up from his early years. Still, the thought of stretching himself made him cringe. That's why he was sitting in my office, clutching the book with its signature oversized red pencil on the cover, trying to figure out how to find nourishment through risk instead of avoidance that was only giving him a false sense of control.

Jeremy knew he wasn't ready for sweeping changes, but the concept of microdosing risk resonated. He began taking small steps to nourish himself through new activities, relationships, and means of healing that included attending a support group for survivors of abuse, drawing, and volunteering at a local dog shelter. These positive changes gave Jeremy the momentum to undergo Eye Movement and Desensitization and Reprocessing (EMDR) therapy with a new therapist. EMDR is an evidence-based trauma intervention, something he admits he would never have thought of or been ready for without those first important microdoses of risk.

Understand the Nuances of Trauma

While the kind of psychological and physical abuse that Westover and Jeremy faced are far too common, there are also as many causes and consequences of trauma as there are items on a Cheesecake Factory® menu.

Gone are the days where we think that trauma is reserved for those serving in combat or experiencing atrocities perpetrated by disturbed people.[3] Researchers and trauma specialists suggest the longer we live, the greater the chance we are going to experience some form of it. According to the Substance Abuse and Mental Health Services Administration (SAMHSA), 61 percent of men and 51 percent of women report having had at least one trauma in their lifetime, even before the global pandemic,[4] which has inflicted trauma in so many shapes and forms, you could fill a library with books on it.

Knowing how different levels of trauma[5] could impact you can help. "Small t" trauma involves circumstances that are disruptive but not a permanent threat to safety or life itself. They are seen as rites of passage that are "easier" to recover from, like:

- Adjusting to challenging life changes such as moving or a new job

- Dealing with conflict within, or the ending of, a relationship

- Struggling through financial or legal battles

The No Big Deal Approach is a common reaction to small t's. These bumps of life become so normalized we don't realize the importance of attending to our emotional healing process. This is what makes them insidious, because when they cluster over time their effects can creep up on us, like an unsuspecting frog in slowly boiling water. They can become a big deal if we completely dismiss the cumulative impact of little ts in our lives without stopping to tap into the right resources. It's not to say that we have to crawl into the fetal position when things go wrong, but it's important not to No Big Deal our ways through moments that are honestly dark and hard to deal with.

"Big Ts" are the louder, more obvious counterpart. They are sustained through big blows that bring about severe distress and disruption, like natural catastrophes, terrorism, and sexual assault. Large Ts are also prolonged stressors like ongoing war, pandemics, abuses of power, violence, neglect, or interpersonal abuse.

Big Ts can be met with a Poor Thing Approach. This involves automatically slapping on a PTSD label, expecting the Worst Imaginable response to trauma as the likely outcome. This Poor Thing Approach is conveyed through sympathetic, patronizing messages to the person(s) suffering trauma, causing more harm than good.

In other cases, Big Ts can also go untended because they can prompt a Total Avoidance Approach, keeping the person unready and unable to face the trauma, remaining in a state of immobilization and disassociation rather than making space for risks worth taking that nourish and grow resilience.

Know the Difference Between PTSD and Acute Stress

Acute stress is generally short term but requires attention to prevent escalation. Symptoms of distress that last three days or more are common within the first month of trauma. This can involve unsettling flashbacks, depersonalization, and avoidance of people and situations. This is prime time to seek out help to prevent the symptoms from escalating.

Post-traumatic stress disorder (PTSD) is generally long term, but its effects can be treated and lessened over time. PTSD involves intense, disturbing, and prolonged thoughts and feelings related to the trauma experience that last for over a month and sometimes years. It can involve reliving the event, avoidance, feelings of sadness, fear, detachment, and/or anger. It can involve involuntary memories, flashbacks, and intrusive thoughts.

PTSD is marked by the significant distress and problems in functioning it causes. Even so, intervention can dramatically improve symptoms and healing can be facilitated, especially when we're supported in expanding our tolerance for risk.

Researchers and clinicians devote endless hours trying to understand why some people seem to remain resilient in the face of trauma, with few "symptoms," while others experience severe disruption and full-on post-traumatic stress disorder. How can someone like Tara Westover who never went to school find her way to Harvard? How do people who've been through the unspeakable find their voice again? In my work, I've seen this consistent theme: being able to reengage with risk is essential to the healing process. No Big Deal, Poor Thing, and Total Avoidance Approaches to trauma not only block healing, but they can make things worse.

Guard Against Unhelpful Responses to Trauma

Negative external responses to trauma are often loaded: sometimes they are because of underdeveloped communication skills and someone genuinely not knowing what to say or do. In other instances, someone may not have your best interests in mind. Disclosing trauma can seem like one of the hardest risks to take, but is worth it. If you've gone through trauma, it can be helpful to know the psychology behind behavior to help you continue self-advocating until you find safe ears. If you are the listener, this understanding can help you avoid common unhelpful responses:

Denial/imperative for protection

This *imperative for protection* involves gross denial. This response has been cited by many studies as equally and often more damaging than the original traumatic event(s) themselves.[6] Too often, those who've endured trauma face serious consequences in speaking their truths.

When the courage to come forward is met with scrutiny and scolding, it perpetuates and reinforces the trauma. Not being believed is a major blow to psyche and soul. This kind of *gaslighting*, a form of psychological abuse where a person's sanity and perceptions of reality are questioned and negated, is rooted in deep primitive instincts to maintain secrecy and "protect."

Leaving trauma(s) unvalidated and unspoken to protect the family name, reputation of a church, image of the perpetrator, agenda of the group, or even the individual affected can seem like a way to avoid pain, but it often makes it worse. The risk of telling is worth it, since the risk of greater shame, regret, and missed opportunities for healing is the tradeoff that comes with secrecy.

It's exactly what Sur-THRIVER Unleashed® podcast host Rena Romano speaks to in her platform for survivors of sexual abuse and assault. Romano emphasizes that "Fear will challenge you, but regret will haunt you." She walks her talk: Romano is a sexual abuse survivor who broke the imperative for protection and bravely came forward, even appearing on Oprah

Winfrey and delivering a TEDx talk to encourage silence to be broken. She asserts that "If healing begins by telling, then we must make telling safe."[7] Too often, people who are abused are met with the exact opposite of what facilitates healing:

You're lying or exaggerating. This can't be true. This couldn't have happened to you/me.

It could always be worse. Or "At least . . ."

It must be your/my fault.

That kind of person would never do that. You/I must have "asked for it."

Don't tell anyone.

Don't bring shame to the family/institution name.

Don't break the silence. This will do more harm than good.

Labeling and exaggerated assumptions

On the other extreme, when people who experience trauma are met with the patronizing Poor Thing Approach, the pity they encounter suggests that the injuries they have encountered are irreconcilable. This approach of grouping people who go through as trauma needing pity is not only contradictory to modern brain science, but a major inhibitor to healing.

Whether trauma is denied, or branded as a stamp of automatic doom, these types of responses serve to reinforce rather than help us work through traumatic experiences. When trauma comes to light, it is essential that the horror of the experiences is validated, while at the same time the capacity to heal is emphasized. These truths must be presented simultaneously; ones that allow for empathy, concern, and proper care. The space to heal must be co-created by the person experiencing the trauma and their support(s), without any whiffs of patronization. Statements like this must be avoided:

You poor thing. I feel bad for you.

Things will never get better.

You're broken goods.

You're doomed for life.

It will never get better.

Your symptoms define and dictate your life.

Oblivion/unawareness of cumulative effect

It's not uncommon for those who are traumatized to interpret their behaviors as strange instead of seeing them as directly connected to their traumatic responses. This is part of why trauma can go untreated for so long. Untreated trauma can impact us on emotional, psychological, and spiritual levels, as well as have negative physical ramifications. In *The Body Keeps the Score,* trauma expert Bessel van der Kolk emphasizes the ways unattended trauma wreaks havoc on our entire system. He underscores the significance of relationships to help us work through the complexity of trauma and keep it from ravaging our mind, body, and soul.[8]

Resilience researchers Ilia Karatsoreos and Bruce McEwen offer hope that we are capable of adjusting to the stressors within our environments, returning to a state of internal and physiological equilibrium, even in the face of trauma.[9] Allostasis helps us to anticipate needs and prepare to satisfy them before they arise. This is good news for us: we don't have to stay stuck in states of chaos and flooding, but to find balance, we must determine which risks are worth taking, to help maximize safety and recovery. Sharing trauma is a risk worth taking: this can be the beginning of growing resilience and optimal healing.

Reach for Resilience

Resilience used to be seen as something we were born with or not, but now we know that it can be cultivated through specific mindsets, behaviors, and activities that help lessen the damaging impact of trauma, especially in the context of safe and caring relationships.

As you think about your own trauma recovery process, whether small t or Big T, remember that we all have forces present in our lives, known as protective factors that help us build resilience and heal. The Search Institute, a nonprofit that researches positive youth development has done amazing work in tracking over six million adolescents to identify "developmental assets" that serve as protective factors that cultivate resilience.

These assets aren't just important in our teenager years. The work at the Search Institute aligns with resilience research that is proven to help us well beyond the early years. These assets include the presence of caring people, therapy, therapeutic activities, positive values, identity, and feeling safe, respected, valued, and valuable.[10]

Another vital way of understanding trauma recovery comes through using a trauma-informed lens. This involves a way of approaching trauma that acknowledges that trauma is everywhere we turn, and that its effects shouldn't be taken lightly.

Trauma-informed specialists emphasize that a trauma-informed lens can make a big difference: within a home, school, community, and society. This lens must be rooted within a sense of safety, trustworthiness, transparency, peer support, collaboration, mutuality, empowerment, voice, and choice that accounts for cultural, historical, and gender issues to help actively resist re-traumatization.[11]

Use Validating Loops to Promote Healing

The way that we speak (or don't speak) about trauma has a significant impact on how we are able to cope with its aftermath. Validating feedback loops, those that provide safety for disclosure, can be a crucial component of healing, like:

I believe you.

I hope you know how brave you are.

I'm so sorry for what you've gone through.

It's not your fault. Perpetrators come disguised in many ways. The most "unsuspecting" can be the most suspect.

Let's get the right help.

Coming out of secrecy is your first step towards healing.

I'm proud of you.

Healing is within reach.

Communication matters when it comes to trauma, and yet many of us (even those with clinical degrees) can struggle to find the right words in moments when someone discloses. One of my favorite sayings is that *awkward conversations can turn out to be the best conversations,* because that's often the turning point toward help.

That was true for me in my undergraduate years. I wasn't exactly the textbook PTSD and depression case study. I was known on my campus for being a bit of a character, sometimes getting in trouble for being too loud and hyperactive, always egging my friends on to do "missions" with me, things like dressing up in costumes on a random Tuesday and going bowling or pitching a tent square in the center of campus to hang out and eat snacks as if we were on a camping expedition. I wrote humor columns for the school newspaper under the alias Garbanzo because I had a low-key obsession with chickpeas (everyone knew it was me: I was the only one weird enough to do this). I had a double major, minor, and four part-time jobs. I was known for being fun, funny, and definitely weird. The fact that I was struggling was well hidden.

Luckily, my A&P professor, Anne, suspected there was something more behind my antics and big smile. She pulled me over after lab one day, and asked simply, "Are you okay?" I was mortified, quickly gave a pat answer, then bolted to my dorm. But soon I realized that I was suffering in silence; her act of caring nudged me to talk to my mom about it, then get a therapist and begin my working on healing from trauma. I often wonder what Anne or my first therapist Patti would think if they knew that their actions had such an influence in not only saving my life, but then going on to influence my whole life's work.

To be validating, we don't need to have a clinical degree. Many times, it's about asking someone if they're okay, and if not, being willing to be present with them, to not to dismiss, patronize, or avoid what they're saying, but to hear pain and help them find their way to the right resources. One of

> In times of pain,
> when the future
> is too terrifying to
> contemplate and
> the past too painful
> to remember, I
> have learned to pay
> attention to right
> now. The precise
> moment I was in
> was always the only
> safe place for me.
>
> JULIA CAMERON

my favorite tools, the V-A-R from Active Minds (a non-profit devoted to reducing stigma), is designed for this very purpose. The V stands for Validate, as in statements such as "It sounds like what you've gone through is really hard." The A stands for Appreciation, as in "I am so glad you had the courage to tell me." R stands for Refer, meaning you help brainstorm possible resources and strategies to tap into and promote healing, as in "I have a friend whose therapist is supposed to be amazing."[12]

Grow Your Resilience

Westover's recovery in the face of significant and repeated trauma defies odds, serving as a prime example of brain plasticity, resilience, and the benefits of microdosing bravery. She started slowly by coming out of isolation, seeking education, and forming community; allowing her to slowly build courage and strength that led her to eventually speak truth to power and abusers.

Still, given the wide spectrum and complexity of trauma and its effects, it is vital to recognize that there is no one size fits all. We can't just steal Westover's playbook for recovery, nor should we romanticize the outcomes of her extraordinary journey.

Healing and recovery are incredibly complex processes that rely on a host of factors that we can leverage over time. Trauma is serious. It is a reality and risk of modern living, especially given the pandemic and resulting aftermath. Whether small t or Big T, we need to understand that, left unattended, it can provoke destructive effects. Healing from trauma is not linear or formulaic, but there are many concrete steps toward it:

Seek proper care. This cannot be emphasized enough. Do not self-diagnose. It is vital to find a licensed specialist who can properly assess and co-create an effective treatment plan.

One of the most promising psychotherapeutic interventions includes Eye Movement Desensitization and Reprocessing (EMDR) therapy.[13] This model helps one to access and process traumatic events safely.

It allows for new associations to be developed to reduce unwanted automated symptoms. EMDR also helps recipients create imagined templates of future events to acquire skills that support ongoing adaptation.

Find community. Healing does not happen in isolation. While finding safe, right-fit relationships can be a challenge in today's modern technology-driven world, it also provides instant access to support groups, meet ups, and forums to safely share the parts of our stories we are ready to share, and receive support. Many groups maintain confidentiality and honor privacy. There is nothing more powerful than knowing we're not alone, and to find meaning and belonging within spaces rife with empathy, solidarity, and collective compassion.

Pursue learning and growth opportunities. Education doesn't necessarily mean following in Westover's footprints and making it to Harvard, but learning can serve as a tremendous healing catalyst. It helps us find organizing frameworks and develop language that helps us make sense of what we've endured.

Learning allows us to develop new skills that help us cope and adapt within the world. It can facilitate increased access to resources that can serve as tools in our healing and growth process. It ties us into intellectual and spiritual communities and networks that can reflect the light of our true potential to us and help us offer ourselves to the world in due time.

Guard against common unhelpful responses to trauma. Don't keep letting denial and imperatives for protection create a blockage towards healing. Resist labels and exaggerated assumptions that assert permanent damage.

Adopt a trauma-informed lens to help you achieve a healthy state of hypervigilance—one that is on its toes without becoming weighed down with anxiety and despair.

Move from survivor to thriver. You are not your trauma. What has happened to you does not define your or your life. Healing takes time. During initial phases of recovery, survival may be all that's possible. Over time, and with the right support, you are capable of healing and avoiding repeated reliving of your trauma. Sometimes this involves removing yourself from certain people or situations in your life. It also can involve a structured way of living that prioritizes self-care, therapy, and therapeutic activities.

Thriving does not mean we can experience a pain-free life or that we have erased what has transpired. But the big and small traumas we have endured can be treated in similar ways to physical wounds. There will always be scars, but the way we experience the pain will keep evolving. Telling is worth the risk: thriving begins here, and secrecy is never a catalyst for healing.

This sweet spot of healing can be found together. It starts by resisting avoidance of trauma and refusing to let it define us. We must come to a place of presence and intentional solidarity, tapping into the resources available to all of us in this present age.

> People who are hurting don't need Avoiders, Protectors, or Fixers. What we need are patient, loving witnesses. People to sit quietly and hold space for us. People to stand in helpful vigil to our pain.
>
> GLENNON DOYLE

We cannot always shield against trauma, but we can lessen its effects. We do not have to resign ourselves to deep, permanent wounds. We can heal and move toward a place that recognizes trauma as part of our human condition, not a stamp of an automatic mental health condition. We can risk exposure to discomfort and begin our process of healing through small microdoses of bravery.

You are not your trauma. You are indomitable.

Move Toward Healing

I swore never to be silent whenever and wherever human beings endure suffering and humiliation. We must take sides. Neutrality helps the oppressor, never the victim. Silence encourages the tormentor, never the tormented.

ELIE WIESEL

Choose Healing Over Secrecy

Move from Survivor to Thriver

When trauma occurs, it can feel like a risk to break secrecy, even though doing so is the very thing that can be a catalyst to healing. Since we will all face small t and Big T trauma across our lifetime, it is vital to understand best approaches to disclosure that promote healing rather than stigmatization or reinjury. Denial and imperatives for protection can project blame onto the survivor, instead of exposing the dysfunctional web of lies and sickness they embody. Labeling and exaggerated assumptions can unfairly brand someone with diagnoses and labels that lead to patronization. Oblivion/unawareness of cumulative effect responses can wreak havoc by keeping issues that need to be addressed in the shadows, allowing for wounds to be trivialized or blatantly ignored, leaving them to fester rather than be treated. Validating feedback loops help prompt access to proper care, community, and opportunities that help us move from survivor to thriver.

Trauma-Informed Check: Reflect

What types of traumas have I gone through?

How have choices to disclose or stay in secrecy affected me?

What responses have I been met with (No Big Deal, Poor Thing, Total Avoidance, Validation)?

Are there opportunities for further steps toward healing?

Who can I trust to open up to about varied forms of trauma?

What trauma stories of people that I know or have read about inspire me to know that healing is possible?

Action Steps: Move from Secrecy to Healing

To move toward healing, we must tune out unhelpful responses and reach for the help we deserve. By seeking community and pursuing learning and growth opportunities, we can shore up protective factors that help us move from survivor to thriver. We do not have to let our wounds fester. They do not define us. How will you make this shift? Consider these steps:

1. **Seek professional help.** Reach out to people you know and trust to help you locate a professional who is experienced in helping people recover from trauma.

2. **Identify right-fit healing activities.** Discover what types of artistic and healing modalities nourish. Trauma responses can be triggered or calmed by a variety of modalities, thus it's important to identify what resonates as a mechanism of relief for your mind, body, and soul. Whether it's time in nature, music, deep breathing, quiet, art, writing, or sports, work to discover activities and experiences that bring comfort and replenishment. Keep track of how many you are using to help you through, and what seems to work best.

3. **Practice self-compassion.** Work to resist feelings that you are overreacting to any form of trauma. Focus on developing a solid inner self-dialogue that involves messaging emphasizing your resilience, strength, and worth. Be gentle with yourself as you navigate a wide range of emotions. Consider journaling to track your progress, and using "I am" mantras as seen on YouTube.

4. **Increase your trauma literacy.** See "Recommendations for Identifying Risks and Growing Resilience" at the back of the book for further suggestions on developing your awareness of trauma and ways you can access healing for you and those you care for.

5. **Develop communication efficacy.** Practice communicating your needs to support your own trauma recovery and those you love and influence. Role-play the V-A-R tool and practice active listening skills to strengthen your empathic responses and self-advocate for what you need to foster healing.

The ordinary response to atrocities is to banish them from consciousness. Certain violations of the social compact are too terrible to utter aloud: this is the meaning of the word unspeakable. Atrocities, however, refuse to be buried. Equally as powerful as the desire to deny atrocities is the conviction that denial does not work. Folk wisdom is filled with ghosts who refuse to rest in their graves until their stories are told. Murder will out. Remembering and telling the truth about terrible events are prerequisites both for the restoration of the social order and for the healing of individual victims.

JUDITH HERMAN

Session Six

You Are Not the Likes on Your Feed

The problem is people are being hated when they are
real, and are being loved when they are fake.
BOB MARLEY

Choose True Security Over Superficial Popularity

It's December 2016. Instagram lights up with orange thumbnails dotted with little flames. Kendall Jenner, along with other models and social influencers, is posting videos set in paradise flaunting a one-of-a-kind, luxury music experience known as Fyre Festival. It's like Coachella, Sandals, and the Met Gala all rolled into one.

The bait's taken: tickets sell out to 5,000 excited fans, ready for their own Instagrammable moments. They are hungry for VIP access to the private Bahamian island flooding their feeds: pristine water, models, celebrity chefs, and cabanas.

When the highly anticipated moment arrived, it was a total bust. "Luxury villas" turned out to be rain-soaked mattresses. "Transformational experience" meant porta potties and no running water. "Uniquely authentic island cuisine" became cheese sandwiches served in foam containers. The organizers frantically hosted "impromptu beach parties" as a last-ditch attempt to buy time and remedy the crisis at hand. Festival organizers Billy McFarland and Ja Rule had promised a once in a lifetime, "on the boundaries of impossible" experience. Talk about foreshadowing. For those who fell for it, it was a cruel irony and hard pill to swallow. Fyre Festival never got off the ground, and participants were herded back to Miami with a cautionary tale of a lifetime.[1]

> Glamour is a beautiful illusion—the word 'glamour' originally meant a literal magic spell—that promises to transcend ordinary life and make the ideal real. It depends on a special combination of mystery and grace. Too much information breaks the spell.
>
> VIRGINIA POSTREL

Fyre Festival was the ultimate bait within our camera-on-at-all-times landscape. Everything has become pomp and circumstance: engagements, birthday parties, weddings, and even Saturday nights are full productions. We can't even go out to eat without broadcasting pictures of our food with clever hashtags and filters, sporting our $276.00 "natural looks" from Sephora. The all-frills, roll out the red carpet everyday Kardashian culture disillusions us into thinking that security is found by building a contrived VIP brand image to strut across our social media accounts.

Gone are the days when popularity contests came around at homecoming dances or class elections. Every day, there is pressure to be our own paparazzi, campaigning for status and showcasing curated images to generate likes. Ironically, we are likely annoying each other with our stunts, wasting energy building false identities that do nothing to foster true security through authentic connection. And this is not just a showoff fest. Just ask the originators of social media. Social media has become big profit.[2]

> We curate our lives around this perceived sense of perfection because we get rewarded in these short-term signals—hearts, likes, thumbs up—and we conflate that with value, and we conflate it with truth. And instead, what it is is fake, brittle popularity that's short term and that leaves you even more, and admit it, vacant and empty [than] before you did it. Because that enforces you into a vicious cycle where you're like, what's the next thing that I need to do now, because I need it back. Think about that compounded by two billion people and then think about how then people react to them to the perceptions of others.
>
> CHAMATH PALIHAPITIYA

In the Netflix movie *The Social Dilemma*, Edward Tufte calls out that the only two industries that call their customers "users" are illegal drugs and software. These vices have become highly addictive. Social media disrupts and impedes building authentic identities that allow us to enjoy the true treasures of life: presence with ourselves and one another. The continual displays of the "perfect life" are getting in the way of meaningful ties. We are so busy chasing the ideal shot that we are missing the organic moments of real life that both scientific and spiritual realms agree tend to be beneficial in creating awe, joy, and true connection. Our feeds are feeding us a lot of garbage, including non-stop advertisements about what will make us lovable, "in," and sexy.[3] What we buy shows what we buy into. Many of us become too afraid to risk being our true selves and instead we miss living an authentic life: a marker of resilience, and the offering the world truly needs from us given all the fanfare at hand.

> We must use our lives to make the world a better place to live, not just to acquire things. That is what we are put on the earth for.
>
> DOLORES HUERTA

The scramble to impress each other and fear of not having what someone else has isn't simply because we are all applause-starved narcissists, but that we are entrenched in a "commodity complex" where our attention has become vital to marketers and institutions who hold us by the jugular and egg us on to continually participate in this highly addictive system that capitalizes on our insecurities, objectifies us, and makes them richer. They are profiting off our malaise. It's all part of a larger system that we need regular doses of bravery to ward off.

Understand the Risks of the Commodity Complex

It may seem like marching to your own beat is too much of a risk, but there are plenty of risks in falling for the commodity complex that we're engulfed in. A commodity complex is the structural aspect within a society that organizes people as disposable things rather than divine beings. It feeds off a culture of excess and overdoing that encourages people to build an identity around social status, achievement, buying stuff, and fitting in. It leads to the relentless chasing of dreams that end up becoming nightmares. It can cause those of us with privilege to forget that most people across the world don't have their needs—never mind their wants—met.

With the growing economic disparities in income and power across the world, where a select few hold the vast majority of resources, it leaves the rest of us clawing to remain relevant and viable. It blocks us from seeing what risks are worth taking, ones that could help us enhance our impact in the world, because we're so preoccupied with pouring our energy into what society is promoting:

The objectification of people. We're at risk of being used and cheapened. Messages include: Looks are social capital. Your body is an object meant to arouse, perform, and please. There is great shame if you don't fit the prototype. You are a disposable pleasure toy. You are only as good as what you do for me. Relationships are transactional, not transformative.

A culture of excessive achievement, overdoing, and hyper-competitiveness. We're taught to be competitive, not collaborative. Messages include: You are what you do. Your net worth is your value. What you produce defines you. Get this thing or that thing to get ahead. Your accolades are you. Take what's yours. More is more. Win at all costs. You are a human doing, not a human being.

The push for copycatting. We're encouraged to conform at all costs. Messages include: Fit in. Get more followers. Be "normal." Fake it 'til you make it. What people think defines you. Keep up with the Kardashians. Why can't you be more like so and so? These messages are reinforced explicitly and implicitly. The culture affirms us when we do what it is asking us to do and punishes when we resist.

Overemphasis on the goods life, not the good life. We're entangled in cycles of overwork and overspending, to the point we neglect ourselves and one another. Constant consumption and materialism are costing us a lot, disrupting us from getting to what positive psychologists call the good life: one characterized by a life of presence, purpose, and meaning.[4]

Illusions of glamour. We're disillusioned from afar. Someone is sexy until you have sex with them. A vacation is a dream until you go on it and it's a nightmare. Being famous is great until you have 376 stalkers and no autonomy. Becoming head of the company seems amazing until it translates into seven-day work weeks.

Take Donna, who was tired from the trappings of the commodity complex. She stopped investing so much time in looking good and worrying about what people think, instead finding ways to let her unique spirit shine. She microdosed risk by setting boundaries with a group of friends who were notoriously "ballers" and spent a lot of money in service of their Instagram image. Donna knew that might risk her standing with her friends, but she found it worth it when she made new friends who had similar values and was delighted that her original friend group started to reevaluate their priorities too.

If we let the quest for excessive status dominate, dictate, and drive behavior, it can become unhealthy and dangerous in this volatile, inequitable market. A market that reinforces these messages that we must fall into place and work and shop 'til we drop at great expense to keep the system profiting. A system that doesn't truly serve or take care of us; one that can keep us from taking risks that nourish and honor our authentic identities to help us grow, connect, and contribute.

> None of us create or do anything in isolation—it's impossible. We are system-bound both physically and psychologically; a continuum. Therefore our view of causality with respect to societal change can only be truly productive if we seek and source the most relevant sociological influences we can and begin to alter those effects from the root causes.
>
> PETER JOSEPH

Know How the Commodity Complex Impacts You

The dangers of the commodity complex are at every turn. It's no coincidence that we are seeing a host of negative consequences, including:

Phobias, anxiety, and collective angst are on the rise. The World Health Organization has declared a mental health crisis writ large. It becomes near impossible to be at ease and feel that you won't be

> I have learned to
> seek my happiness
> by limiting my
> desires, rather
> than in attempting
> to satisfy them.
>
> JOHN STUART MILL

replaced, disregarded, or marginalized if you are not doing what everyone else is doing and working yourself to the bone to climb to the top professionally and personally. Anxiety is one of the biggest threats to us taking risks that nourish, since it gives us the constant signal we are in danger and can't handle anything new or provocative—even when, in fact, strategic risks can help us change our circumstances in positive ways.

We are trapped in cycles of overworking and overspending. Consumerism and the sense of never being satisfied is seen everywhere. Our debt outweighs our earnings, and we are carrying heavy workloads to try and stave off our heavy financial burdens to make ends meet and/or maintain excessive lifestyles. It is worth risking having the best of the material world in favor of having less and enjoying it more. Financial burdens and overwork are major disruptions to resilience.

Creativity and purpose are undermined. There is relentless societal pressure to acquire "marketable skills," climb the corporate ladder, or choose from a handful of "esteemed" professions that are often the most apt for burnout and dissatisfaction. We're unable to fully express our true selves without scrutiny and penalty if we do not engage in cookie-cutter thinking and behavior that position us to be "successful" and "do well" in the market. Ask any artist how many times they've been told they shouldn't pursue their true calling because of concern they "won't make money."

This is similar to when people are dissuaded from helping and healing professions like teaching or social work because they are not lucrative, even though these roles are invaluable to society and embody a deep sense of sacred identity, purpose, and offering incredible contributions to the world.

Creative risks are amongst the most important to take. They are what help us to enjoy life, engage with novelty and variety, and to express our authentic identities. Stagnation is a dead-end street.

Creative risk-taking can help us build pathways to resilience, making for a fun and interesting journey. Similarly, when we select work that honors our true identity, we are apt to enjoy what we do, even if it's a risk to what people see as esteemed.

Generate experiences, not stuff. Travel with an open mind and heart. Do not over explain yourself. Seek aligned partnerships that get it. Engage with healing and performing arts. This will help you tell your stories and sing your songs and do your dances. Your life is art. Art should be appreciated, not picked apart or requiring lengthy explanations. Do not let anyone take this from you.

Learning and growth are cheapened. We've made learning about test scores and grades and a means to an end, rather than a treasured opportunity and dynamic process of discovery. For many, punitive grading and narrow measures of defining "intelligence" have been damaging. Higher education has become big business, with many institutions seeing students as customers rather than contributors to the learning environment.[5] Taking academic risks can include pursuing unique subjects and interests that may not hold the same value that to other people, or trying things that are hard for you and risking not seeming smart in honor of deeper growth and learning.

Love and relationships are misconstrued. In our shopping for partners, and swipe-left culture, love becomes transactional. We have precise checklists and impossible expectations. We rate people and call them "full packages," cheapening their true worth according to metrics of attractiveness, affluence, and desirability that someone else has determined as trusted indicators rather than true chemistry and synchronicity. We become more concerned about showing off conquests and partners as a means to boost status. I call this "wifey propaganda," a type of showing off when people post gushing images and videos of their perfect romance, the heroic figure that they cannot be a whole person without.

Some people spend an entire lifetime searching for "real love" for their very own "you complete me" *Jerry Maguire* moment.

Idealized Hollywood romance and fairy tale folklore can cause us to think that our identity comes from a precise type of partnership.

> The voice of our original self is often muffled, overwhelmed, even strangled, by the voices of other people's expectations. The tongue of the original self is the language of the heart.
>
> JULIA CAMERON

This can cause us to overlook people who do not meet scripted criteria, overriding the laws of deep, meaningful connection and organic attraction in favor of superficial, curated feelings that we're "supposed" to experience with someone who looks good on paper or an Instagram story. Love becomes like an episode of *The Bachelor* meets fifth grade gym class, where we pick according to superficial measures based on who's watching. Love is meant to be a binding force of light in our lives, not a showoff contest. Laws of attraction reveal deeper spiritual ties that we often miss within the cheapened, "post-worthy partner" climate of love.

It is worth taking the risk of asking yourself whether you are apt to pick or stay with a partner for their image, or for deeper reasons that are important to you. It's worth risking what people think in favor of what you feel.

Microdose Bravery:
Risk Looking Good to Feel Good

Love for the sake of image can make us look good, but feel bad. The kind of connection being sold in the larger commodity complex culture leaves us disillusioned and disappointed. Try avoiding these common traps:

1. **Pining for the imaginary perfect partner:** That elusive, Michael Bublé "I just haven't met you yet" partner: meets all checkboxes, will do everything for you, be a master linguist in all your love languages, and never let you down. Markers include the belief that finding this person will solve your problems entirely.

2. **Putting all the eggs in one basket approach:** All effort is invested in one person, forming an insular couple identity, foregoing all other friendships and connections or forms of identity outside the relationship. Markers include your health and stability relying on someone else, and the majority of time spent with them or thinking about them.

3. **Displaying the trophy that you cling on to and showcase:** How you look is more important than you feel. Partnership takes on an arm candy approach versus loving a partner or varied partners because of their intellectual, spiritual, and chemical attributes that you are truly magnetized toward.

When we resist fabricated love, we take the risk of reducing status or being alone. Sometimes this means finding a partner(s) that you really like versus someone who is more "display-worthy." Other times it can mean creating non-traditional relationship structures in which you develop varied partnerships and connections without the pressure of one person being the end all be all. True connection comes in many forms, and we cannot risk authentic connection to appease social pressures that promise happiness or popularity but deliver discontent.

From every realm, there is increasing pressure to create the perfect brand image of ourselves and hide our imperfections, even though they are part of what ties us together in our shared humanity. Our constant propagation of what isn't real can get us into real trouble.

Fabrication has no place in true connection. Finding real requires us to resist chasing what's superficial over what's truly beneficial. We must abandon the cliché, collective, trophified model of so-called connection. When relationships are solely for display, we may look good, but feel bad. The disproportionate reliance on a sole idealized relationship that completes us can prevent us from building our own structures that help us cast unconventional characters in our lives with whom we co-create epic experiences marked by soulfulness, chemistry, reciprocity, and synchronicity, not superficiality.

Search for Real

Searching for realness in all things, whether friendships, romantic love, familial bonds, our experiences, goals, creativity, or careers, is a risk worth taking. Otherwise, we can risk getting hooked into the commoditized models of love and happiness showcased and have trouble seeing when real arrives. In Margery Williams Bianco's classic *The Velveteen Rabbit*, the rabbit is trying to decipher the meaning of real. He consults with the Skin Horse for answers:

> "'Real isn't how you are made,' said the Skin Horse. 'It's a thing that happens to you. When a child loves you for a long, long time, not just to play with, but REALLY loves you, then you become Real.'
> 'Does it hurt?' asked the Rabbit.
> 'Sometimes,' said the Skin Horse, for he was always truthful.
> 'When you are Real you don't mind being hurt.'
> 'Does it happen all at once, like being wound up,' he asked, 'or bit by bit?'
> 'It doesn't happen all at once,' said the Skin Horse. 'You become. It takes a long time. That's why it doesn't happen often to people who break easily, or have sharp edges, or who have to be carefully kept. Generally, by the time you are Real, most of your hair has been loved off, and your eyes drop out and you get loose in the joints and very shabby. But these things don't matter at all, because once you are Real you can't be ugly, except to people who don't understand.'"[6]

This powerful tale can help us be and seek Velveteen Rabbits who are not ugly throwaways, but precious comforts we can form deep attachments with. We do not have to live a life of surface or manufactured connection. Instead, we can redirect our quest to find true security over superficial popularity:

> **Seek real connections.** When we take on an Uncurated Self, Velveteen Rabbit approach, it can feel vulnerable, but this can help curb the loneliness surging in our culture of contrived connection. Sociologist Sherry Turkle characterizes this as being "alone together."[7] Data is emerging that alerts us to the risks of loneliness as "the new smoking."[8] Loneliness seems ironic, given all our modern tools for connection, but quantity is not a substitute for quality. Fake connection pales in comparison to real.
>
> Loneliness is exacerbated by intensive schedules and the fact that people are less apt to nest into family and community structures in our transient global world. The increasing opportunity for choice and movement can make for complexity. Finding real bonds and community can take time. It can be challenging to connect our inner world with our outer world and to foster trust and reciprocity.
>
> It's hard to open up under the pressures of time, and not always having the luxury of go-to people in our immediate reach. Many of my students from around the world tell me how lonely they feel when they study in the US, and even when they go back home, it often makes things worse because with the changing they've done, they now feel like they don't fit in anywhere.
>
> This is also true of third culture kids (TCKs), people raised in a culture other than their parents' or the culture of the country named on their passport (where they're legally considered native) for a major part of their early development years. This exposure to a wide range of cultural influences can make them feel like they fit in everywhere and nowhere all at the same time.[9]
>
> Even though technology and social media can help us build and sustain relationships, it is important to make sure it's not a substitute for the unplanned, organic moments of human connection. Science

reveals that the simple act of listening to each other's stories and experiences in real time can positively impact the length of our telomeres—the caps at the end of each strand of DNA that serve to protect our chromosomes and help our cells do their jobs to keep us healthy and spry.[10]

When we intentionally come up for air from our screens to seek connections where we can be ourselves and truly tune into one another, there are many benefits. Trading likes for likes or maintaining social relationships for status alone can leave us lonely and unfulfilled. When we seek real moments, we are more likely to manifest closer relationships and bonds that help us avoid stalking the likes on our feeds as a measure of worth.

Seek true security within simple moments. Science shows that it's not the grand gestures and manufactured moments that are beneficial, but those when we're fully present with ourselves and one another.[11] We are more likely to enjoy our lives when we create awe and joy in small things. It's often the organic nooks and crannies of life that are most gratifying, not the contrived, grand-scale, Hallmarky Hollywood ones. Often, the things that are not necessarily post-worthy cultivate a sense of renewal and security in our lives. While pomp and circumstance has its place, we cannot let it interfere with our recognition of the simple pleasures as treasures in our lives.

> To be nobody but yourself in a world which is doing its best, night and day, to make you everybody else— means to fight the hardest battle which any human being can fight; and never stop fighting.
>
> E.E. CUMMINGS

Choose beneficial over superficial. We must avoid selecting friends and associates based on status over substance. Social climbing is a prime example. While it might be fun to hang with the "in" crowd, these relationships have complicated dynamics and can fizzle out. Seek quality of experience and relationship with people you value and who value you. Choose people who want to help you grow and be willing to do the same. This strengthens self-esteem rather than hanging out with people purely to strengthen your social status that you'll never feel like you measure up to.

Know the difference between a true VIP and superficial VIP.
Popular leaders and influencers are not always prime examples
of consciousness or substance. It is important to stay on guard
against those who appear to hold their own selfish interests in
mind, rather than demonstrating humility and values-aligned
behavior. Many of us have been conditioned to rate people
according to superficial metrics rather than honor the everyday
heroes in our world who give of themselves with no expectation
for recognition or reward. True security comes through actions
of intentional service rather than enhancing one's own status or
followership.

Within today's display-case world, we don't have to lie down and
accept a fate of not feeling good enough. Instead of basing our worth
on the attributes and accolades being offered, we need to rise against
the extremes of the commodity complex ramping up our insecurities.
If not, we run the risk of chasing superficial validation that will
ultimately be of no lasting value. Instead, we can become conscious,
true VIPs who contribute positively, securing a better future for
ourselves and one another.

You are not the likes on your feed. You are secure.

SESSION SIX WORKSHEET

Search for Real

Choose True Security Over Superficial Popularity

Focus on Your Nature as a Divine Being, Not a Disposable Thing

Social media culture is baiting us to constantly strive for a VIP depiction of our lives, seeking validation and popularity that interfere with, rather than enhance, our sense of security. A commodity complex encourages building an identity centered on social status, achievement, acquisition of material goods, and fitting in. This contributes to the objectification of people, competition over cooperation, and copycat behavior. These structures lead to an undermining of creativity and purpose, cheapening of learning and growth, and a misconstruing of identity, love, and relationships. Given the significant escalation of mental health issues that are bred within cycles of overworking, overspending, and displaying a likeable self, it is vital to reject the commodity complex. We can strive toward this by searching for real connections and reimagining our definitions of VIP.

Real Check: Reflect

How much time do I spend per day posting on and viewing social media?

Am I enjoying moments and people without considering their postability?

What types of accounts do I follow?

What percentage of them are depicting real people and/or noble causes?

What kinds of advertising tempts me to fall into the commodity complex?

What's it like for me when I encounter "perfect" neighbors or coworkers?

What types of social phenomena or goods am I most likely to buy into?

How have I typically defined "VIP"?

Who or what are my Velveteen Rabbits, which provide me a sense of true security?

What societal dreams am I chasing? Are any of them becoming nightmarish?

What can help me move towards becoming a VIP who contributes positively instead of seeking popularity and recognition?

> There are no odds to beat anymore, just some real junk to dump. You dump your junk. After you dump it, you don't sort it in your mind. You dump your junk and you walk away. You wear all one color on the outside, swirl with every color on the inside. You walk forward. You keep your head angled up so that you see over the fray. You protect yourself and all the little weirds that make up who you are.
>
> JENNY SLATE

Action Steps: Move from Superficial Popularity to True Security

We often wish for friends and status. We spend time making ourselves look good and hustling for approval. We are subject to messaging that we are to gauge our worth based on likes on our feeds and other metrics. We want to stop hyper-competing, but if we are not careful about how we define VIP, we can get sucked into the vortex of excessive achievement and overdoing that marks the commodity complex. Here are some ways to move away from superficiality:

> **Find your Velveteen Rabbits.** Make a list of all the real people in your life who you can be your true self with. Make a conscious effort to spend time with them outside of social media. Thank them for being real to you, and vow you'll do the same.

Do a social media audit and cleanse. Evaluate the amount of time you spend on social media and which "VIPs" you follow. Consider reducing your intake and feeding off inspirational examples of people found in literature. Track your screen time and document how you're spending it in other uplifting activities.

Embrace your divine self. Evaluate your emotional and spiritual gifts and talents. Rather than drawing upon the metrics of beauty that society prescribes, make a list of your soulful personal characteristics that make you unique and equipped to contribute thoughtfully and creatively to the world. Consider creating an artistic piece from this (poem, painting, drawing, vision board).

A statue isn't built from the ground up—it's chiseled out of a block of marble—and I often wonder if we aren't likewise shaped by the qualities we lack, outlined by the empty space where the marble used to be. I'll be sitting on a train. I'll be lying awake in bed. I'll be watching a movie; I'll be laughing. And then, all of a sudden, I'll be struck with the paralyzing truth: It's not what we do that makes us who we are. It's what we don't do that defines us.

RAPHAEL BOB-WAKSBERG

Session Seven

You Are Not Your Accomplishments

One of the saddest lessons of history is this: If we've been bamboozled long enough, we tend to reject any evidence of the bamboozle. We're no longer interested in finding out the truth. The bamboozle has captured us. It's simply too painful to acknowledge, even to ourselves, that we've been taken. Once you give a charlatan power over you, you almost never get it back.

CARL SAGAN

Choose Being Over Doing

The COOP, an iconic landmark bookstore in Harvard Square, is the ultimate literary haven, buzzing with booklovers who go as far as to call themselves "bibliophiles," and there's almost always a tourist snapping selfies on its signature spiral staircase. The bit of elitism in the air is mostly counterbalanced by the whiff of salted caramel lattes and patrons wearing Doc Martens. Hipster clerks instinctively pluck "selections that likely suit you" if you're "equal part fan of Jonathan Franzen/Pablo Neruda/Isabel Wilkerson/Pema Chödrön/Samantha Irby" with uncanny ease and minimal smugness. I am in my glory. Until I land in the College Admission Section.

There's clearly some tense energy as anxious patrons thumb through twelve-inch-thick guides on mastering the ACT, PSAT, SAT, and TOEFL.

There are titles for every workable angle on writing the "fresh and unique" essay and landing the coveted acceptance letter from the admissions committee who has ALREADY.SEEN. that same essay 67,852 damn times. Well before the test prep books enter the scene formally, the Get Into College memo is LOUD and CLEAR:

Attention: All Students

CC: Your parents (start that U fund now, folks: your family's collective nervous breakdown=expensive!)

PAY ATTENTION!!! There is a good chance you have ALREADY fallen behind and DESPERATELY FAILED despite all the homework we've assigned (the kindergarteners cry). Here is your formula for success:

Before you lose your first tooth, select your first-choice top-tier college. By third grade, read minimum four grade levels ahead, and play at least three sports and/or instruments. By high school, stack your schedule with enough AP classes and co-curriculars that allow for only three hours sleep and NO.TIME. to actually taste food. Because Gawddd Forbidd you turn twenty-one without your own nonprofit or startup. Oh, and don't forget your sunny disposition to get those volunteer hours in.

To help you with this, we invite you to take advantage of our Grueling Treadmill Lifelong Membership Club. Join now for 24-7 access to our specially formulated machines, locked at 15.0 incline, maximum speed. Your feet will be strapped in to help you fight off any temptation to stop running. Proper use of this membership can lead to achieving profound levels of socially constructed success. While there are reports of exhaustion, injury, and death, we recommend you do not dismount and risk letting anyone see any sign that you are actually sweating.

Welcome to The Club!

Yours truly,
Modern Problems of Privilege

To the soldiers standing in the COOP's test prep section who've maintained impressive sprint paces marathon over marathon and haven't yet collapsed, bitten off every last fingernail, or drowned in anxious tears, I see you. The books you are clutching are NOT the Holy Grail. You are on your way to endless cycles of testing retakes, laborious attempts at a poised, yet unpretentious application, more sleepless nights, and panic attacks.

Once you get in, you will quickly realize everything before this was just a warmup drill. Everyone else will seem in wayyy better shape than you. The race for GPA, a stacked resume, acing grad school exams, and landing the ideal job with equally inhumane and exhausting standards will leave you locked into your Grueling Treadmill Lifelong Membership Club, a contract that feels impossible to break once you've clocked in so many hours.

I want to interject, but none of the students and their parents have a "please share unsolicited advice" look on their faces. Maybe I should call the manager over to suggest replacing the College Admissions Section with one called Sanity 101, stacked with titles like *You Are Not a Robot*; *Enjoy Life, Even if You Feel Your English Isn't Great*; *Damn You Are Already Impressive*; *You Are Not Your Test Scores*; *Your Mental Health Is More Important Than Social Constructions of Success*; and *You Are Not Your Accomplishments*.

I know damn well this would be a highly unwelcome change for the book publishers, test entities, and the institutions of higher education, corporations, and forces of capitalism making big business on treadmill memberships that are driving students and families to a state of panic, frenzy, and exhaustion even before kindergarten graduation day.

I can't bear to watch. I head downstairs away from the test prep section when a small table brimming with expletives grabs me: *The Subtle Art of Not Giving a F*ck, F*ck Feelings,* and *You Are a Badass.* Maybe this modern-day literary trend isn't a coincidence, perhaps it's the rebuttal to the Cult of Overachievement that infiltrates every inch of our lives. There's plenty to swear about, with all the Grueling Treadmill Lifelong Membership Club memos being circulated. We've all memorized the bullet points:

- Leisure is taboo. Actual rest=laziness.

- Everyone MUST GO to college.

- Worth=scores, letters after names, titles, likes on feed, accolades, and image.

- Buck up, suck it up, grin and bear it, run like hell.

The memos leave off the part about the risks of irreparable damage from the Grueling Treadmill Lifelong Membership Club. And that for far too long, this club has been exclusive for whites and the upper class, with unfair rules, worse pressure, and less access for BIPOCs who have additional pressure to make it look easy, as if they're not constantly fighting the battle of systemic racism.

> It's better to make a change now than to keep living your mistake simply because you worked hard to get there.
>
> ALEXANDRA ROBBINS

At every turn, we must remember that we are not our accomplishments. We can take pride in what we do, without it defining or owning us. None of us can sustain a never-ending treadmill, locked on warp speed, full incline. Accomplishments give us a sense of pride, but they are only parts of us.

Guard Against the Cult of Overachievement

The Cult of Overachievement breeds this: people who are doing EVERY-THING but think they are NOT EVEN CLOSE to doing ENOUGH. Underperformance Dysmorphic Disorder (UDD) is everywhere we turn:

The most educated, advanced, accomplished group of society suffers from an obsessive focus on the perceived faulty belief that they are *Unaccomplished Letdowns* who are failing miserably even when they are doing THE MOST. They spend hours ruminating and compulsively comparing themselves to fake and inhumane standards of success. They are consumed at every waking moment with being seen as flawless and exhibit extreme signs of mistake aversion. Perfectionistic thoughts and behaviors are frequent and unrelenting. UDD is marked by a loss of sleep, peace, serenity, sense of self, and sanity. Highly contagious. Disruptive to meaningful social connection.

Treatment protocols include taking the risk of going against the grain of a hypercompetitive global market marked by greed and fierce individualism; intermittent technology fasts; heavy doses of self-compassion; and repeating this deprogramming mantra: overachievement is dangerous.

Nothing is worth getting sick over. It's better to give up some trophies than to not be able to enjoy the ones you earn.

UDD will sabotage the quality of our lives if we do not resist. There is so much more to life than SATs, raises, promotions, letters after our names, likes on feeds, and cars we drive. Maybe we don't need six-year-olds spending hours on homework like their PhD candidates, becoming walking Wikipedia pages by eight, or amassing a collection of trophies by the time they've hit puberty. And maybe there's something highly dysfunctional about how many "successful" adults are too busy to even enjoy the fruit of their labor. Or that across the world, so few even have these opportunities to begin with.

The Cult of Overachievement has bred an epidemic of romanticized success and Underperformance Dysmorphic Disorder: we look in the mirror and somehow walk away thinking we have not done enough, even when we are doing the most. Identities that are constructed around goals and roles are a form of disillusionment that becomes erosive. Within a capitalistic, greed-oriented model, we have fallen for the lie that we are commodities and must work ourselves to the bone to be viable and worthy, and that it is "normal" to be flooded with constant anxiety and exhaustion because "it's the only way" to get ahead, which is code for having an exorbitant level of material possessions to give us status and allegedly make us feel "secure." We need to write this so-called normal off before it writes us off. Maybe we need to fall behind to discover wholeness through being, not doing.

Combatting UDD requires significant shifting from a cultural paradigm that encourages unhealthy overwork and stigmatizes leisure and fun. We need to take the risk of being less productive in favor of sanity. Our to-do lists need revision (or to be shredded). To stop calling ourselves "lazy" when we aren't being "productive." Rest and respite are productive ways to ensure we don't fall into long-term patterns of UDD that suck the pleasure out of life. Also helpful is a complete shift of priorities, and the realization that our energy could turn instead toward more substantive problem solving when offering ourselves to the world through our authentic identities and commitment to social change.

The energy we invest in becoming "successful" needs to be better spent on solving root issues. UDD doesn't simply spread because we're all a bunch of try-too-hards sipping Dom Pérignon, feigning for YSL handbags, red bottoms, and Teslas. If we can unlock from the disillusionment of the treadmill, we might be able to free up space to devote time to critically think through critical issues that perpetuate such behavior. Many of us fall into the trap of spending as much as we earn on lifestyles modeled by the 1% that we can't afford. If we get sucked into identities around what we have to show off, we are more likely to spend the money we earn on things we don't need instead of using our time and resources

> Until we know the assumptions in which we are drenched, we cannot know ourselves.
> ADRIENNE RICH

to help change a system that allows zero accountability to corporations, all while poverty leaves far too many seeing three meals a day as a luxury, never mind complaining about not having enough sushi or the latest Nikes (first world problems).

Resist Imposter Syndrome

Imposter syndrome, a form of intellectual self-doubt, is common amongst high achievers. It is experienced with greater intensity by groups who are marginalized and discriminated against due to race, class, gender, sexual orientation, and other non-dominant, non-majority social identity categories. It makes you worry you are a phony or fraud, that you're not as smart as people think. When we spend our energy locked into this cycle of self-sabotage and anxiety, it blinds us from seeing our true strengths and worth. To foster wholeness, we can focus our energy on how far we've come, what we do know, and the excitement over our potential for ongoing evolution.

You'd think all the hardcore exercise would make for confidence in our fitness. Yet, imposter syndrome manages to weasel its way into our internal dialogue. Its unruly cousins—perfectionism, social comparison, and social anxiety—relentlessly crack their knuckles at us, putting pressure to stay in the Club. You'd think we'd be less intimidated, but the Cult of

Overachievement's greatest accomplishment is its ability to turn us into our own bullies. We question whether the admissions committees made a mistake to let us in, if employees should have promoted us, and whether we are deserving or truly belong in the spaces we are situated in.

Strive for Healthy Achievement

Treadmills are far from new. Overachievement has ramped up in the past decade, but even in the 1970s, during the time of snail mail and rotary phones, when work from home meant chores, burnout was already on the radar.[1] With all that's been added to the mix since, the risks of its telltale symptoms—emotional exhaustion, depersonalization, and depletion—have grown exponentially.

> What haunts me is not exactly the absence of literal space so much as a deep craving for metaphorical space: release, escape, some kind of open-ended freedom.
>
> NAOMI KLEIN

There seem to be no escape doors from back-to-back Zoom meetings, text messages, social media feeds, gorged inboxes, multiple sign-ins, and non-stop news cycles. Burnout has taken on a whole new meaning in this age of pandemic PTSD, "infobesity," and "technostress." Burnout is being called the "new normal," increasingly seen as a public health and occupational risk.[2]

In 2019, The World Health Organization (WHO) made a bold statement. In their International Classification of Diseases (ICD-11), they changed burnout from being a medical condition to an occupational one.[3] EVEN!PRE.PANDEMIC! they were actively working on a set of workforce guidelines to protect well-being, warning of imminent danger from stress-related illness.

When we put in twelve-to-fifteen-hour days on the treadmill without any emergency stop button in sight, we are risking quality and longevity of life. We must microdose bravery instead to renegotiate our Club membership contracts, setting needed boundaries that allow for a more humane pace and striving for healthy achievement, not anxious overachievement. New memos need to be sent ASAP to:

CC: Parents who spend more time with their kids than any generation prior: You are not a GIANT FAILURE if you show up to the soccer game without Pinterest brownies that won't upset any allergies. (Not saying you should bring the tree nuts recklessly, either!)

CC: Students who have access to more educational opportunities than any ever before: As do not define you. Your mental health is more important than your grades.

CC: Employees who are doing the work of multiple people: It's time to see beyond receiving "exceeds expectations" in every category. It's riskier to stay locked on the treadmill than to dismount.

Your mind, body, and soul will thank you.

Sincerely,

The Voice of Reason
(Backed by data, countless therapists, health experts, and the annals of long-term treadmill users.)

Too many people fall for the idea that abandoning society's definition of success isn't a risk worth taking. But this is the very thing our world needs: for our time and talent to be devoted to offering ourselves in creative and conscious ways, rather than for the sake of personal gain or wealth.

> The planet does not need more successful people. The planet desperately needs more peacemakers, healers, restorers, storytellers, and lovers of all kinds.
> DALAI LAMA

Know the Difference Between Anxious Overachievement vs. Healthy Achievement

The anxious overachiever:

Misses chances to take risks that show authentic identity.

Holds unrealistic standards, then stews in self-criticism when said standards are not met with immediacy and precision.

Perseverates over mistakes. Engages in toxic self-analysis and criticism.

Has contingent self-esteem, relying on outside validation to fuel self-worth.

Barely takes breaks—constant urge to run, run, run without stopping for air.

Is dissatisfied with performance. Minimizes progress, neglects to celebrate wins.

Is consumed with nagging concern over what's to be conquered next.

Take Susan, who had a 4.0 in college and went on to work at a big firm, clocking eight-plus hours weekly. She barely has time to sleep or have any kind of life outside work. She has accomplished a great deal, but instead of relishing in all she's done, she's always on to the next thing. Susan is certainly pleasing her parents, but in the meantime, she dreams of devoting her time and attention to things that have more meaning to her.

The healthy achiever:

Takes risks that nourish and support authentic identity.

Sets a pace that is sustainable over the long haul.

Recognizes worth is built on their ability to contribute positively, not perfectly.

Take a long marathon, not sprinting, approach to life.

Is not shy to ask for help.

Engages in self-compassion and self-care practices.

Avoids mental self-sabotage, constant comparison, and hyper-competitiveness.

Seeks to serve the greater good.

Ned is the embodiment of a healthy achiever, and this isn't to say it didn't come the hard way. Ned's burnout and overload prompted him to take a risk and talk to his academic advisor about a more reasonable load, including courses he loved outside his program of study. In doing so, Ned realized that he didn't have to stay in a major that was too intense and unsatisfying. His new, more reasonable pace is allowing him more time to nurture relationships and give back to the community. He feels gratified that he's no longer climbing and crashing off the ladder of "success."

Use Self-Care to Sustain Yourself

Sometimes when people hear "self-care" they think they have to spend twenty-five dollars on a yoga class or orchestrate a royal *Parks and Rec*-sy "Treat Yo Self" day—Donna Meagle and Tom Haverford style. But you don't need Gucci, Chanel, and trips to Canyon Ranch or Rodeo Drive to practice it. While we work toward institutional change, we have to take matters into our own hands to intentionally protect our minds, bodies, and souls from the damaging treadmills littering our world. This is not selfish, superficial, feel-good stuff, but what's necessitated. Scientifically grounded strategies are critical to keep us from normalizing treating people like human doings, not human beings.

Scientifically based self-care is substantive. The intentional, deliberate process of protection of mind, body, and soul is not superficial or selfish. In this age of anxiety and burnout, it is something that we need to ritualize into our daily lives to protect us and to cultivate resilience. The opposite of self-care is self-neglect, which is not only inhumane and illogical, but a recipe for disaster. We must move past the popularized myths of it to be able to apply the science toward protecting well-being.

- **Myth:** Self-care is selfish.

- **Fact:** Every human is at risk for burnout, particularly those in leadership, human work, and caregiving professions and roles. We all benefit from and deserve needed respite and replenishment.

- **Strategy:** Give yourself permission to dismount the treadmill and take time to recharge.

- **Myth:** Self-care needs to be "big" and/or expensive.

- **Fact:** It is inadvisable to wait for the next big break or vacation to include self-care on your checklist. Research shows that small daily rituals can significantly improve our health bottom line.[4]

- **Strategy:** Invest in activities like being in nature, taking a walk, and focused breathing. They don't cost money but provide a big payoff.

- **Myth:** Self-care is solo.

- **Fact:** The efforts you invest in yourself can pay dividends for those you love and are connected with.

- **Strategy:** Sometimes "me time" and solitude might be just what you need, but self-care can also involve time with friends, family, and accountability partners.

- **Myth:** Self-care won't actually help.

- **Fact:** Prevention is less costly than repair. Regular, intentional self-care will help sustain you. There is a cumulative effect on our well-being when we put it into practice. Small things can make a big difference.

- **Strategy:** Track your self-care efforts and notice their impact on your energy, outlook, and well-being and tweak accordingly. Gathering such data can be a tremendous call to action and holds us accountable towards our change goals.

Architect Your Self-Care Strategy

Self-care comes in many variations—there is no one-size-fits-all formula, so it is wise to try out a variety and identify which are most high resonance for you. It starts with giving yourself permission and resisting any guilt that may pop up. We all need and deserve time to refuel. Here's a few starters:

Self-advocate. When we are in environments that always keep their treadmills dialed up, we need to find ways to ask for a reasonable, sustainable pace. Consider enlisting people you trust to help craft a strategy to ensure a rhythm that helps you to do well and be well. This may mean taking turns with chores at home, a more flexible work schedule, finding opportunities to collaborate, or adjusting expectations of response times to emails beyond work hours.

Develop break rituals. When our brains are overstimulated and unrested, we are more likely to fall into the trappings of automated unhelpful thoughts. Having some go-to "break rituals," short routines infused throughout the day, can be highly beneficial. While there is no one-size-fits-all approach, selecting a short ten-to-twenty-minute activity to recalibrate can help us avoid wasteful allocation of our precious cognitive resources.

Here are some options:

Feet on the wall: Slide your body as close to the wall as you can get and put your feet up into a V formation. Lie with your palms face up. Close your eyes and focus on your breathing. Notice the new energy you've generated after a few short moments.

Walking: Walking has many health benefits and is a proven mood booster.[5] Select a pace that's right for you. Take a cue from Thich Nhat Hanh and "walk as though your feet are kissing the earth." Breathe deep and tune into the beauty around you and notice that your feet are grounding you, and helping you get out of your head.

Dancing: Studies reveal that dance fosters a synchronization in low theta frequency in the brain, linked to emotion and memory processes central to interpersonal interaction and self-understanding. When we engage in partnered dance, the two brains become attuned to one another's frequency, which has been described as a "function of any empathetic community." Solo dancing also boosts limbic functions and provides numerous benefits to the mind, body, and soul.[6]

Meditation: Close your eyes and focus on an object. Concentrate on your breathing and when your thoughts wander, bring the object and your breathing back into focus. Notice your thoughts as they happen, but do not cast judgment on them. Consider using a guided meditation, song, or one of the many apps available such as Calm, Headspace, or Buddhify to help you develop foundational skills.

Advocate for Organizational Change

Getting to a place of healthier achievement isn't simply a matter of individual behavior change. It needs to be nurtured within societies, organizations, and institutions to ensure policies and practices that support, rather than diminish, human well-being. Whenever I consult with organizations to help them improve culture, the burning question is, "How do we strive for excellence and rigor without burning out?" The answers are never simple given the realities of the bottom line within a world rife with crises and volatility.

Unfortunately, many organizations perceive an emphasis on well-being as "touchy-feely," worried that they will have to outfit offices with kombucha taps, weighted blankets, and Yogibo loungers. Many are still operating from a 1950s command-and-control lens that believes no-nonsense, always-on culture will drive the best outcomes. Without realizing it, they are balking at modern brain science, which shows that organizations that prioritize well-being generate better productivity and retention. Workplaces who don't treat people like people are much more likely to breed high rates of presenteeism, absenteeism, and turnover.

Work cultures and societies that value people know that well-nurtured brains perform better. Showing people that they matter and aren't just another body on a treadmill goes a long way. It allows for building trust, which in turn creates a sense of psychological safety that brings out the best in people. The old paradigm of top-down leadership and work 'til you drop approaches do not align with modern brain science discoveries: people need time for rest, creativity, movement, and connection to do well and be well. There is no one that can endure a long-term stint on maximum incline and speed without injury or consequence.

We don't have to throw away the treadmill altogether, but we do need to make sure the settings are adjustable and calibrated to protect and sustain people and the organizations and institutions they are part of. Organizations that prioritize people know the difference between healthy achievement and anxious overachievement.

We must question work and societal cultures where inhumane paces have become normalized. When people buckle under these circumstances, we can't turn to them and shame them for their lack of strength. We need to question the settings and include people as a priority in our visions for what success truly looks like. This kind of momentum can be directed toward social impact. When the parts of the whole are healthier, both individual and collective progress can be achieved.

Move from Me to We

Collective efficacy, a construct that emerged from my grounded theory research, emphasizes collective accountability to one another. It helps us move from *me* to *we* by recognizing that an injury to one is an injury to all. That when one suffers, we all suffer; when one does well, we all do well. It helps us to adopt a global lens of conscious citizenship, rather than climb the ladder for the sake of self. Collective efficacy has no room in its heart for oppression and discrimination. Science reveals this approach as one that helps us construct an intentional and shared identity, versus a selfish, individualistic, cutthroat, territorial approach to success.[1]

> Treat yourself as if you were someone inexpressibly dear to you.
> AGAPI STASSINOPOULOS

Even more important than reclaiming our individual sanity and identity is our effort toward collective efficacy. Modern problems of privilege like not getting into an Ivy League school or receiving a mediocre performance review distract us from the significant problems at hand that require attention. Poverty rates and wealth gaps are escalating. When societies do not ensure fair minimum wages and provide a decent standard of living, overwork becomes a matter of survival, not choice, for far too many. If we are in a position where we have resources, sharing them can help us take on a role in society that is desperately needed and begin restoration and reparations through collective efficacy.

Enacting collective efficacy doesn't mean we need to undertake mass treadmill destruction or cancel memberships entirely. Achievement for the sake of one another is a way we can channel our talents, drive, and resources. When healthy achievement is fueled by a desire to actively contribute toward collective efficacy, we become better positioned to stave off the burnout and demoralization that can seem inevitable during complex times. When we take agency for our own responses to the Cult of Overachievement, we become more effective as voices for change. This can feel like a risk when we stand up against such forces, but it is one worth taking.

You are not your accomplishments. You are a whole being.

SESSION SEVEN WORKSHEET

Reject the Cult of Overachievement

A thoroughly good relationship with ourselves results in being still, which doesn't mean we don't run and jump and dance about. It means there's no compulsiveness. We don't overwork, overeat, over-smoke, overseduce. In short, we begin to stop causing harm.

PEMA CHÖDRÖN

Choose Being Over Doing

Focus on Your Dature as a Divine Being, Not a Disposable Thing

The Cult of Overachievement invites us to mount treadmills at an early age, keeping an inhumane pace and steep incline to earn coveted spots and roles in life. We end up risking our well-being and chances to own our authentic identities. We are taught that leisure is taboo, and that our worth is based on test scores, letters after our names, accolades, and image. Despite all that's being invested, rates of imposter syndrome, perfectionism, social comparison, and social anxiety are escalating. To combat the effects of Underperformance Dysmorphic Disorder, we can architect a more expansive identity to recast ourselves as human beings, not human doings. We are not commodities to be thrown away who fall for the lie that working ourselves to the bone makes us viable and worthy. It is worth the risk to forego winning all the prizes so that we can become healthy achievers who stave off burnout and work toward collective efficacy.

Being Check: Reflect

What are the settings like on my treadmill?

How often do I adjust them or dismount altogether?

On a less productive day, am I inclined to feel guilty and call myself "lazy?"

What is the relationship between my self-esteem and roles and goals: the things I do vs. who I am?

In what situations have I experienced imposter syndrome?

Which behaviors of the anxious achiever do I exhibit? Healthy achiever?

Is the school or work culture I'm part of one that values well-being?

Have I ever fallen for any of the myths of self-care? Which ones?

In what ways do I self-advocate? Is there room to improve in this area?

Which break rituals and self-care practices work well for me?

Who might make a good partner to enjoy activities with and/or hold me accountable?

Action Steps: Microdose Bravery: Redefine Success

Success is sold to us as a formula of meeting goals and taking on roles that look good but can feel bad. When identity is derived from external metrics propagated within the Cult of Achievement, we can grow weary and even face injury and burnout. Rather than succumb to the bait across our lifespan, it can be helpful to move from me to we and see that becoming healthy achievers for the sake of one another can bring about collective efficacy and optimal outcomes for all. Here are some ways to resist the pressures and seek wholeness:

1. **Calibrate your own treadmill.** You define your own settings, and how long and for what reason you invest in goals. Work to stop basing your worth on comparing yourself to what someone else

is doing and instead determine your own metrics for success as a whole person. Resist comparison, perfectionism, and roles that seem prestigious but leave you locked in 24-7 with no reprieve.

2. **Enact your self-care plan.** Include break rituals and self-care practices as part of your daily life. Pick activities that are simple and sustainable and build them into your schedule. Resist any guilt and grant yourself permission to take the time to nourish and sustain your mind, body, and soul. What are your favorites? How often are you getting them in?

3. **Move from me to we.** Consider your role in advancing collective efficacy. Think about ways you can influence the world through conscientious behavior. If you are in a position where you have resources or privilege, look to utilize that in ways that bring about positive outcomes beyond your own benefit. Write it all down and ask for feedback from those you trust are committed to accountability and social change.

Perfectionism is the voice of the oppressor, the enemy of the people. It will keep you cramped and insane your whole life, and it is the main obstacle between you and a shitty first draft. I think perfectionism is based on the obsessive belief that if you run carefully enough, hitting each stepping-stone just right, you won't have to die. The truth is that you will die anyway and that a lot of people who aren't even looking at their feet are going to do a whole lot better than you, and have a lot more fun while they're doing it.

ANNE LAMOTT

You Are Not Your Label

If you are walking on a path thick with brambles and rocks, a path that abruptly twists and turns, it's easy to get lost, or tired, or discouraged. You might be tempted to give up entirely. But if a kind and patient person comes along and takes your hand, saying, 'I see you're having a hard time—here, follow me, I'll help you find your way,' the path becomes manageable, the journey less frightening.

ELYN R. SAKS

Choose Solidarity Over Stigma

One of my favorite bumper stickers reads: labels are for jars, not people. Unfortunately, labels are overstocked across the world, pre-printed and slapped on the second we arrive: girl or boy, light or dark skinned, high or low class. Soon after, it's gay or straight, normal or abnormal, popular or outcast, well or unwell, smart or stupid, successful or loser. The labels don't peel off easily, manufactured with a glue that's toxic and hard to scrub off. The distributors of the labels are trying to keep their system working by imprinting us with a mark that dictates who is seen or unseen, heard or unheard, who's likely to be well and do well, who gets to live or die. Labels perpetuate stigma, stereotyping, and discrimination, increasing risk for depression and anxiety, especially for marginalized and underrepresented identities. It's no wonder that we are in a full-blown global mental health crisis. This requires our full attention to move to a place of safety and solidarity.

When mental health issues hit us personally, it can feel like there's no way out. Consider the story of Fred Frese, who at twenty-five was poised for tremendous success. He was on his way to becoming a Marine Corps captain when it became clear he was suffering from something beyond the usual bad day. Frese was diagnosed with schizophrenia: complete with delusions, psychotic episodes, and hospitalizations that lasted an entire decade.

Schizophrenia is commonly seen as a label that is damning, an insurmountable diagnosis that generally gets in the way of even basic functioning, never mind what Frese pulled off. Despite this, he managed to earn his doctorate, marry, and unhook from the delusions and paranoia that were holding him hostage. He received and complied with a strict treatment protocol to help him regulate his mind and emotions and defy convention with what many would characterize as the most stigmatized, unhopeful of labels.

Against the odds, Frese achieved an epic breakthrough: he went from being a psychiatric patient to becoming the director of psychology at Ohio's largest state hospital. Eventually, he became a professor of psychiatry at Northeast Ohio Medical University and department chair of their medical school. This is a feat on many levels. The automations that come with schizophrenia do not typically lend themselves to such a dramatic recovery that allows one to not only stabilize, but to help others to do the same. And he didn't stop there.[1]

It was only a few hours into the National Alliance on Mental Illness (NAMI) conference in Denver, Colorado, when I met Dr. Fred Frese. If you've ever been to any other, non-NAMI conferences, you know the drill: there's the guy tweeting his head off trying to win Best Hashtags; the underwhelming continental breakfast with unripe honeydew and no watermelon in sight; and awkward, contrived networking with proverbial business card hand-offs and LinkedIn stalking. People wear their best Normal Disguises: business casual (there's something about those khakis, Sperrys, and pearl earrings that screams "I'm totally fine!"). Everyone is wearing lanyards and giving their best impersonation of Normal, which is very, very boring.

NAMI conferences are nothing like this. They are like what you'd get if you combined a Bob Marley concert with a doggie park (minus the poop), and filled it with characters cast by Dan Levy, all supervised by the love children of Marianne Williamson and Deepak Chopra. It is come one, come all: there are No Normal Disguises Allowed. Everyone is breathing a sigh of collective relief, showing up as their gorgeous selves, with no pretentiousness in sight. It feels like home: *minus irritable roommates and never-ending messes to clean up.*

I made the rounds with people who have been through the worst of the worst and who make you feel safest of safe: like you're wrapped in a million Snuggies with Enya on repeat and lavender oil wafting through the air. There were therapy dogs casually stopping by my book signing table with their owners and there was ZERO POSTURING or need to over explain ANYTHING. Most of what was said did not require words. We had stories and scars and were there to end stigma and discrimination, and to send The Memo to policymakers: You need to do wayyyy more toward mental health prevention, integration, and access.

The solidarity at NAMI was EVERYTHING: there were no snake-oilsy Pretending to Be Normal People (P2BNPs) who generally infest the hallways at such events, begging to become LinkedIn friends to drum up likes and evangelize their three-step programs.

When Fred approached me, I could tell he wasn't a P2BNP, so I put my phone down, meeting the eye contact he'd initiated. We were braving the frigid air conditioning and stiff hotel chairs with tacky gold embossing and a grandparental, putrid green pattern in the social influencers lounge. He nonchalantly told me about his schizophrenia recovery story as we sipped ice cold water out of 1970s goblets. I got chills, and it wasn't from the hotel elements.

Frese asked about my credentials but was more interested in my backstory. I told him of my trajectory with public disclosures in my writing and speaking. I recounted the time I'd been invited to give a book talk and share my research on human resilience at the university where I teach: It is Thattt Snowy Monday: the kind of situation where you are actively wondering if too much pizza has been ordered and trying to manage the very possible scenario that it might be you, the tech crew, and your die-hard besties for the next hour. But just as I have resigned myself to this very fate, I am hit with the be-careful-what-you-wish-for moment when EVERYONE shows up. Heads at the university. Students galore. My bosses. People from the community. My heart thumps. People had trudged through some serious New England tundra to be there. The energy in the room gives me the nudge I need to go rogue.

Five minutes in, I abandon my PowerPoint and go for it. I can feel the stare of the pizza guy all the way in the back of the room as I spill out the details of my chronic battle with depression and anxiety in non-academic, not-at-all clinical terms. Even though I am dead against stigma and all about seeing mental health from a scientific and biopsychosocial lens (one that accounts for genetics, cognitive factors, and social context[2]), telling my story in full color in front of EVERYONE is A LOTTT.

The walk of shame on the way back to the office is unsettling. It feels like I've committed professional suicide. *Have I watched too many Brené Brown talks? Aren't I supposed to be able to KEEP IT TOGETHER since this is my area of expertise? Maybe I should go straight home.* I worry that there will be some variation of shunning, awkwardness, or micromanagement greeting me when I arrive at my desk. But instead of the anticipated stares and whispers, my colleagues pull me aside with hugs, high fives, and their own disclosures.

Our conversations were a needed reminder that our reactions were "normal" given the demands of our work, with all the pressure educators face of attending to everyone but ourselves. Burnout is highest amongst those in teaching and human service professions.[3] Academics and clinicians face pressure to be all knowing and resilient. We take pride in what we do and who we are. Maybe we think we can outsmart mental health issues. Or it's just A LOT to admit we need help too.

Even so, we all knew we needed to cry uncle: accepting a fate of burnout wasn't exactly what we signed up for. My colleagues and I were finding a new sense of solidarity. We were not at NAMI-conference comfort level, but it was a breakthrough, and there would be no truncating of details or airbrushing my story moving forward.

Eventually, I decided to dial it up and gave a TEDx talk called "The Risk You Must Take" that highlighted Thattt Snowy Monday when everything changed. I acted it out on stage, along with a scene with my therapist Lyla giving me some reality checks on my tendency to overdo everything and not cut myself a break. The day the talk was released online, I went into a catatonic state for at least two full days. Public disclosure, even knowing its tremendous value, can be jarring and provocative. This is why I love NAMI, with its quintessential solidarity and support which helps us take risks to liberate ourselves and one another from stigma.

When I recounted that Monday to Frese, he smiled and gave me a knowing look. He told me that the sense of solidarity he experienced was a vital factor in his incredible journey of recovery, advocacy, and impact. His wife and peers were what got him through. He pointed me to an article that he coauthored with colleagues who also had lived experiences of schizophrenia and went into work devoted toward preventing and treating mental illness.

> You either walk inside your story and own it or you stand outside your story and hustle for your worthiness.
>
> BRENÉ BROWN

As we said goodbye, Frese wished me well on my talk and promised he'd send people my way. When he left, I Googled him and saw that the article he had casually mentioned was the most frequently hit on in the Schizophrenia Bulletin.[4] Frese was a legend in the field, known for his recovery story and convening people who also had severe struggles yet still went on to make significant leadership contributions in mental health disciplines. Astonishingly, he wasn't one of a kind.

One of the coauthors of the article is Dr. Elyn Saks, another epic thought leader who lives with schizophrenia. She is an esteemed professor, lawyer, and psychiatrist and is the Orrin B. Evans Professor of Law, Psychology, and Psychiatry and the Behavioral Sciences at the University of Southern California Gould Law School.[5] She has written extensively on the impact of coercion and excessive force against persons with psychiatric illnesses. Since age eight, she has suffered major episodes, with her first full blown episode while studying at Oxford.[6]

Increase Your Mental Health Awareness to Avoid Internalizing Labels

Disparaging labels that society assigns according to race, class, gender, sexual orientation, age, ability, and country of origin are destructive. In the mental health realm, proper diagnosis by a licensed practitioner can be life changing, but unfortunately, diagnosis can move at turtle speed. Stigma, fear, and desensitization to symptoms, along with lack of access to the most knowledgeable doctors, can severely impede getting the right help. The average time to treatment from initial onset of symptoms ranges between eight to ten years.[7] That's a big ughhh and a whole lot of unnecessary suffering and trudging. It can also be dangerous.

Basic 101 mental health hygiene protocol, suicide prevention, symptom awareness, and evidence-based strategies have typically been left off society's teaching agenda.[8] We are taught to floss, memorize the periodic chart, and properly spell too, two, and to, but most of us were never taught the difference between a bad day and a manic episode, or a proportionate reaction to stress versus a sign it's time to hit up a therapist. We don't know what a "panic attack" is until we are in the ER, or that there are many universal precautions we can take to prevent an escalation of symptoms and protect our brains.

There is always a reason for behavior that goes beyond what meets the eye. Diagnostic frameworks can provide an individual and their loved ones with invaluable tools. When we remain in the dark over the root causes of issues, it can lead to improper, old school characterizations of behavior. Difficulties are mislabeled as moral failings, lack of will, signs of low intelligence, or even a matter of laziness or craziness. Getting the right assessment of what's happening can lead to identifying aligned strategies to help. There is no good reason to stay in the dark: the risk of ignoring symptoms and not knowing far exceeds the risk of making these discoveries in the first place. Either way, the underlying issues will affect us, and when we know why, it can generate needed insights and momentum to make improvements.

Diagnosis can serve as an important organizing tool that explains behavior and phenomena which can otherwise be incredibly perplexing and hard to make sense of. For anyone who has struggled or watched a loved one endure mental health challenges, you know that finally getting an answer can be cathartic. There is tremendous relief when we can get to the bottom of things with trained and caring professionals. The benefits of this cannot be overstated.

Even though there's growing consensus that we all show up on diagnostic spectrums and vacillate in and out of mental health episodes across our lifetime,[9] we are currently entrained to see diagnosis solely from a deficit framing. We shudder at the implications of diagnosis, even when research shows that people who show up on spectrums are also likely to show up with incredible strengths.

Bipolar disorder spectrum has been associated with high levels of empathy, creativity, and artistry.[10] People with ADHD often have incredible entrepreneurial abilities, a zest for life, and boundless energy.[11] People on the autism spectrum are often highly observant and gifted.[12] As Drs. Frese and Saks' lives illustrate, people with lived experiences of schizophrenia can be highly intuitive and brilliant. This is not to romanticize mental illness, overgeneralize experiences within spectrums, or oversimplify recovery processes, but to honor and hold space for the paradoxes, and to be able to devote just as much attention to cultivating the strengths inherent within lived experiences as well as addressing the disruptions. BOTH are critical in bolstering outcomes.

We need a revolution in mental health awareness to help us grasp the wonder and complexity of human behavior, health and functioning, and the nuances and intersections of brilliance and madness. This starts with dismantling myopic myths that prevent us from seeing the simultaneous wonder and complexity of our fullest selves. It involves providing access to the tools that mitigate being overtaken by the ravages of burnout and mental decompensation: the very risks of living in the modern world. Our sense-making approaches need to be comprehensive—grounded both scientifically and medically, steeped in love, and presented in ways that account for the multidimensionality of emotional and spiritual essence. Those things that go beyond what the mind can first conceive of.

This new mental health imperative relies upon universal precautions and a vehement resistance to linear checklists and binary labels that frame our gorgeous spirits solely as either complex and fraught or indomitable and wondrous. It also relies not on good will and best practices but the moral courage of policymakers to treat human beings like human beings. Dogs are often treated better than people. This is our new imperative: to radically change the way we care for ourselves and one another. We cannot extricate ourselves from the fact that the lines we walk are incredibly thin and blurry, and our only hope is to rewrite and navigate them together in solidarity, with every measure of creative reason and conscious community that can be mustered . . .

Diagnosis can begin the important process of sense-making and help pinpoint specific, evidence-based strategies and develop a comprehensive treatment plan for a person and their support system to draw upon. A prognosis can similarly be beneficial in that it can provide an expected course of what the recovery process might entail, including possible outcomes.

Still, diagnosis and prognosis are not the end-all-be-all. Allen Frances, prominent rogue psychiatrist and author of *Saving Normal: An Insider's Revolt Against Out-of-Control Psychiatric Diagnosis, DSM-5, Big Pharma, and the Medicalization of Ordinary Life,* warns against diagnostic inflation and overtreatment of the "worried well." His work is a reminder of the importance of seeing oneself in context and understanding the difference between proportionate reactions to stressors versus clinically significant difficulties. Over-medicalization of the human condition can prove detrimental.[13] Here's what to look out for:

- **Rigid diagnosis.** Diagnosis has come a long way since the days of Freud. We have evolved to see that there's a continuum of symptoms that can lead to a range of mild, moderate, or severe disruptions that can influence our lives on the daily and in the long run. Diagnosis should consider biopsychosocial factors, strengths, and caveats of each person's experience. It is important to unhook from stereotypical views of a particular disorder based on popularized myths, anecdotal information, or cautionary tales. There are no two people on a spectrum that have identical experiences. We all have unique variables and protective factors.

- **Damning prognosis.** The outlook we cast on the future bears heavily on outcomes. Because so many people remain in the shadows before accessing help, initial impressions can be grave. We are wired for resilience, but if we've hit rock bottom or gone through a long and uphill battle with repeated cycles and patterns, it can diminish hope. Mental health issues are infamous for hosting that toxic inner critic that taints our outlook. When we are engulfed in difficult moments, or simply exhausted by all the climbing we've done, it's generally best to avoid sweeping overgeneralizations of what's to come, and instead focus on the now, building blocks as catalysts for small wins. Over time, those small victories can have a positive cumulative effect and bring us much further than once envisioned or what has been put on us.

- **Unilateral treatment protocols.** Medicine can save and dramatically improve the quality of our lives but is not a one-stop solution. Brain science is constantly unveiling vital discoveries that help us to stay calibrated. The world of functional medicine, integrative health, and epigenetics has revealed myriad possibilities that can be leveraged. Research shows that learning coping skills, engaging in community and meaningful activities, lifestyle medicine (proper sleep, nutrition, exercise), pursuing creative endeavors, and creating solid relationships are essential protective factors for mental health. Psychoeducation and supervised skill practice (people and places that provide accountability and support) are powerful forces in recovery.[14]

Frese's and Saks' stories of recovery started with proper diagnosis and treatment and landed in a place nothing short of inspirational. When I met Frese, it was hours into the NAMI conference, and I was already floored. Later that day, when it was my turn to present my research, *all Frese's friends showed up*, which is to say that *nearly the entire conference* had descended upon me. I hadn't had the chance to update my friend Elizabeth, who had come along on the trip to help me out, about my Frese encounter. She'd just spent the last hour on a wild goose chase across the streets of Denver searching for the very precise blend of non-gassy green juice I'd asked her to grab for me: *"something with cucumber . . . celery . . . apple is fine, but not a lot of kale because I never drink too much of it before a public talk."*

When Elizabeth, who's up for at least five nominations in The Most Patient Friend Ever category, unsuspectingly arrived back still upbeat from this *only best friends do this kind of favor* excursion, with the special edition, minimal-gas green beverage I'd sent her scavenging for, she gave me the *what's with this crowd* look. There wasn't time to explain. I was already completely encircled by Frese's comrades.

I was standing eye to eye with people who had recovered from schizophrenia and other major mental illnesses. The solidarity was palpable. We immediately gave each other The Great Gift: seeing each other in full splendor, both in flaws and beauty. We skipped over the inconsequential and got to business. The safety and energy of the moment brought out an even more dramatic mutation of my Thattt Snowy Monday self, and I started yelling out cryptic one-liners like "there's no such thing as normal," "we all struggle," "human condition, NOT mental health condition," "it's society that's messed up" and "we cannot pretend." People were crying and cheering and hugging, and then it was dinner time and Elizabeth and I stood alone quietly for about .06 seconds until we both burst into uncontrollable tears.

Burn Your Normal Disguise

The highlight of the NAMI experience was that people did not have Normal Disguises (NDs) in their wardrobe—they'd long since thrown them out. NDs are handed out early in life. We are told that the LAST THING we want to do is to let people know our struggles, vulnerabilities, and truths. Just suck it up, fake it 'til you make it, don't make a scene. Normal Disguises are said to protect us against scrutiny. To make people like and accept us. To keep us "safe" and "unexposed." To keep them from thinking we are crazy, weird, uncool, or weak. And for those in some religious communities where there's scientific dismissiveness, mental health issues can be conjured as a lack of faith and spiritual attunement. The pressure is laid on thick: pray harder, be more spiritual, have more faith so you will be immune to such struggles. It MUST BE something you're doing or not doing.

> I don't go crazy.
> I am crazy. I just
> go normal from
> time to time.
> AUTHOR UNKNOWN

Professional communities and corporate environments have their own version: work ridiculous hours, endure back-to-back meetings, do the work of multiple people, sacrifice sleep, eat at your desk, do not take ONE

SECOND to breathe, and *Gawddd Forbidd* you ever let anyone see you sweat. *Keep that Normal Disguise on—even if it is squeezing the life out of you.*

At home and work, Normal Disguises are heavily required artillery across the gender spectrum with serious consequences resulting for everyone. The foundational piece of clothing in the ND is the straightjacket. Men and women are taught that normal is attractive to the opposite sex. Anything but straight is seen as deviant, even though sexual orientation and gender are now understood as a fluid spectrum, rather than fixed.

Men (male identifying) are taught to layer up on toughness and to limit emotional responses to anger. Normal is code for masculine, and worth is defined by size, strength, force, and The Trophy you sleep with. Ironically, if you are brave enough to reject the forced disguise, exposing your real self, you will be called a pussy, sissy, or baby. Even when doing so is The Great Act of Courage.

> When the whole world is silent, even one voice becomes powerful.
> MALALA YOUSAFZAI

Women (female identifying) receive their own disguise wardrobe too. They are taught to masquerade their real needs, put on the cloak of guilt, and spend inordinate amounts of time focused on presentation, appearance, eating ridiculous amounts of salad without being gassy, and making everyone else happy. Normal is code for quiet, doing endless emotional labor to hold everyone together, submissive, thin, and desirable. Normal equates to fuckability—and there is nothing less sexy than being too bossy or talking about how uncomfortable and unfitting the disguises are, and how irritating the scratchy labels are. They are supposed to be worn or you will be called high maintenance, hysterical, or endure gaslighting when you stand up and speak truth to power. Even when doing so is The Great Act of Courage.

Even though both transgender and nonbinary identities have long been recognized by cultures and societies across the world, they have to fight perceptions that they are following a fad. They deal with constant microaggressions, unsolicited questions and stares, and emotional and physical attacks on their identity and human rights. The misconceptions, violence, and hate are endless and atrocious.

NDs are hard to shed: standing up to these so-called societal "norms" bears consequences. But it is a risk worth taking. Otherwise, we are subject to dangerous unintended consequences. We can run the risk of being passive bystanders who watch when things like bias, oppression, discrimination, and violence are normalized. Passivity allows society to wear its own disguise, pretending that the automations of deficit and labels perpetuated by racism, sexism, classism, heterosexism, ageism, ableism, and xenophobia are "normal."

How are we supposed to be normal within such an abnormal world? None of the conditions that cause us to struggle come even close to being normal. Abject poverty. Racism. Discrimination. Greed. Disease. War. Humanitarian crises everywhere we turn. Lack of basic resources for the majority while elites hoard. The root problems for mental health are being grossly overlooked and underaddressed. You'd think that given this, we might have the moral decency to at least provide the right kinds of services and safety nets. Yet, funding for mental health is all crumbs.

Taking care of people should not be controversial, nor should it be a novel concept—PLUS we have the resources and knowledge to do so. But instead, across the world, there is a critical shortage of practitioners and services. Rural areas are especially scarce when it comes to finding help. Like most everything in life, if you don't have money, you are far less likely to get the help you need. Plus, there is very little effort exerted toward prevention and mitigating the factors that ramp up mental health risk. Research shows that if we improve schools and communities and have a decent standard of living for families, including safe housing and access to healthcare, it significantly improves mental health outcomes. The work of the Robert Wood Johnson Foundation, along with the Centers for Disease Control and Prevention (CDC) and the World Health Organization, emphasizes that social determinants of health (the conditions in the places people live, learn, work, and play) impact a wide range of health risks and outcomes, particularly for mental health.[15] Social determinants play a significant role in health inequities—the unfair differences between groups based on where they live in the world.[16]

We cannot for another split second accept the Normal Disguises
of unjust systems. They will only continue to divide and alienate
us. These costumes need to burn if we want to see us move
from a place of pathologizing people to prioritizing them. As

individuals, when we internalize deficit labels, we might be less inclined to call into question the social issues that are affecting our well-being. On micro and macro levels, we need to remain hypervigilant and brave in overcoming entrenched paradigms that assign labels on people instead of addressing the systemic forces that bring harm to begin with . . .

Move From Stigma to Solidarity

Life has NEVER BEEN NORMAL, why are we expecting ourselves to be? When we're afraid to risk letting people know our truths, we can end up losing a vital community who would get it and help usher in a whole lot of needed relief. Instead of connecting over our shared humanity, we end up isolating further. I am not suggesting that we should strip down and bear all to everyone. Not everyone has the bandwidth or ethics to hold proper space that keeps us safe. But exiting the set of the Normal Show that society casts us for is a profitable risk that outweighs the perceived benefits of hiding. Here are some ways to shed the stifling Normal Disguise and move from stigma to solidarity:

> If you want to keep a secret, you must also hide it from yourself.
> GEORGE ORWELL

Microdose bravery through disclosure. Asking for help doesn't have to be a public play-by-play dumping of what's in your head. It can start with reaching out to someone you trust and who gets it. While asking for help is arguably the hardest, it's also the most important. Hiding only exacerbates mental health conditions, and stigma blocks us from finding a community of safety and solidarity. Reaching out in manageable doses helps us tap into the many channels of healing available.

Don't let your label define you. Labels can help provide an organizing framework for understanding emotions and behaviors, but they should never become parts of embedded identity. Every label carries a connotation; thus, we need to approach our analysis of ourselves and one another with great caution and intentionality. It is vital to know the difference between using diagnosis as a tool versus adopting it as a fully internalized identity. We are so much more than our labels.

Refuse to wear a Normal Disguise: Be your own wardrobe designer. Putting on airs and pretending to be someone we're not only exacerbates isolation. Let yourself show up in full splendor: that kind of energy becomes infectious and magnetic. Rather than conforming, take exception with pressure to suit up and instead design your own sweet spot that is unique and unconventional.

Identify your supports. Work to build a proper TEAM—Trusted Energizing and Mentoring Relationships with people who will get you, see you, nurture, and co-inspire. Solidarity is a vital component of healing and recovery. We need people who have the emotional maturity and with-it-ness that we can be ourselves with and experience reciprocity.

Advocate for new social paradigms. Do not fall for 1950s depictions of mental health that label people as crazy, lazy, stupid, and pathological. Modern brain science shows that all of us are likely to vacillate in and out of mental health episodes across our lifespan. It is just as vital to consider ways to leverage our talents, resources, assets, and strengths as it is to understand what underlying factors might be impacting us and interfering with the quality of life.

Resisting labels is as much a collective effort as it is individual. We cannot stay silent and risk suffering and complacency. Even pre-pandemic, the World Health Organization (WHO) projected depression as the leading cause of disability by 2030. Given the critical shortage of mental health practitioners worldwide, we need an all-hands-on-deck approach to fighting stigma and improving access to prevention and treatment.[17] We need leaders and citizens with the moral courage to prioritize and protect mental health. As WHO points out, there's no health without mental health.

Mental health relies upon physical, economic, institutional, and societal structures that support individual, familial, and community mental health. This starts with teaching ways to adopt a universal precautions lifespan approach (meaning we are all prone to suffering at various junctures in our lifetime) to mental health, to putting funding dollars toward early intervention, integrated services, and comprehensive treatment for all ages. Especially for vulnerable populations—those marginalized due to race, class, socioeconomic status, gender, sexual orientation, ability, religion, place of origin, or otherwise. We need to work collectively to strive toward societies where discrimination and stigma are things of the past.

Assessment and diagnosis have a vital place in providing understanding and setting the course for often lifesaving and life-altering treatment, and there is no reason to wait almost a decade to find relief. Prevention and adequate services must happen early on. We need to address the critical shortage of trained mental health practitioners. We also must avoid the over-pathologization of normal and honor the fact that we are human beings, with names and stories, who should never be defined merely by a diagnosis.

The stories of Drs. Frese and Saks' are proof of the extraordinary capacities we have to heal and move beyond damning labels. This starts with taking the risk of asking for help and linking arms with those who have longed since burned their Normal Disguises. The Great Gift, seeing ourselves and one another through a more loving and humane lens, allows us to move from scrutinized "mental health condition" to "human condition." This kind of community is how we move from stigma to solidarity.

You are not your label. You are so much more.

> What mental health needs is more sunlight, more candor, and more unashamed conversation.
>
> GLENN CLOSE

Redefine Normal

The power to label is the power to destroy.
ALLEN FRANCES

Choose Solidarity Over Stigma

Seek Community Over Cover-Ups

Even the most damning circumstances can lend themselves to healing and recovery. Labels are not fixed parts of our identities. Posturing and pretending to be normal can lead to loneliness and disconnection from our true selves and each other. Taking the risk of revealing ourselves requires courage but is one we must take. Solidarity allows us to move from a place of stigmatizing mental health conditions to seeing ourselves as part of the human condition. The Great Gift we can give to ourselves and one another is seeing each other in full splendor. When we burn the Normal Disguises society ties us up in, we begin to heal. Our risk is no longer fear of stigma, isolation, and alienation.

Labels Check: Reflect

What labels have been assigned to me?

Are there ways these have become lodged into my identity?

What is my relationship to Normal Disguises?

Who are the people that I can give and receive The Great Gift (of seeing each other) from?

What forms of healing in my life have proven beneficial?

Action Steps: Move from Stigma to Solidarity

You are not reduced to a label that you have been assigned. We can form communities to overcome internalized negative views of ourselves and generate a strong sense of solidarity.

Focus on finding spaces where you can be yourself and ask for the help you need. Know that you are not alone and that your own story has infinite power and potential to be a healing offering to the world.

> The greatness of a community is most accurately measured by the compassionate actions of its members.
>
> CORETTA SCOTT KING

1. **Reach out.** Consider who you feel safe enough to take this risk with. Resist the urge to self-diagnose or ignore symptoms. Find a licensed practitioner who knows what they're doing. Help them get to know you fully. Your strengths. Your passions. Your backstory. Your health and family history. Unique stressors and life stage. Your social roles and responsibilities. What's working well. What's not working well. This is an essential step to recovery.

2. **Redefine normal.** Resist old-school framings of mental health and develop your identity around your values, strengths, contributions, and relationships. Not everything is a full-blown disorder. And even when there's something major going on, there's still plenty of room for healing and resilience to be cultivated. New research reveals that we all fall on the mental health diagnostic spectrum, and that we vacillate in and out of various episodes across our lifetime. Season's of life, losses, trauma, isolation, and stressors can overwhelm our thresholds for coping—it's part of being human.

3. **Seek community and solidarity.** Work to identify and add new forms of community where The Great Gift, seeing and being fully seen, is present.

4. **Leverage comedy as a therapeutic tool.** Watch Gary Gulman's HBO special *The Great Depresh* as well as Neal Brennan's *3 Mics* and Wanda Sykes' *Not Normal* Netflix specials. Watch performances and learn more about the backstories of comedians Pete Davidson, Jordan Carlos, and Chris Gethard.

You Are Not Unguided

Synchronicity: a meaningful coincidence of two
or more events where something other than
the probability of chance is involved.
CARL JUNG

Choose Synchronicity Over Control

Y ou shouldn't have done that." I could feel the scolding bubbling up in my friend Dee. "She's a big name, you know."

I wasn't convinced I'd committed the mortal sin Dee thought she'd just witnessed.

Dee went on. "She's renowned. You can't just go up to her like that. Plussss, she's A-r-i-a-n-n-a Huffington's sister."

Dee had just watched me dash to the front of the room, fish my book out of my handbag, and hug Agapi Stassinopoulous like she was my long-lost mama, all while spilling out the tangential details of my quest to disrupt the Cult of Overachievement. After twenty years as a therapist, I'd been working nonstop to get the word out that success isn't success if we're too sick to enjoy it. That overachievement is overrated. That mental health is EVERYTHING.

I didn't notice Dee was watching in horror, trying to flag me down with her side-eye because she thought I was starting to sound like a creepy sales guy with a too-tight suit and salami breath.

"You're an established professor in behavioral science. She's a celeb . . . you gotta go through the right channels. You don't want to risk giving off a book peddling vibe."

I wasn't trying to overstep boundaries, but something had drawn me to Agapi's magnanimous energy. Her name literally means "love," which is very fitting. My instincts screamed at me to approach her. It was her light, not her fame, I was drawn to.

Plus, I believe that when we take small risks like this, it opens the door for amazing experiences and human connection, especially when we are being genuine.

When Agapi hugged me, that 1,000-year best friend feeling came over me. It didn't matter that she was "big." Her realness was what mattered. The next thing I knew, we were laughing and exchanging telephone numbers.

Dee made me pinky swear I wouldn't repeat my socially awkward actions. I was her personal guest at the Virgin Pulse Thrive conference we were attending in Boston. She didn't want any further fanfare.

The next morning, Agapi approached me in the foyer of the hotel. "Daaahhhling. I read your book last night and loooooved it. Next time you're in New York, be sure to visit me. And you muuuust blog for us at the Huffington Post . . ." Agapi kept using words like "synchronicity" and "manifestation" as she hugged me, and we snapped selfies. Dee finally cracked a smile. I was glad I'd trusted my instincts.

Two weeks later, my inbox greets me with another gem: "Congratulations. Your book *Reset: Make the Most of Your Stress* has won the Next Generation Indie Book Awards Motivational Book of the Year. Join us in New York." Whaaat? I book the trip and email Agapi in one fell swoop.

My then nineteen-year-old daughter Tori and I pack our bags for the ceremony held at the Harvard Club in New York, a fancy venue where I apparently missed the thirty-five warning emails NOT to take pictures in the foyer. We are glammed up in the highest of heels and longest of lashes and didn't realize we were under surveillance. The foyer incident isn't my only faux paus of the night.

Upstairs, the room is filled with authors of all different genres, equally enthusiastic about their own awards, wishes, and dreams. I find it interesting that everyone I am bumping into keeps using the word "synchronicity," just as Agapi had a couple of weeks ago. It's not exactly the kind of language we toss around freely in academia.

A guy straight out of *Harry Potter* wearing a fedora finally gives me the skinny. He waves his hands dramatically and tells me about "alignment," "intention," "manifestation" and how our "energy is all connected." That things are supposed to happen in certain ways. That we need to be open to the laws of destiny to seize what the "universe" wants to deliver to us in divine orchestration and timing. "*S-y-n-c-h-r-o-n-o-c-i-t-y*," he tells me, "is a thiiing."

At first, I'm not so sure. It sounds like the kind of magical thinking counter to my behavioral science training. My colleagues in academia would frown on this kind of thing, and if there is anything my work has taught me, it's how susceptible we are to believing what we want to believe. But then I remember the Agapi thing.

The speaker comes to the podium, breaking up the mystical conversations. Time for business. She introduces Marilyn Allen, the no-nonsense New York literary agent and cofounder of the book competition.

Marilyn gets up and gives an animated speech about the last winner of the book competition: work went viral, six-figure deals, gigs on all the shows. Everyone is salivating and planning their outfits for their own tours and appearances. The collective energy is palpable. Marilyn has done her job. We are hyped.

They corral us to line up for pictures to meet the contest heads. When Marilyn shakes my hand, I don't even say a proverbial hello or thank you, I just blurt out, "I'm going to be next." She smiles politely, hands me her card, and tells me to email her.

My daughter yanks my arm and gives me a much fiercer version of Dee's side-eye. "Mommmm . . . too much. . . let's go." You cannot argue with a nineteen-year-old.

The next day, Agapi calls in response to the text I'd sent the night before. "Dahhhhling . . . come and see me. I have only two hours. Trust synchronicity. Believe you will get a cab, and it will manifest."

She rattles off the address of the Huffington Post. Tori and I are making silent scream faces and jumping up and down until we realize it's five o'clock rush hour in New York City.

We give it our best, but maybe we were missing a step in the laws of cab manifestation. A guy pedals up on a rickety bicycle taxi that my dad would call a "death trap": the kind that looks romantic in Central Park but not the best judgment during NYC downtown rush.

I YELL no thank you as politely as I can and then feel Tori's signature no-nonsense first-born grip tightening on my arm. "C'mon Mom—this is the only way!" She isn't having my not-so-low-key-panic attack, despite my pleadings.

We jump in, and I let out a little scream as we weave in and out of traffic. The guy tells us not to worry. He promises to get us there in one piece, flashes a smile and tells us that he is a believer in *synchronicity*.

Agapi greets us like it's a holiday and we're her long lost relatives. She introduces us to the entire Huffington Post staff, an impressive group of savvy New Yorkers with enough brain power to run the world. We eat baklava and talk about our mutual passions to stop the madness of the Cult of Overachievement.

Arianna Huffington is a few feet away, filming a video on burnout. She comes out to greet us and sign *Thrive: The Third Metric to Redefining Success and Creating a Life of Well-Being, Wisdom, and Wonder,* her latest book. She introduces us to her chief of staff, who sets me up on the spot with my blogger portal.

It's day three. My head is spinning from all the *synchronicity*, but there's still work to be done. Tori heads to meet her friend Sarah for cheesecake at the iconic Junior's. I head to the New York Book Expo, armed with copies of my book, business cards, and big dreams.

> Nonsense is that which does not fit into the prearranged patterns which we have superimposed on reality. . . . Nonsense is nonsense only when we have not yet found that point of view from which it makes sense.
>
> GARY ZUKAV

My heart drops when I see the thousands of authors, agents, and publishing houses swarming. Brenè Brown and Adriana Trigiani are headlining. I'm trying to use the laws of synchronicity, but there's way too many tabs open in my brain, and I need air.

I see a staircase and take it. At the top, there's an escalator filled with people heading toward the food court with seventeen-dollar sandwiches. I'm hangry, my feet hurt, and I want to be eating cheesecake with Tori and

Sarah, not trying to keep my head above water in this sea of literary chaos.

A petite woman is coming down the escalator. Something nudges me. She has a similarly exhausted I-need-cheesecake look. I reach out my hand to her, which feels completely natural at that moment, but by ordinary measures is weird and random.

She gives a knowing look and says, "This is overwhelming—do you want to sit down with me?" We make our way to a table with coffee stains, remnants of stale dessert crumbs and coffee rings all over it. There's a huge wad of napkins underneath it, failing to do its job of keeping it from wobbling every time we so much as gestured towards it.

I'm trying to be covert as I try to make out her name tag, but subtlety is not my game. She lets me off the hook: "I'm Lybi Ma, editor at *Psychology Today.*" She asks to see my book, flips through it, and says, "I'm not going to beat around the bush. Send me your headshot and bio, I want you to blog for us."

Was this synchronicity? It seemed so: 20,000 people, plus me resisting the urge to run out the building, plus arriving at the escalator at the precise time Lybi was coming off, plus her willingness to entertain a quirky stranger, cannot equal "mere coincidence."

On the train home, Tori and I stared at each other in disbelief as I gobbled up leftover cheesecake and processed everything that just transpired.

It was like we were live characters in one of those weird math word problems: A mom and her daughter take a train to New York. In three short days, two major publication outlets and a five-star literary agent are secured. What is the probability of such manifestation? Is this the universe's magic? Or random luck?

Synchronicity didn't have me at hello, but it was growing on me. My quest to bring impact through my writing and public platform was strong, but as

> Abandon the urge to simplify everything, to look for formulas and easy answers, and to begin to think multidimensionally, to glory in the mystery and paradoxes of life, not to be dismayed by the multitude of causes and consequences that are inherent in each experience—to appreciate the fact that life is complex.
>
> M. SCOTT PECK

hard as I was working, things were moving at a snail's pace. Before all this, my publisher advised me to "get in" with *Psychology Today* and Huffington Post, but despite multiple emails, I was like Forrest Gump with a net full of rusty sea artifacts, no shrimp. The only reason I'd been at the Virgin

Pulse conference was that my original trip to Dallas had been called off days before, creating a never before, never since three-day opening on my calendar when Dee invited me. When I returned home and told my publisher about Agapi, Marilyn, and Lybi, he congratulated me on "my hard work paying off." But I knew that what happened wasn't me being the love child of Leslie Knope and Will Farrell's *Elf* character. Hustle mattered, but so did listening to the nudges to take risks, ones cringeworthy from a proper social etiquette lens, but somehow helped by something beyond my mind's conception.

These epic experiences were affirming and provocative. I'd always believed "timing was everything" and beliefs are powerful. My science-oriented brain was trying to connect the dots between it all. I scoured books about quantum physics, metaphysical forces, and energy medicine to try and make sense. I began meditating on the regular and exploring various intersections between science and spirituality. Like any good inquiry, I have more questions than answers, but have come to realize that the little risks we endeavor at the right timing can turn us up with some incredible experiences and opportunities. Especially when our intentions are aligned to what we want to offer in the world.

> The quantum field responds not to what we want; it responds to who we are being.
>
> JOE DISPENZA

Synchronicity isn't simply about waving a magic wand to get what you want. It's also about paying attention to moments that align with your authentic identity, looking for chances to connect, and taking the risk to say yes to opportunities when they present themselves, even when you are first afraid or apprehensive.

This isn't to say that everyone has equal opportunity when it comes to risk taking and resilience. Privilege provides an unfair advantage, encouraging those who hold it to be bold and go after their dreams. For BIPOC and underrepresented groups, these ideas of manifesting whatever you want can collide with the harsh realities of inequality, racism, and violence. This makes it critical for those holding privileged identities to remain accountable and earnestly work for collective success.

Shift Your Question

Wishing for what we want is a natural part of being human. We've all blown on candles, gazed wistfully at shooting stars, tossed pennies into wishing wells, and rubbed Buddha bellies on our quest to make our wishes come true. Prosperity psychology and spiritually hype us up into thinking the world can be our oyster if we just believe, willing whatever we want into existence. Manifestation has become big business, selling easily because of the human tendency to believe we can get what we want when we want it through set steps. It's no wonder we fall for it, given the yearnings of our psyches and souls to believe that we have full control over our destiny.

This is not to say that we must forego our longings altogether. But we must recognize that superficial wishing can leave us underwhelmed and caught in a leaky bathtub: no matter how much warm water we pour in, we eventually end up shivering, wrinkly, and naked. It's natural to seek comfort and highs, but overreliance on the external environment to soothe leads to letdown. This is known as the *hedonic treadmill* in psychology, *dopamine chase* in brain science, the *hungry ghost* in Buddhism, and *Keeping up with the Kardashians* in pop culture.

Life brings intermittent comfort. We cannot expect to be enveloped by a salty lavender 112-degree bath at every turn. We also need to do the work of attuning our mind, body, and soul to being what we want versus constantly chasing it down.

When we adopt a microdosing bravery approach to life, we embrace what is possible, and architect a life of substance and vision to offer ourselves fully to the world. This begins with shifting our question from:

What will the world offer me?

to:

What will I offer the world?

This adjustment is more than semantics, or a JFK speech spin-off. The first question positions us as receivers, who are in "control" and need something. The second invites us to take the risk to embody what we want, without guarantee of receiving in equal measure. When we ask what we can contribute rather than receive, it is a way of acknowledging our inter-beingness, rather than operating in silos or in selfish interest. This helps us do the work of microdosing bravery to contribute positively without an expectation in return, something that is very counterculture.

What do you ask for the most? Is it love, protection, or someone or something to provide you with a form of deliverance? Is it jewels, money, shiny wheels, and the oohs and ahhs of the audience you're carefully curated yourself to? Stop begging the universe for more of what you don't need. Change your proposition from what you can get to what you can give, and you will find gains beyond wildest imagination and measure.

Be What You Want to Receive

Shifting our question from receiving to being what we want brings us to a new level of connection and engagement with life. To find what we're seeking, we can work to microdose bravery so that we can connect more and offer ourselves to the world by exuding what we're looking to receive. For example:

- If we want love, we keep an open mind and heart and display kindness.

- If we want to be more mindful, we focus on the now, relish in moments, and resist mindless behaviors.

- If we want healing, we seek healing resources and actively work to grow resilience.

- If we want fun, we become more playful, joyful, comedic, and fun.

- If we want creativity, we see ourselves as artists and live accordingly, engaging in flow and expression.

- If we want joy, we cultivate it by means that spark zest and enthusiasm.

- If we want peace, we engage in meditation and grounding activities.

- If we want abundance, we appreciate what is. We avoid scarcity mindsets and hold what we already have as sacred.

- If we want liberation, we work to break free from the cages of society.

listen: there's a hell of a good universe next door; let's go

E.E. CUMMINGS

Instead of clutching onto control, we work with synchronicity to be the embodiment of what we desire. We strive to be love, light, mindful, healed, fun, creative, joyful, at peace, and to find abundance and liberation. We position ourselves as an offering who exudes what the world needs.

Develop Your Soulful Savvy

I'm skeptical about the ways spirituality is packaged and sold. You wouldn't know this by visiting my house, The Land of Spiritual Paraphernalia, where you'd find my unironic placement of essential oil diffusers and Himalayan salt lamps in every room, fridge full of kombucha, the distinctive whiff of sage in the air, and a rainbow dream catcher hanging over my bed.

As we let our own light shine, we unconsciously give other people permission to do the same.

MARIANNE WILLIAMSON

You might find it contradictory when you see my *Thinker's Guide to Scientific Thinking* collection situated next to books like *Frequency: The Power of Personal Vibration* and *Stepping into the Aquarian Age*. I wear Buddha bead bracelets and have a growing collection of crystals. Even though I lament about the #!@?* ridiculous cost of Lululemon yoga pants, I have a growing Spiritual Gangster t-shirt collection with words like SHINE LIGHT, GRATEFUL, and LOVE IS MY RELIGION. My penchant for burning palo santo wood has evolved to low-key obsessiveness. My Google search history reveals my fascination with shamanism, my quest to find retreat centers with Ayurvedic food options like marinated birch tree bark infused with antioxidants, and healing art sessions with clever titles to align every last inch. And yet, you'll still catch me saying things like, "I can't believe how commercialized this has all become," even though I've been to my fair share of Wanderlust festivals and thirty-dollar

SoulCycle classes. Getting our Zen on is leaving our wallets in need of their own coping strategies.

Commercializing sacred practices is problematic in many ways. Misappropriation can cheapen the true intent of deeply held ancient cultural traditions. It's also another horrendous example of resources that are out of reach and inaccessible for those who need it most. Contrived spirituality is packaged with a focus on sensory comfort rather than helping us connect to our childlike spirit. As kids we instinctively:

- Hum, without realizing it was "om" the universal vibration.

- Bang on drums without calling it a "sound healing."

- Do somersaults and handstands without expensive yoga classes.

- Love the woods without having to take a forest bathing class.

- Ride bikes and sing songs without bougie playlists and strobe lights.

- Pick up pretty rocks without paying big bucks in a healing arts shop.

Besides losing money, marketed spirituality can divert us from a path of organic love to one of a long list of dos and don'ts, superstitions, and expensive practices. In our quest to find community and a sense of belonging, we can end up in groupthinky circles that fail to deliver on their promise to uplift and help us to spread love. It is worth taking the risk to develop our own organizing framework rather than relying on commercialized spirituality or organized religion to satisfy all the cravings of our soul.

> Stop acting so small. You are the universe in ecstatic motion.
>
> RUMI

Spirituality and faith can be linked to resilience, but they can also bring harm if we get hooked into contrived models with their own interests dominating. Healing and spiritual practices should be accessible to all and prioritized for those in greatest need.

Recognize the Significance of Your Contributions

We don't need to have gone through years of seminary or to be quantum physicists to be able to make significant contributions to the world. We do not need to go off the grid and live in the woods to receive our true calling.

We don't need to hire a personal shaman, set ourselves on fire with sage, rub essential oil over our bodies, and drown ourselves in kombucha to be enlightened. While all those things might be very helpful spiritual practices and even make for a delightful sensory experience, we don't need these things to be enlightened.

We also don't need big titles and fancy letters after our names or to hold esteemed positions of status. We can contribute positively through small, consistent gestures: acts of kindness, a smile, offering to help someone even when we're already stretched, looking for similarities and sources of intersectionality, speaking up, raising consciousness, demonstrating empathy, being an accountable ally, valuing people, telling truths, participating in democracy, not accepting conditions of violence, war, racism, sexism, heterosexism, xenophobia, religious bigotry, and economic and social injustice. Every time we speak up and take such steps, we are helping to dispel darkness.

Know the Difference Between Contrived Spirituality vs. True Essence

Commercialized spirituality and prosperity religion bait us with promises of protection, belonging, and peaceful states of bliss and immunity. They have something to profit from your participation (power, money, control, reinforced identity that they are "good" or "evolved"). Some encourage groupthink and compliance. They portray those who do not follow and believe as the "other," someone to try and save, worry about, be afraid of, or fight against.

True essence is fostered within loving spaces that allow for one's unique expression of their soulfulness to live life as art. They honor individuality and cherish co-inspiration without power-over dynamics. They are inclusive, welcoming spaces that reflect being awestruck by the human spectrum. Ones that promote discovery and expression of true essence as sacred, not something to be controlled.

You do not "become" more spiritual by engaging superficially with religion or spiritual practices. Rituals alone do not give us a direct connection to source, or guaranteed protection. Nor do rules and restrictions. No matter how many steps you follow or ceremonies you attend or penances you make, how much sage you burn, chants you do, or namastes you say, it is not the contrived, feel-good-look-good, cheapened, stolen, watered down, power hungry versions of spirituality that will bring you back to truth. True connection to source can only be led by your own heartbeat. It is through the elements of fire, water, air, earth, mountain, movement, song, drum, dance, sensuality, story, touch, and community that we rediscover our truest essence. This is where we find our greatest sources of love, light, and elation in the highest vibration.

Define Your True Soul Activities

The shiny apples of prosperity spirituality are tempting. There is no shortage of snake oil and five-step programs baiting us to buy in and manifest whatever we want. The apples might seem appealing but can be filled with poison and sidetrack or sideline us.

> Hunger only for a world of truth . . . all that you have is your soul.
>
> TRACY CHAPMAN

We can bang our heads against the wall, pushing an agenda with forced timing that leaves us in a state of frustration and perceived control. We cannot fall for the formulas being sold, based on someone else's imagination or agenda. To be in sync with our soul, we allow for synchronicity to work in tandem with our own practices that help us stay in tune with the path we're supposed to be on, rather than be led by ideals that others have manufactured. The rhythm of our own souls must define our dance with life.

It is better to risk uncertainty than to go along with pre-packaged, misappropriated, inaccessible trends. To discover our true soul and manifest what is meant to be, we cannot just make passive wishes or go along with the latest trends. Even when we decorate ourselves with rose crystal quartz, burn sage, turn on our salt lamps, attend services regularly, and religiously stick with the formula, we might not come close to the kind of comfort that is possible

when we tune into the unmanufactured. We can move beyond fears, superstitions, and formulas and instead find activities that help us to connect to
a deeper state of total engagement and presence with life's moments. Both
modern brain science and ancient wisdom reveal many evidence-based activities that help us sync up and find healing and resonance:

Writing. Writing is enriching on many levels. It allows for deep
reflection, contemplation, creative expression, and positive
contributions to the matrix of humanity. It helps us develop a
profound understanding of ourselves and our purpose in the world.

Brain science reveals that handwriting in particular has positive
effects on learning and memory. Whether you journal, write poems,
songs, or messages to facilitate healing, connection, learning, and
growth, writing is a sacred practice with high therapeutic value.

Unfortunately, this may be difficult for anyone that was shamed
in school or told they weren't a "good" writer:
whether they were critiqued on structure,
content, or even had their handwriting picked
apart. So many of my students carry shame
because at one point they have been told that
they're not good at something or only really
good at one thing.

> Creativity is the
> most valuable
> resource in
> the world.
>
> DANIEL Z. LIEBERMAN
> AND MICHAEL E. LONG

Painting, drawing, and other art modalities
that engage fine motor skills and ignite the right brain also reap high
benefits. Similar to writing, some are told that they are not good at
art, inhibiting us from doing it for the joyful, therapeutic value. It's
worth revisiting these practices to reestablish a positive relationship
with them and reap their benefits.[1]

Seek aligned partnership(s). Today we have the opportunity to love
in new ways and to seek partners that are aligned with our soul, not
society's projections of what makes for a "full package" or all the
"right" check boxes. True love is one of the most sacred connections
we can experience.

There are too many roadblocks that interfere with us finding
relationship alignment. We are taught to go for the "hot" trophy partner;

the "ten" that looks good to the outside world but leaves the soul cold.

Before we can fully and freely love, we must love ourselves. We must confront any self-loathing and insecurities. If we feel unworthy, we will not be able to attract people who truly lift us up.

There are other things that can stand in the way. Between body image issues, attachment issues, fear of rejection, pressure for monogamous commitment, and conformity to gender roles or heteronormative behaviors and relationships, we can end up missing out on the full spectrum of love available.

Picking a partner who looks good on paper or to show off on your Insta feed might sabotage you from connecting based on organic chemistry and divine orchestration. Some of us find love in one person but need to be careful not to see that person as a savior and sole focus. Some of us are drawn to non-traditional forms of connecting, where multiple friendships, partners, and surrogates meet our wide spectrum of needs.

> My darling girl, when are you going to understand that 'normal' isn't a virtue? It rather denotes a lack of courage.
>
> STOCKARD CHANNING

It's important to realize that the old way of viewing one soul mate per lifetime has now been overturned. A soul mate is not necessarily reserved for a romantic partner. Connection has many manifestations. Love is inexplicable, and so are we. Each of us needs to microdose bravery to open our minds and hearts to discover what type of partner(s) most align with our souls and values.

Connecting with surrogates and divine messengers. There are times when partners, friends, and biological family will let you down. We often put enormous pressure on these relationships, expecting one heroic partner, friend, or family member to meet all our needs. This blocks us from seeing the significance of the many surrogates who bring love and light.

Life is constantly providing divine messengers to affirm that we are loved and protected and to encourage us to keep being the manifestation of what we seek. These confirmations can come in the form of someone you bump into on the street, your

Uber driver, or the co-worker in the cube next to you who has responded to the nudge to deliver something you need.

We must listen to the many people who show up throughout our day with something that has been placed on their heart. Look for that through line in the messages that keep coming to you through multiple sources. There is often a running theme that emerges. Start paying attention and listening in new ways that allow you to rethink whether someone's words are random or "out of nowhere."

Meditation/prayer. You don't have to sit for hours and empty out your mind to be a "successful" meditator. Even five-minute pauses to focus on breathing, enjoy presence in the moment, and notice your thoughts instead of dissecting and judging them, can be highly beneficial. These are moments when you can find meaning and guidance.

Prayer is a form of meditation where one seeks to directly communicate with their source of light. Both prayer and meditation have been cited as highly effective in reducing reactivity to traumatic and negative events.

> To live on a day-to-day basis is insufficient for human beings; we need to transcend, transport, escape; we need meaning, understanding, and explanation; we need to see overall patterns in our lives. We need hope, the sense of a future. And we need freedom (or, at least, the illusion of freedom) to get beyond ourselves, whether with telescopes and microscopes and our ever-burgeoning technology, or in states of mind that allow us to travel to other worlds, to rise above our immediate surroundings. We may seek, too, a relaxing of inhibitions that makes it easier to bond with each other, or transports that make our consciousness of time and mortality easier to bear. We seek a holiday from our inner and outer restrictions, a more intense sense of the here and now, the beauty and value of the world we live in.
> OLIVER SACKS

Dr. Daniel Spiegel, associate chair of psychiatry and behavioral sciences and medical director of the Center for Integrative Medicine at Stanford University, explains that the medial prefrontal cortex and posterior cingulate cortex (mid-front and back portions) of the brain are activated during prayer and meditation.[2]

When these parts are activated, we move from reactivity to reflection, allowing for stillness that nourishes adaptability.

Enlightenment is not about being a rock star physicist or spiritual guru. It is not about power, control, personal evolution for the sake of self, neurotic attempts for protection, or the revelation of all the "truths" all at once. True enlightenment is the reimagination of primitive and conditioned divides; the chipping away, the unlearning, the unbecoming, the yearning for growth, rejection of passivity, the eradication of fear and "territory." It is the tapping into the consciousness of our collective energy; co-creating a matrix of intentionality, intersectionality, and solidarity. Enlightenment is the resistance of isolative tendencies and the dismantling of groupthink for power and privilege's sake. It is the recognition of the tremendous influence our beliefs and behaviors bear on the collective. It allows us to hold one another in highest accountability, fullest reverence, and deepest regard. In short—to be holders of the new frequency; transmitters of love and light.

Tantric practices. People think human intimacy is just a good feeling, but it also has the power to be epically healing. Sexual desire is one of the most intense forms of energy that exists. Sexuality is one of the most sacred paths and expressions of soul and spirituality.

Tantra emerged in India six thousand years ago, initially as a rebellion against organized religion which advocates for abstinence and celibacy. Tantra asserts that sexuality is a doorway to the divine. Tantra means "to manifest," "expand," "show," and "weave." Its practices seek to expand consciousness and unite masculine and feminine energies.

This isn't reserved for hetero connection: we all have a blend of masculine and feminine energy to share. Tantric sex, or "sacred sex," involves an ecstatic co-creation of life force energy that transcends time and space. It is healing, allowing for expansion of intuition and getting lost in time and space.[3]

It's a shame that the most divine expressions of our spirituality end up distorted and perverted for capital and personal gain. What a travesty that such a powerful, luminous, sacred expression of love and vitality has been cheapened, distorted, commoditized, and in its worst form manifests as violence in the form of abuse, assault, and rape. This makes for deep trauma, heartache, and confusion.

Tantric sex is emblematic of the deep spiritual nature of sex, which should be upheld as a sacred source of bonding and energy exchange. It is a practice that allows for experiences of euphoria that can bring us to states of enlightenment and transcendence.

> A creative life is an amplified life.
> ELIZABETH GILBERT

Integrative health practices. In addition to the healing that sexual intimacy can bring, there are many forms of touch that elevate the mind, body, and soul. Integrative health modalities such as massage, reiki, qigong, yoga, breathwork practices, and sensory deprivation tanks are demonstrating increasing efficacy in reducing stress, increasing creativity, and enhancing well-being.[4]

Music and performing arts. There are a wide range of activities involving music that provide pathways for self-discovery and creative expression. Neurologist Oliver Sacks described the effects of music as inexplicable because of "the fact that it reproduces all the emotions of our innermost being, but entirely without reality and remote from its pain."[5] Engaging in performing arts as a performer and participant can connect us in ways beyond imagination.

Invoke humor, fun, and childhood spirit. Life's heaviness can lead to bitterness if we can't access humor as a healing tool. Artist Georgia O'Keeffe was said to embody this: "Georgia's capacity to laugh at herself was crucial. It protected her from emotional pain, emboldened her, and allowed her to receive pleasure in taking risks. The risks she was taking in her art were important ones, reflected and embodied by the risks she was taking in her emotional life. Both kinds of risks thrilled and energized her. Her exuberance was infectious and highly visible."[6]

Nature and travel experiences. Travel and time in nature are highly elevating activities. Whether you are getting up from your desk to get a breath of fresh air, or traveling across the continents, these shifts can be highly transformative. They allow for adventure, new discoveries, and bonds that static space lacks.

Being in different places allows new perspectives to emerge. Seeing new things and spending time in nature are highly beneficial and nurturing for the mind, body, and soul. When you do so, fully immerse yourself in the elements. Stand in the rain. Play in the snow. Touch the rocks. Swim in the ocean. Taste the food of the land. Let yourself become part of the scene. Air, water, fire, and earth are amazing soul and sensory experiences that cue our brains to experience deep, lasting joy.

> You are not unguided. You are aligned. If your everyday practice is to be open to all of your emotions, to all the people you meet, to all the situations you encounter, without closing down, trusting that you can do that—then that will take you as far as you can go. And you will understand all the teachings that anyone has ever taught.
> PEMA CHÖDRÖN

Attune yourself to the seasons. Consider applying principles from Ayurvedic medicine, which focuses on three life forces or energies called *doshas*. They include *vata* (space and air), *pitta* (fire and water) and *kapha* (water and earth). Every person has a unique blend of these, but there are typically predominant doshas within all of us. When out of balance, it can leave us susceptible to illness.

There are many Ayurvedic rituals and practices including eating local foods according to when they are in season, yoga, meditation, *abhyanga* (massage with warm oil), and using a scraper to clean the tongue and a neti pot to clean the nostrils.

Form a soulful, spiritual, creative family. Good things in life are best shared. Hang around with people who feed your creative, soulful energy. Hold space for each other. Break bread together. Co-inspire. Oftentimes surrogates and divine messengers become spiritual and creative families.

Rather than chasing manufactured peace and serenity, we can focus on seeking synchronicity and divine timing. We can work toward being the embodiment of what we want, rather than trying to control outcomes.

SESSION NINE WORKSHEET

Offer Yourself to the World

We read to know we are not alone.
WILLIAM NICHOLSON

Choose Synchronicity Over Control

Focus on Being What You Seek

The laws of timing and synchronicity can orchestrate us to places beyond imagination. Commercialized spirituality tells us we can manifest what we want when we want it. It disillusions us to think we are at the center of the universe rather than working toward a life of substance, vision, and timing beyond our control, or what's meant to be. It is natural to yearn for wishes to come true, but if we're not careful, we can become like leaky bathtubs chasing serenity, or stuck on the "hedonistic treadmill." Shifting our question from "What can the world offer me?" to "What can I offer the world?" helps us move from a position of taking to contributing. Given the intermittent comfort life brings, we must microdose bravery and give up control in order to become what we're seeking.

Offering Check: Reflect

In what ways am I demonstrating compassion, affection, and kindness?

What sources fill me with light and allow me to exude brightness, clarity, and purity of intentions?

What helps me focus on the now and appreciate what is? What gets in the way?

What signs of growth and resilience do I demonstrate?

Do I see myself as capable of progression and evolution?

What type of energy do I emit?

To what extent is my uninhibited spirit showing up? What forms of play and fun am I engaging in?

Do I see myself as an artist? In what ways?

What helps me to relish in the positive and cultivate awe and zest?

What are my strengths? In what ways am I showing ownership of them? How can I wield authentic power without falling for the trappings of ego?

Do I appreciate varied points of views and experiences? What helps me put myself in someone else's shoes?

What am I grateful for? In what ways am I appreciating what I have and using it to contribute positively?

What aspects of society do I find myself entrapped by? What might help me unhook and forge a path toward liberation that inspires expression and freedom?

In what ways can I help advance the human condition?

Action Steps: Move from Commercialized to Attuned

Manifestation is packaged to us in ways that distract us from deeper spiritual attunement. To find our true essence, we can engage with practices that both modern science and ancient wisdom affirm as healing. Even when the shiny apples of prosperity spirituality tempt us to engage in superficial wishes, we can attune ourselves toward syncing our souls with the Dance of Life. When we move beyond fears, superstitions, and formulas, we can find our way to a deeper state of channeling and divine flow that brings us to total engagement and presence with life's moments. Choose at least three evidence-based activities from this session to help you sync up. Circle/highlight them below and commit to devoting at least twenty minutes a day to implementing them into your daily practice:

Writing

Aligned partnerships

Surrogates and divine messengers

Meditation/prayer

Tantric practices

Hands-on healing

Music and performing arts

Humor, playfulness, fun

Nature and travel experiences

Attunement with moon cycles and seasons

Forming a spiritual or creative family

Session Ten

You Are Not Alone

A human being is a part of the whole called by us the universe,
a part limited in time and space. He experiences himself, his
thoughts, and feelings as something separated from the rest, a
kind of optical delusion of his consciousness. This delusion is a
kind of prison for us, restricting us to our personal desires and to
affection for a few persons nearest to us. Our task must be to free
ourselves from this prison by widening our circle of compassion to
embrace all living creatures and the whole of nature in its beauty.
ALBERT EINSTEIN

Choose Connection Over Isolation

It's four forty-five on a Friday afternoon and I've skidded into the
Boston Public Library with my notes tab open on my iPhone, on a
mission. Ever since New York, I've been working to give up control
and allow for synchronicity. When four different people who didn't know
one another have separately told me that I have to read the same list of
books, I figure I'd best listen. Plus, I've been reading white papers all week
and my social calendar isn't exactly popping. The least I can do for myself
is have something interesting to read.

The library is my haven, but the usual serene vibe cannot survive Boston Accent Intercom Guy. "The libraaa'y clowses in fifteen minutes. Take yah books to the neahest desk." *Check out? I still need to get to the fourth floor to see why people I barely know have insisted I read this list of woo woo books.*

I look like I just came from spin class once I make it to FC2395.M3. The announcements are still blaring, along with my anxiety. I'm in a full yoga squat scouring the bottom shelf when "something" tells me to look up. I see turquoise and am squinting to make out the yellow san serif letters that read *Aquarian Age.* I try to get back to my original search, but my eyes are pulled back. The book seems to be moving; I chalk it up to a long week.

Intercom Guy gives me my final laaahst caahhwl warning to check out. I give up on the books I came for and hustle to the desk with the book that found me. There are sighs and side-eyes. Lesson learned. Don't mess with librarians at five o'clock on a Friday.

The magic of this turquoise book is not lost on me. I carry it everywhere I go. I recite passages to friends. They are too polite to pry, but they can tell I'm lonely. Nancy Privett's *Stepping into the Aquarian Age: A Guidebook for the New Evolutionary Cycle* is like Xanax for the soul. I read it twice, return it late (more side-eyes), and finally buy my own copy.

Privett emphasizes that we are not alone, even when we feel lonely. Rather, we are part of a dynamic and complex ecosystem of inter-beingness. Her premise is that we are at a moment in time where we are capable of manifesting love, peace, collective compassion, and wisdom and global community. I'm all in on this because: 1.) the bickering in our polarized socio-political landscape is A LOT, and 2.) my life was starting to feel like a scene from Lemony Snicket, with a series of unfortunate events that included divorce, empty nest, job pressures, a move, and the death of my sweet dog Coconut.

The urge to lock myself into the fetal position slowly lets up as *Stepping into the Aquarian Age* reminds me that I am not alone, even though I am lonely. It's not that I'm the type of person who needs constant companionship, but there's only so many weekends you can spend tucked away reading without losing your mind. Privett describes the "Law of One" which reminded me how similar our experiences are as humans.[1] I stopped feeling as much of a walking disaster, realizing it was time to muster the courage to start dating, find new friends nearby, and embrace my Queerness, something I'd kept hidden for a large portion of my life. It was like I had a wide-open canvas with a large stock of paint, and Privett had just handed me a brush. Empty canvases tend to be simultaneously terrifying and exciting, but if life has taught me anything it's that messiness is unavoidable whether we hold back or lay lots of color down. I knew I needed to start microdosing bravery if I were going to do more on Friday nights than annoy librarians.

You Are Not the Only One

It's Thursday, six o'clock in the evening at Ruka Restobar, a trendy theatre district hotspot in Boston. I'm elated that I'd listened to my hunch to invite Ying, who's sitting across from me, for dinner. It'd been a while since we first met at Trident Booksellers, a hipster Boston local favorite known for its collection of indie books, whimsical RBG gear, fresh squeezed carrot juice, and unparalleled veggie tempura. Ying and I hit it off instantly and became "friends" on LinkedIn, vowing to get in touch, but between life and schedules, it took a few months before this moment when we're devouring Peruvian fusion tapas and swapping notes on our shared interests. Ying is an attending psychiatrist at Harvard McLean, who's as obsessed with integrative medicine, psychology, and spirituality as I am. Five minutes in, it's already clear we're kindred spirits. The clincher comes when I order my detox special: hot water with lemon. Ying tells me that my drink choice is "very Asian," teasing that my last name is Lee and we may be related. This is the icebreaker that leads us to talking about our dating life.

Ying is the embodiment of what people would call the "full package," even though I hate that term because really, should we just start putting barcodes on people? Ying is a brilliant engineer, creative entrepreneur, and skilled psychiatrist, who's in the running for the world's best conversationalist. Her relationship resume is stacked: she went to MIT and Harvard, owns a brownstone on Commonwealth Ave, and has her own private practice. She's a big ball of energy who is well read, always up for adventures, and smells like daisies. She definitely uses a Sonicare and probably even flosses. She meets all the checkboxes without even trying; it seems like there'd be no shortage of suitors breaking down her door.

When Ying reveals she's having difficulty, I instinctively summon all the muscles in my face to hide the total state of shock I'm in. The Kakuni pork belly and salted edamame beans have gone totally cold on the table as we, in predictable fashion, go on to psychoanalyze every last inch of modern dating: we cite research on the ratio of professionals in the dating pool, perils of swipe-left culture including no-shows and ghosting, long work hours, and how we both would NEVER date colleagues, patients, or students; plus, the Boston bar scene is known for its distinctive "Masshole"* breed.

Ying tells me she's taken to dating apps, the ultimate human behavior experiment you'd hoped never to participate in. She's had a range of experiences: some of her stories are like a Hulu special concocted by Samantha Irby and Lindy West; others give me slight hope that maybe it's worth the risk.

When I tell Ying I've been relying entirely on *organic approaches*, have never tried dating apps, and have no intentions to, it's her turn to try and suppress her surprised facial muscles. I try to sound convincing as I tangentially name no more than three instances when *luck was on my side* at the doggie park, in the rent-a-car office, and *that fateful day I ran into a postal truck*. Ying smiles politely, gives me her *if you risk driving you can risk dating* look, then opens her phone and shows me Coffee Meets Bagel, her app of choice, along with Bumble. Luckily, Ying is a seasoned psychiatrist who can smell my looming panic attack a mile away, so she quickly intervenes and tries her best to reassure me while I pepper her with questions like, "Who gets to be the coffee, and who's the bagel?" and "What about creepy stalkers?" and "What's the worst that's ever happened to you?"

A few weeks later, I have a rare three days off; perfect timing since my *organic approaches* have brought me to a near lethal limit of loneliness. I decide I would rather die of embarrassment than loneliness, so I take the risk of activating my profile and see almost no daylight for a full seventy-two hours until my eyes look like I'm auditioning for a Visine commercial, and a message flashes, "That's everyone: You've seen all the people nearby. Change your filters or check later."

I take a deep breath and check the "People who like you" feature, only to discover my very first suitor is a childhood friend with a

---

* Masshole=Massachusetts Asshole, a local word fusion describing Bostonian cultural behaviors at their finest, such as carrying a large Dunkin Donuts iced coffee at all times, "r" omissions, overuse of "wicked," and aggressive driving habits.

well-documented-girl-next-door crush on me even through my braces, bad hair, and excessive black eyeliner phases. *OMGGG! Now everyone's gonna know how desperate I've become* . . . I think about deleting the app and embracing my destiny to live a life of no coffee and bagels. But I teach resilience and taking risks, so figure it's best to hang in a bit longer.

When I first set up my dating profile, it took me a while to tell Ying, and even longer to tell even close friends. You'd think that since I've told vivid details of my mental health story publicly, come out as Queer, and take a let's-not-make-things-taboo-or-judgy stance to life, that fessing up to the significant loneliness I felt, especially with all the transitions I was going through, wouldn't be such a big deal. Between my dinner with Ying and the number of people on the apps, I knew I wasn't the only one.

Avoid the Trappings of Loneliness

When life delivers Lemony Snicket seasons, and comfort totally goes MIA, it's easy to bubble up with embarrassment and internalize a cautionary tale identity. There's something about it that feels so hermit-y and seventh-grade-lunchroom-outcast awkward. We think our discontent reveals a character flaw or is some form of punishment, rather than recognizing it as a very common human experience. Loneliness is being called the "new smoking" as a health risk of today.

Certain vulnerabilities are hard to admit. As a world, we've made some progress in destigmatizing struggle and we're inching away from a 1950s deficit-oriented "mental health condition" framing to a more evolved, modern "human condition." Even so, loneliness can elicit shame, even though it's a natural part of our existence. We don't have to be out on the street, broken bottle, alone and cold to experience loneliness. It's a part of life that often lives in the shadows but is real to all of us.

We don't even have to be alone to feel lonely. Loneliness especially stings when we have people around us, but they don't get and can't see us as we really are, without their own projections and agendas pressuring us to change and conform in ways that directly oppose our core essence and values. Invalidation and scapegoating are excruciating driving forces of loneliness. If we succumb to living a fake life to please everyone else, it will come at a great cost to our psyche and soul. The risk worth taking is being real. Loneliness feeds off inauthenticity, inauthenticity breeds resentment. Sometimes this means setting boundaries and not letting people in our lives have their way with us. Going along to get along may at first seem like a way to handle conflict, but can breed resentment and false connection, leaving us to feel lonely because we're not being genuine in who we are and what we need. Being real may create waves but will help lead us to a community that aligns with and accepts our true selves. It takes persistence to find, but authentic connection is epic. Connection to uplifting practices and humanistic values can also bring about a sense of meaning and connection when loneliness threatens us.

While we seek meaningful ties, it can be hard to resist the feeling that there's a big L imprinted on our forehead. The need to belong and be seen is fundamental to our existence. Loneliness can bring out the worst forms of self-loathing, with our Toxic Inner Critic chirping at us that we're flawed, unlovable misfits. Internalized shame can be paralytic, right at the moment when taking the risk of putting ourselves out there is crucial.

Instead of marinating in worry over perceived flaws, or trying to win the approval of people who may never give it, it can be helpful to take inventory of the various factors that drive loneliness, so we can account for the significant forces at hand, rather than beat ourselves up:

1. **Untreated mental health issues have a dramatic effect on relationships.** The depression and anxiety spectrum can hold us and those we love hostage. Mood dysregulation has a significant impact on how we perceive ourselves and one another. When mental health issues are untended, it can disrupt healthy communication and connection. Untreated mental health issues can leave us at a greater risk for misunderstanding, disappointment, and conflict. Getting help can be a powerful catalyst for understanding strengths and struggles, assessing underlying issues, identifying patterns, and improving interpersonal skills and relationship quality. It is worth taking the risk of asking for help, versus risking further spiraling and unnecessary suffering.

2. **There's enormous pressure to conform.** Groupthink is a powerful force. Being "different" and expressing our true

identities can position us to be misunderstood. Rejection can
cause us to internalize negative views of ourselves, making it
seem like a massive risk to put ourselves out there as our true
selves. Conformity is only a quick fix; one that doesn't foster true
belonging. It takes persistence to find accepting, safe forms of
community. Think the "Ugly Duckling" tale. Embarrassment isn't
lethal. It is worth taking the risk to march to your own beat versus
living under the scrutiny of an unsafe community.

3. **Trauma can result in depersonalization.** When we undergo
   traumatic circumstances, it can create a sense of detachment
   from one's mind and body, which can create major barriers in
   connecting with people around us. When we feel out of sync
   with ourselves, it's hard to stay in sync with the opportunities in
   the world for connection. Addressing trauma can help facilitate
   better connection within one's inner and outer world, and to be
   able to experience deeper presence and integration of mind, body,
   and soul in the moment. It is worth taking the risk to address
   unresolved trauma versus letting it erode the quality of our lives.

4. **We are busy creatures.** Time crunches and competing
   priorities are real. With barely enough time to breathe, it takes
   intentionality and nothing short of a miracle performed by The.
   Actual.Scheduling.Gods. after seventeen texts and five reschedules
   to spend time together. Evaluating priorities, setting boundaries,
   and avoiding technology overload and distractions can help make
   way for more quality time so we don't lose touch. If you have
   high quality relationships, try to nurture them to every extent
   possible. It is worth taking the risk of spending precious time on
   relationships that matter versus risking being lonely because of
   unsatisfying or scarce connections.

5. **Transience.** We're in a constant state of motion: physically,
   energetically, and situationally. Proximity and convenience are
   powerful forces. If we are not running in similar circles, we can
   easily lose touch. We've all had best friends we pinky swore we'd

always stay close with, until life takes over and then we're not. Think of a colleague you adore but they get a new job and it takes eight months to make one forty-five minute lunch happen, or the soccer game post-hangs that disbanded even though it seemed like those Fridays were too good to ever not be a thing. Or the friend who gets coupled and goes MIA, or the one who has a kid and pulls a Houdini except for major occasions. Staying nimble and keeping an open heart and mind towards new relationships can help us cope with the inevitable losses we contend with across our lifetime. It is worth taking the risk of putting yourself out there for new relationships, even though you might risk rejection.

6. **Change is the only constant.** People come and go. We are continually evolving, outgrowing, wanting different things, and expressing varied parts of our identities. Even when we think we've got ourselves or each other figured out, something shifts. There are times when it becomes clear that a relationship has run its course. Relationships, like all of life, are impermanent. When we leave communities and contexts of origin and return, it's not uncommon to feel we don't fit in anywhere. Think Third Culture Kids, and those who have shifted away from or outright rejected cultural and or religious ideologies of origin. Embracing impermanence is difficult, but necessary: it helps us be present and enjoy the positive moments and be able to ride waves of change, recognizing new possibilities as they unfold. It is worth taking the risk of letting go when times have changed, rather than risking rumination and staying stuck in grief.

7. **Sometimes *people* flake.** And when I say *people*, I mean me and you. We take turns being weird with each other and playing the role of ghost and ghostee. Mess ups and let downs happen. We are not perfect, and sometimes, even with good intentions, we drop balls and burn bridges. We can work to be more conscious in our flaky behavior and avoid over personalization when it happens to us. It is worth confronting when we need to confront and forgiving when we

need to forgive, versus over personalizing every disappointment that occurs (whether we or someone else is the inflictor).

Loneliness is a big horse pill to swallow. The grief that arises when eras end, someone passes, a relationship runs its course, when we face rejection, or someone moves, flakes, or ghosts, can be brutal. For nonconformists and those holding multiple identities within varied affinity groups and cultures, the dialectical tensions between not wanting to go along to get along, all while not wanting to be a lone wolf, are intense. For whatever reasons loneliness is showing up, it can cause us to:

- **Yearn for past comforts.** Longing for earlier times when we felt more attached and connected to and protected by someone or something that brought solace and happiness.
  - › **Statements include:** Things will never be as good as they were back in the day. Everything was way better then. Being with this person or in that situation is the only way I could ever be happy.
  - › **Behaviors include:** Idealizing and romanticizing the past. The struggle to appreciate and enjoy the now. Ruminating over the "what ifs" you perceive as the key to a better outcome, all while ignoring "what is."

- **Have trouble connecting our outer world with our inner world.** The worry that no one will "get" us, that the things we truly think and feel would be perceived as "weird."
  - › **Statements include:** I am not worthy or valuable enough. If I reveal my inner world, it won't make sense to most people. No one else looks at things this way. I'm an outcast who will never fit in anywhere.
  - › **Behaviors include:** Shutting down, social anxiety, pretending to be someone else, conforming to so-called "norms."

- **Wish for a guarantee of absolute allegiance.** The persistent fear of abandonment. Wanting people to have your back unequivocally. Worrying you'll be left out, left behind, forsaken, and betrayed.

> › **Statements include:** Even though I'm loyal to people, it's inevitable that they will let me down. It's hard to trust anyone.
> › **Behaviors include:** Giving up, seeking attention and validation, needing stimulation, jockeying for control. Overcompensating by doing disproportionate amounts to stay in someone's favor, coupled with a persistent insecurity that if you stop overdoing they will not be loyal to you. Taking it personal when someone becomes less consistent in their availability.

The consequences of loneliness are everywhere. We are seeing crises of mental health, burnout, addiction, obesity, and suicide. Resilience research overwhelmingly points to the critical nature of relationships and healthy attachments for our well-being.[2] But relationships are complicated. They come and go. They are often unlikely to live up to our expectations, creating perpetual cycles of conflict, stress, and disappointment. Many of us perseverate when relationships disappoint us. We kick and scream and proposition the universe to ask for deliverance, wishing:

• For Cupid's arrow to strike

• This didn't have to end

• For a more understanding partner, friend, sister

• That my partner, friend, brother didn't pass on, move away, abandon me

• So and so wasn't so annoying

• My boss was more understanding

• Family wasn't their own form of a reality TV show

Who can blame us for not wanting honeymoon phases to end, and good times to last forever? The realities of transience and impermanence are harsh. Understanding the psychological phenomenon known as locus of control can help.

Architect Your Locus of Control

Locus of control refers to the extent we believe we have control over the events that influence our lives. Psychologists posit that we fall on a continuum of perception regarding what falls in or outside our hands. Think serenity prayer.

Internal locus of control holds the predominant belief we have control over outcomes, which ramps up motivation and initiative to try and change situations. Take Jade, who approaches life through this lens. She demonstrates strong self-efficacy: the belief she can reach the goals she sets. She takes responsibility for her actions and is not overly porous to people's opinions. This position helps Jade take strategic risks rather than passively waiting for change.[3]

External locus of control sees external variables as being the primary influence on outcomes. This can lessen the drive to work towards change, and even devolve into learned helplessness: a state of giving up and accepting a difficult fate due to the belief that negative outcomes are unavoidable. Take Winnie, who falls predominantly on the external end of the locus of control continuum.

> Don't grieve. Everything you lose comes around in another form.
>
> RUMI

When bad things happen, she tends to blame outside forces, experiences a sense of powerlessness, and views change as out of reach. Winnie is risk averse and less apt to ideate possible solutions.

Psychologists agree we all fall on a continuum regarding perceptions of locus of control.[4] Different situations can elicit varying beliefs about locus of control. The locus of control framework can help us evaluate when to act and when to let go. When it comes to the battle of loneliness and relationship complexity, there are things that fall within and outside our locus of control. When we realize the complexity behind it all, we can become clearer on what to accept and what not to. When connection is no longer available in the places we once found it, the resulting agony should not be minimized or oversimplified. Still, we can work to accept the things that fall beyond our control and then take new steps to get unstuck from the mire of isolation and loneliness to expand our vision on *what is possible.*

Search for Surrogates

It was mid-June in New England when Gina sat in my office, visibly shaken. It was the early part of our session, and she got right into it. She'd just left CVS where she was trying to pick out a Father's Day card. She told me that after reading through a good two dozen cards "gushing with wind beneath my wings, you are the backbone of the family bullshit," she stood paralyzed in the middle of the aisle. There were no such vibes in her family: her father's abuse was something out of a horror—not a Hallmark—movie.

Gina refused to buy a "fake" card, so she left in a tizzy. We talked about "gaslighting": the perpetuation of abuse when one's personal sanity and perception of memories are called into question. Gina was bewildered and enraged that her mom and siblings were treating her like she was Pinocchio and her father was Bob Saget. She was fed up and exhausted by the fights she was having with them out loud, never mind the ones in her head that left her in cycles of agitated rumination for hours.

Gina's CVS breakdown led to a breakthrough. She told me that when she got to her car, she started thinking about the many "surrogate" figures she has in her life that bring significant comfort and joy: her dynamic father-in-law, her jokester best friend, a close coworker. It wasn't that these relationships erased her trauma or replaced her father, but they were important family-like figures to Gina, nurturing her to see her worthiness. Despite the seriousness of the abuse she endured, she realized she was loved and protected. Gina knew she wasn't alone, despite having far from ideal family circumstances.

Gina's story illustrates the power of moving away from a *what if* life, marinating in anguish and lamenting over the letdowns of family and other relationships, toward being able to see the *what is* life: that the definitions of family and love can be expanded. Her ability to confront her feelings was a risk worth taking: it allowed her to properly grieve and move toward forging meaningful connections that nourished her. I have yet to meet anyone with perfect families, despite the propaganda on our feeds telling us that everyone is one big happy fam even though you know damn well everyone has drama. Wishing for ideals that rarely exist is a big energy drain and totally counterproductive to us building a dynamic and creative ecosystem of support.

Benny, a patient of mine who was forty-three and never married, was working in similar ways to unhook from social pressures and ideals.

He'd had some long-term relationships where he'd "put all his eggs in one basket" and found himself sorely disappointed when things didn't work out. He described himself as a "romantic at heart," explaining his hopes to find his "true soul mate" and have children. He confessed that watching Facebook marriage proposals and seeing pictures of his friends' kids was "heartwrenching." As time went on, Benny became more aware that some of the freedoms he had were coveted by his coupled friends. Some even admitted that the honeymoon had ended and now they felt smothered. Others experienced a loss of identity. Benny started appreciating the many people and activities in life he was invested in and began to recognize that it was becoming unhealthy to make his happiness entirely contingent upon having this socially constructed ideal that might not be so ideal after all.

Letdowns and disappointments are inherent. Maybe your biological mother could not fully be present for you, but in the meantime, life has delivered more than one surrogate mother who has mentored, nurtured, and seen you in ways she was unable to. Maybe your difficulties with siblings have led you to find a chosen family without the drama of sibling rivalries and family hierarchies. Friends can disappoint us too: sometimes we have to renegotiate boundaries when there are constant letdowns, like cancelling plans at the last minute or flaking on us in other disappointing ways.

Maybe you wanted your son or daughter to take on a certain path and they completely went against it. This can breed parenting regret, shame, and guilt. Or you haven't procreated and you long for your "own children" instead of seeing the endless opportunities to nurture and impact kids as aunts and uncles, coaches, teachers, therapists, mentors, and other service roles. Sometimes life delivers us from roles we thought we should have to open up space for other opportunities in our lives. When we find people who are like a mother, brother, daughter, or grandfather to us, it can be extremely healing.

Gina and Benny were among many patients I worked with who found relief in expanding their definitions of love and happiness. Their examples remind us not to overlook the forms of family, love, and joy that show up in our lifetime. Even if it feels a bit cobbled together or "unfair" that we don't have what everyone else allegedly has, surrogates often provide us with more than what we need to thrive. Surrogates can help us take major steps in our healing, helping us to architect new structures that don't rely on hitting the family jackpot, having the perfect soul mate, doting parents, the overachieving son or daughter, or the BFF straight outta Hallmark. Love and family dynamics are complicated, calling upon us to microdose bravery and unlearn ideals that teach us to be dependent on that one figure or structure in our lives for us to be okay. We can still be okay architecting our own structures and avoiding basing happiness on constructed ideals that have their own set of problems.

To see love as limited to one form within the framework of an idealized partner, special someone, heroic figure, or golden child, is to miss the countless manifestations of it that are always available. This requires a giving up of control—an expanding of imagination that is counterculture. One that recognizes kind gestures from alleged strangers. That is able to receive nurturing from surrogates who are nudged to step in and be that person we need. That allows us to receive the continual microdoses of love and empathy, sacred gifts, and cherished deliveries that arrive. We cannot allow the continual signs of protection evidenced in our ecosystem to remain untallied, to be taken for granted. When we only count the actions/inaction of the "perfect" partner, parent, child, or friend, it is a setup for disappointment and dysfunction. We must move beyond singularity and duty. We must reimagine these structures. Become porous to the abundance of love and light that permeate our lives. This is what carries us. It's what protects and delivers us from our deepest fears of aloneness and abandon. We must retrain ourselves to relish in the simplest acts of regard, which arrive from the hands, mouths, ears, and spaces of sages, surrogates, healers, and lovers—those that are led by reverence and resonance, not obligation.

Microdose Bravery: Risk Putting Yourself Out There

It can feel easier to hide under a rock in a fetal position than to crawl out and work toward resolving loneliness. The biggest lie that loneliness tells is that we are the only ones, and that the risk of opening up again will be met with jarring rejection. It also doesn't mean that every time we take a risk, violins will play and flower petals fall from the sky. The law of averages is always at play: some risks land well; others require us to go back to the drawing board.

Microdosing bravery is a process of putting yourself out there in ways that allow you to show up more authentically and intentionally to initiate deeper bonds and possibilities. Consider the following:

1. **You are not alone.** As Privett reminds us in *Stepping into the Aquarian Age,* we are interconnected. Loneliness isn't unique to you: it's a condition of today's modern world. Stop marinating in stigma and shame.

2. **Risks are unavoidable, whether we choose action or inaction.** Whether trying dating apps, inviting a colleague to lunch, attending a social event, or initiating conversation with someone who fascinates you, there's always a risk it won't land well. The adage "nothing ventured, nothing gained" reminds us that by doing nothing, we'll get nothing, but when we take chances, we increase the probability of finding a meaningful connection, and at minimum, continue to learn what we need and value.

3. **We are wired for connection.** Relationships are cited as amongst the most protective factors that cultivate resilience. We are not meant to be alone. We are also not meant to live a fake life surrounded by superficial, non-reciprocal relationships that help us feel a semi-sense of belonging. Be diligent about seeing spaces where you can show up as your real self, in full splendor. This is one of the most impactful microdosing bravery actions to take toward dispelling loneliness.

4. **Trust yourself.** You are a wondrous creature with distinctive qualities, perspectives, and experiences living in a complex world. Decipher what you can control, and what to let go of. You have the wisdom and resources to make decisions that help you maneuver your way toward connection. You have the discernment to set the boundaries that help you do and be well in life.

We must resist instincts to internalize loneliness as a failing on our part. Microdosing bravery to find connection can be provocative, but helps us truly find incredible surrogates, friendships, and partners to help us stay and do well. You are not alone. You are connected.

If you cannot trust yourself, you cannot even trust your mistrust of yourself—so that without this underlying trust in the whole system of nature you are simply paralyzed.

ALAN WATTS

SESSION TEN WORKSHEET

Strive for Connection

All the lonely people, where do they all come from?
All the lonely people, where do they all belong?
THE BEATLES

Choose Connection Over Isolation

Focus on Inter-Beingness

Loneliness is being called "the new smoking" as a health risk, but when we're going through it, it can seem like we're the only ones. The Law of One emphasizes human inter-beingness, and our capacity to manifest love, peace, collective compassion, and global community. While loneliness leads to internalized stigmatized views of ourselves, we need to remember the similarities of the human condition and identify risks worth taking to avoid the trappings of loneliness and understand the driving forces behind it. Whether it stems from untreated mental health issues, pressures to conform, depersonalization resulting from trauma, busyness, transience, constant change, or human flakiness, loneliness can truly be paralytic and a big horse pill to swallow. Instead of yearning for past comforts, thinking no one will ever get us, or demanding "guarantees" for absolute allegiance, we can leverage our locus of control to identify what we can take agency to change, and what we need to accept.

Loneliness Check: Reflect

To what extent am I relying on organic approaches vs. strategic ones to expand my current circle? Are there opportunities to tweak?

Of the various loneliness trappings described, which ones am I most prone to fall into?

What do I want my relationship life to look like?

Where do I fall on the locus of control continuum? Am I more apt to favor internal vs. external?

Who am I close with in my family or community of origin?

Who are the surrogates in my life? What role do they play?

What helps me to put myself out there? What makes it hard?

How apt am I to trust myself to take strategic risks to be myself and find real connections?

What steps can I take today to work toward connection?

Action Steps: Move from Isolation to Connection

Finding meaningful connection within today's world requires intentional microdoses of bravery. We need to trust ourselves in architecting the kinds of risks that help us be more real in how we show up and connect. It can help when we recognize that we're not alone, and to identify ways we can remedy disconnection and isolation. Consider which of the following steps might help you increase your risk tolerance and find a deeper sense of connection to your true self and others:

Write short poems or essays about yourself to clarify various identities and then seek affinity connections

Reach out to friends/fam you've lost touch with

Consider using tools like Meetup to join interest groups, or apps to find friendship and love interests

Reflect on your current surrogates and send a small gesture of gratitude

Invite someone interesting for coffee

Attend in-person or virtual networking events

Ask friends to introduce you to new people

Commit to at least one this week and note how doing so impacts your loneliness. Keep building strategically.

Session Eleven

You Are Not Like Anyone Else

Your problem is how you are going to spend this one odd and
precious life you have been issued. Whether you're going to spend
it trying to look good and creating the illusion that you have
power over people and circumstances, or whether you are going
to taste it, enjoy it, and find out the truth about who you are.
ANNE LAMOTT

Choose Inner Acceptance Over External Validation

S*aturday Night Live* was *the* sacred ritual of high school weekends
with friends: Naz loved Dana Carvey; Heidi, Adam Sandler; I
was officially obsessed with all things Chris Farley. Netflix and
smartphones weren't a thing in the 1990s, so when midnight arrived, we
had our ritual down like clockwork: clad in pajamas three sizes too big with
matching scrunchies, eyes glued to the tube TV, stuffing ourselves with Bagel
Bites, Crystal Light, and big bowls of Breyers ice cream with ACTUAL!
nuts, dairy, and maraschino cherries chanting "Live from New York . . . it's
Saturday Night!" in unison like we were on set. This always elicited the *Keep
it Downnnn* cough signal from my parents' bedroom, which inevitably led
to obnoxious red-dye laughter followed by more disciplinary coughs.

Reenactments of Farley's iconic air quotes bit and motivational speaker skit were mainstays in the majority of our teenage interactions, much to the chagrin of our teachers and parents. We weren't the only ones: the world couldn't get enough of his comedic brilliance. His film career was skyrocketing to the point that the role of Shrek was written specifically for him. Even with all this, in private, Farley unironically asked close friends, "Am I funny?"

You'd think Farley would be THE.LAST.PERSON. to ask this question, especially at such a career pinnacle. Yet, he's not the first superstar to be blinded by his own light. Farley's entanglement with addictions and his inability to internalize his level of giftedness led to total ruin. On December 18, 1997, at age thirty-three, he died of a drug overdose. The stories of him consuming massive amounts of food, drugs, and alcohol with multiple attempts at rehab are heartwrenching. While we might not ever reach such highs and lows, Farley's life and death are sobering lessons on the human struggle to internalize our strengths, leaving us with a gnawing hunger for outside validation and inviting harm in all kinds of forms.

I still get choked up about Farley, *the* funny man who didn't know he was funny. Twenty years as a psychotherapist introduces you to a lot of Chris Farleys: *the overachiever* who feels perpetually under accomplished, *the pretty* who thinks they're ugly, the *gives you goosebumps* singer who's too shy to perform, the teacher who *gives everything* but thinks it's not enough, the student who has no clue how savvy they are. It's a repeated, consistent pattern I've seen play out in my therapy room and classroom. I call this the Brilliance Blindspot: the inability to internalize the very thing we shine at. Consider the following examples:

1. Stet worked his way to become principal dancer at a premiere ballet company. You'd think such an achievement would be enthusiastically celebrated, but Stet struggles with the haunting itch to continue to rise to new pinnacles. His situation is a classic example of the struggle to choose a *what is* life vs. *what if* life. While this drive is an admirable part of what's propelled him to such heights, it prevents Stet from internalizing his massive legacy contribution to the arts. When the curtains go down and the applause fades, Stet is consumed with what he

could become, rather than enjoying who he is. Stet decided to microdose bravery and share his insecurities with his director and fellow principal dancer. They helped remind him of the nature of the level of competition and of his extraordinary journey and impact. This helped prompt Stet to begin the needed work of taking the risk to see himself in greater favor, practicing self-compassion and acceptance.

2. Bob has spent a good portion of his life kicking himself for not attending college, despite his extraordinary success as a businessperson. He constantly engages in negative self-talk, downplaying his accomplishments and impact in his community. His close friend Ben reminded Bob of his highly valuable and sought-after skill set that many with even advanced degrees have not acquired. Bob slowly started to realize that it wasn't a degree that defined him, but the sense of accomplishment he experienced through hard work and entrepreneurship. As his shame lessened, he began to re-envision himself more holistically, and take risks accordingly.

3. Stella's Brilliance Blindspot prevents her from seeing herself as the amazing, kind soul she is. Her friends watch in horror as she seeks validation through underwhelming partners who pay little attention to her and don't have her back. Stella is so fixated on her perceived shortcomings, which were reinforced in her upbringing, that she remains totally oblivious to her strengths and beautiful essence, thus settling for far less than what she gives. Stella's entanglement with outside validation intensified with the proliferation of social media. Eventually, she deleted the majority of her accounts and risked missing out on the latest. She started a gratitude writing practice to redirect her attention more productively.

4. Banji dreamed of getting into Ivy his whole life. When he arrived at Harvard freshman year, he found himself in an instant hole. As he looked around at his exceptional classmates, he was

filled with imposter vibes, wondering whether the admissions committee had made a mistake. For the first semester, Banji didn't let on that he was struggling. Once he finally reached out to a therapist, he started recognizing his worth by tapering his comparison behaviors within such a competitive arena. Over time, Banji began to shift his focus toward taking risks that led to positive contribution, not just personal advancement.

> What are you going to do? Everything, is my guess. It will be a little messy, but embrace the mess. It will be complicated, but rejoice in the complications.
> NORA EPHRON

Brilliance Blindspots (BBs) impact all of us in varied forms throughout our lifespan, across circumstances, roles, and walks of life. While humility is a needed attribute in this world, being blind to strengths can lead to unwelcome behavioral patterns and outcomes. It can cause us to miss opportunities to take risks that nourish, since we don't recognize our ongoing capacity for growth and further impact in the world.

Architect Humility and Confidence

Know the Difference Between Owning Strengths vs. Arrogance

Owning strength doesn't mean we need to walk around with sunglasses at night because we are so blinded by our own light. Humility in a world of vanity is beautiful to behold.

Still, owning strengths is about recognizing our infinite possibilities as humans, and knowing that we are wired creatively and intricately with gifts, talents, and capacities that are one of a kind. There's no such thing as a human without strengths. Owning them reflects that we have undergone a process of self-assessment and are working toward self-compassion and recognizing the ongoing potential in our developmental process. This helps us shift focus on contributing positively, versus chasing superficial metrics of success.

BBs disproportionately impact high achievers: those whose minds are wired to imagine elaborate goals, then lament unless they're met in a precise, grandiose fashion. This tension leads to states of self-disparagement, inability to enjoy successes, and low insight on the actual progress that's been made. BBs are marked by:

- Getting stuck in *what if* vs. *what is* mode

- Inability to truly see one's own dynamism

- Perfectionistic behaviors: including hyper-performance, compulsive overwork, extreme self-doubt, and criticism

- False humility: minimization of strengths and potential for growth coupled with romanticization of someone else's abilities and trajectory

- Settling for less in relationships, jobs, and life roles

> We should not minimize our sacred endeavors in this world, where, like faint glimmers in the dark, we have emerged . . .
>
> ANDREI SAKHAROV

- Persistent sense of under accomplishment, despite what's been achieved

- Entanglement with imposter syndrome: a form of self-doubt, of being a phony and less than people think

- Belief you are a "has-been": that you've already "peaked," are washed up, past your prime, and/or it's too late in life to turn things around

- Belief you are a "wannabe": that you're not "legit," and never going to be as "good" as everyone else

- Tendency to hyper-focus on perceived deficits rather than strengths

BBs come from a host of conditions in our life. The global hyper-competitive market coupled with Instagram culture is propagating unattainable standards of success, illusions of perfectionism, and images of beauty and status that create the perfect storm for despair. Signature behavior traps include:

1. **Unquenchable thirst for validation.** Working compulsively to validate false identities based on social metrics such as likes on feed, attention, being coupled with a trophy partner, degrees from prestigious institutions, letters after names, and outside symbols of status such as designer clothing, cars, and homes. As in *if you're not covered in Gucci and Fenty, you're trash.*

2. **Numbing to escape the pain of inner unrest and insecurity.** Living a life marked by a contingent self-esteem that shifts constantly, relying on external validation and maladaptive coping through means such as food, alcohol, drugs, shopping, beautifying, social media, and anything else that provides temporary relief. As in *you're nothing if you don't drop your entire paycheck at Sephora.*

3. **Not being able to enjoy success.** Compulsively moving from task to task, climbing the ladder tirelessly without stopping to take in the views. Struggling to enjoy the now without constantly fantasizing about the big break that's ahead, while neglecting to stop and bask in the afterglow of what's been accomplished because there's the inevitable perpetual dash to the next project. As in *if your letters after your name and resume aren't as long as the Bible, you're damned.*

4. **Shoulding and musting.** Cursing at ourselves that we should have been further along with our goals, expecting that we should and must meet inhumane standards of performance with tangible results, or else we are failures. Living with deep regret, steeped in unproductive hindsight bias over what we could or should have done. As in *I'm going to kick myself foreverrrr over mistakes I've made.*

5. **Decontextualizing ourselves.** Ignoring the global mental health crisis that's bearing down on all of us. Personalizing our perceived flaws and shortcomings as moral failings, not proportionate reactions to our intensive environments. As in *I'm the only one that feels like a hot mess,* even though we all do.

6. **Selling ourselves short.** Not bossing and leveling up in relationships and aspirations. Settling for less because we don't own up to who we are and what we want. Playing it "safe," hesitancy to set boundaries or ask for what we want because we think we don't really deserve it. As in *everyone else is running the show but me, I have no say.*

Overcoming Brilliance Blindspots and their trademark contingent self-esteem starts by microdosing bravery to let go of external validation as a sole measure for our self-worth.

Owning brilliance and true power can feel counterintuitive, and even terrifying. Consistent microdoses of uncoupling from outside means and metrics of feeling good can be temporarily uncomfortable, but over time we can become more comfortable with the uncomfortable. Instead of playing small because of fear, we can build the resilience to come into a deeper place of acceptance: for not only ourselves, but one another.

> Our greatest fear is not that we are inadequate. Our deepest fear is that we are powerful beyond measure. It is our light, not our darkness that most frightens us. We ask ourselves, Who am I to be brilliant, gorgeous, talented, fabulous? Actually, who are you not to be? You are a child of God. Your playing small does not serve the world . . . We were born to make manifest the glory of God that is within us. And as we let our own light shine, we unconsciously give other people permission to do the same.
> MARIANNE WILLIAMSON

Microdose Bravery: Risk Letting Go of External Validation

I saw the efficacy of microdosing the risk of letting go of external validation exemplified in Camu, a high achieving student, who set out to slowly and consciously pull away from what others expected so she might honor her true soul talents. Camu had put in her time at an elite university, worked several corporate jobs, and despite much outside praise, felt misaligned and depleted. She wanted to pursue writing, but at first felt paralyzed even at the thought of putting herself out there. Still, not doing so felt like a greater risk: an abandonment of her true desires. Camu didn't want to end up steeped in regret and the feeling she'd always be a wannabe writer. She noticed that as she took deliberate micro steps towards her goals, she felt exposed, but despite her discomfort, it eventually gave her needed momentum and increased risk tolerance. It was a newfound energy that helped her stop fearing what people would say or think. When she hit "publish" on her first grassroots blog, Camu felt cathartic relief, and she began internalizing her identity as an artist. Camu went on to publish a podcast, then her first book, delighted that her risks were paying off. Her momentum was contagious: several friends and family who were initially skeptical of Camu's choices began taking microdosing bravery toward their own dreams.

> If I didn't define myself for myself, I would be crunched into other people's fantasies for me and eaten alive.
> AUDRE LORDE

At first, letting go of outside validation can be provocative, leaving us unsettled and even anxious. It's a tough risk to sit with. We are wired to want social acceptance and positive feedback, and the resistance that arises when we take the "non-conventional" path can be stressful. But when we base our inner worth on external validation, which is often laced with limiting, fear-based thinking and steeped in social comparison, we risk missing opportunities to live out our brilliance in full splendor. When we define who we are and what we want, it helps us begin living freer and bolder. This begins with examining our social comparison tendencies and making needed adjustments.

UNDERSTAND THE FORCES BEHIND SOCIAL COMPARISON BEHAVIOR

Social comparison is a hallmark driver of Brilliance Blindspots. While social media is creating more traps than ever, it's not a new phenomenon. The human tendency to base worth on the characteristics of others was first explored by social psychologist Leon Festinger in the 1950s.[1] Since then, scientists have presented explanations of why we do it, ways it can benefit us, and trappings to avoid. Social comparison is driven by our need for:

- Identity (a sense of who we are)

- Validation (that we are okay)

- Security/reducing uncertainty (that we are protected)

- Gauging one's opinions and abilities (that the way we're thinking is on point)

- Enhancing ourselves (that we can achieve upward mobility)

Social comparison types include:

- **Upward comparisons**: Comparing ourselves with people who seem to be better off, or "superior" than us.

- **Downward comparisons**: Comparing ourselves with people who seem to be worse off, or "inferior" than us.[2]

Social comparison isn't all bad or good. It has two sides. In some situations, comparison can serve as a motivating force, but this depends on our baseline self-esteem.

When we have high self-esteem, we're more likely to be motivated when we compare ourselves to people who seem to be "ahead" of us. When we see someone else's achievements, it can motivate us to set and reach our own goals. Social comparison, in its healthy form, can provide us a point of reference from which to check our own progress and our own unique path.

But when our self-esteem is shaky, deriving its metrics solely from the extremes of the commodity complex, upward comparison can result in a negative effect. This is because people with low self-esteem tend to engage in downward comparisons instead of upward comparisons.

Downward comparisons have been shown to help improve mood, motivation, and hopefulness. This doesn't necessarily imply someone is sadistically salivating over someone else's misfortunes. For example, studies have shown that patients confronted with breast cancer fared better when they compare themselves with someone less fortunate.

Architect Security: Know the Difference Between Healthy and Unhealthy Social Comparison

Healthy social comparison allows us to see the big picture, using others' successes as examples that motivate us to strive toward our own goals. When we can tune into the gifts and strengths of others, we can recognize our own positive attributes.

> People who say they don't care what people think are usually desperate to have people think they don't care what people think.
>
> GEORGE CARLIN

Paying attention to the types of behaviors and attributes of people we admire or look up to can help set a fire under us to strive toward our own substantive dreams. Instead of feeling bad that we're not "as accomplished," we can recognize the power of our own potential to do extraordinary things—including a broad range of creative, professional, personal growth, service, and healing endeavors. Healthy social comparison is contingent upon a healthy self-esteem that recognizes we can use our energy and gifts to make progress and bring impact.

Unhealthy social comparison is driven by an obsessive desire to beat others and to advance oneself. It leaves us more susceptible to falling for someone's presentation of themselves and setting that as our baseline standard, rather than realizing that what they have on display is only a superficial glimpse of their full story.

Unhealthy social comparison can also leave us more porous, or open to other people's views and standards. When we absorb this kind of negative feedback, we are more apt to conform to avoid being pegged as "different" or "weird." We are also more likely to have a "contingent self-esteem," one that is based on external feedback rather than a deep confidence in one's purpose, capabilities, wholeness, and creative processes.

Avoid the Trappings of Unhealthy
Social Comparison

Unhealthy social comparison can hold us hostage. Since we are wired for validation, when we feel as though we're not keeping up, it can feel threatening to our core identity. It's hard not to feel like a loser in our Cult of Overachievement which can make us feel like we're *failing at life* if we don't have our top-tier college picked out by the time we lose our first tooth, post a viral TikTok video every eight seconds, read five grade levels ahead, take thirteen AP courses in high school, ace the standardized test, launch a start-up by age twenty-two, and land the perfect job, partner, family, car, and house to strut across our feeds.

While social comparison has always been a thing, now there are the pressures of judgment from a sea of billions of social media users. If it wasn't already hard enough dealing with the peanut galleries of family, town, city, school gossip, and bullying, now any sense of privacy has gone out the window and been replaced with a constant chirping when we make or miss the mark. Mental health issues are skyrocketing between ages 15–44, the prime years where demands for academic, family, and professional achievement are highest.[3]

> To know what you prefer, instead of humbly saying 'Amen' to what the world tells you you ought to prefer, is to have kept your soul alive.
> ROBERT LOUIS STEVENSON

Avoiding the trappings of unhealthy social comparison requires a critical look at our inner monologue and how it is being influenced by the Cult of Overachievement and the constant feedback we're subject to. Here are some ways to avoid letting social comparison blind you from seeing your brilliance:

Blow the whistle on perfectionism. To unlock from the vices of unhealthy social comparison, we must recognize perfectionism as a form of unhealthy behavior that manifests from our unhealthy, excessive, in-your-face, on-your-feed achievement culture. It beckons us to stay on the hunt for superficial popularity rather than investing in what brings true security. The culture baits us to offer things it doesn't need, creating obstacles for us to offer what it does need: our active contribution to advance the human condition.

Perfectionism is a way of engaging with life which holds the view that anything short of "perfect" is unacceptable, an indicator of personal weakness; that we're washed up or doomed. Research over the past decade shows perfectionism is on the rise by 33 percent with social comparison identified as the number one driving force.[4]

Remember life is awkward, not you. Social anxiety is the fastest growing anxiety spectrum disorder, marked by irrational anxiety, fear, self-consciousness, and embarrassment within everyday social interactions.[5] When we look at so-called "norms" in society, it becomes clear that fact is stranger than fiction. Work to avoid internalizing negative views of yourself if you're not cookie cutter, or a bit clumsy. Molds of conformity were designed by antiquated, dominant groupthink, and do nothing to help us embrace the quirks that make us unique.

Be the enigma you are. Social comparison can cause us to be afraid of ourselves, forcing us to stay in hiding on who we are, rather than offering the world our dynamic truth and expression. Brilliance Blindspots can be overcome when we see ourselves as enigmas, not has-beens or wannabes. The word *enigma* means a person or thing that is mysterious, puzzling, or difficult to understand.[6] Embracing an enigmatic mindset helps us avoid the traps of having to explain ourselves, or stuff ourselves into the stifling boxes of tradition. This identity positions us to resist the judgment of others who might try to characterize us as troublemakers, hard to get along with, and not "legit" because we don't go along to get along. If people are talking about you, it might just be a good sign. They are trying to figure out what you've already figured out. Don't let their judgments interfere with your capacity to see your brilliance and ongoing potential for growth. Embracing your complexity and enigmatic identity can help you fully enjoy expressions of your true self, leading to deeper joy, greater adventure, and increased resilience.

> I'm just an individual who doesn't feel that I need to have somebody qualify my work in any particular way. I'm working for me.
>
> DAVID BOWIE

You do not owe any explanations about your "variances." You are a beautiful mystery, an enigmatic soul. Your fiber and fabric are epically unparalleled. When people misunderstand you, it is not about you. Do not be porous to punitive, questioning, stigmatizing, and discriminatory energies. Resist systems of oppression and othering. You are not a puzzle to be solved. Hold your magic sacred. You are a ball of energy with infinite possibilities.

Celebrate your genius. When we stop comparing ourselves to inhumane, false standards, we begin to mine for our own strengths and brilliance. Research shows that people who can own their strengths are more likely to engage in activities that cultivate joy, allowing for *psychological flow*, a state of full presence and full immersion in the now without being consumed with the competing distractions and illusions that surround us.[7] When you find your genius, don't let people objectify you or treat you like a consumable good. Let your inner acceptance and values be your guide, not superficial validation.

Unhooking from external validation can be vulnerable, especially as we're working to learn the skills and practices of self-acceptance. That's why microdosing this form of bravery is so vital. Slowly, we can take steps to embracing our multidimensional nature and true identities to avoid being governed by what people think or say. The risk is worth taking so that we can come to appreciate our infinite potential for growth and progress at every stage of life.

You are not a wannabe or has been. You are inexplicable.

Explaining yourself is like trying to capture the magic of a rainbow with your old phone's camera in black and white with no panoramic button. Any pioneer, innovator, leader, sage, healer, artist, writer, dancer, lover, healer, and/or philosopher will tell you they've had to endure a grueling breakout from the cages of convention and popular opinion. The burden of having to over explain and prove oneself. The maneuvering through painful periods of self-doubt, rejection, and alienation. Then, if they are finally seen and recognized for their genius, they risk being put on an awkward pedestal that commoditizes them and cheapens the essence of their soul and voice. This is the truth of the road less traveled. It is the inherent tension of conscious, creative, enigmatic living . . .

SESSION ELEVEN WORKSHEET

Move to Self-Acceptance

Don't you ever let a soul in the world tell you
that you can't be exactly who you are.
LADY GAGA

Choose Inner-Acceptance Over External Validation

Focus on Seeing Your Brilliance

It can be difficult to recognize strengths and internalize the aspects of ourselves where we shine bright. We must carefully choose our sources of external validation to avoid the trappings of Brilliance Blindspots: the inability to recognize dynamism, leading to entanglement with perfectionistic tendencies, false humility, settling for less, a sense of under accomplishment, imposter syndrome, believing we are has-beens or wannabes, and hyper-focusing on deficits. We must uncouple from social pressures that lead to behavior traps such as an unquenchable thirst for validation, numbing to escape pain or inner unrest, not being able to absorb and enjoy success, shoulding and musting, decontextualizing ourselves, selling ourselves short and hardcore social comparison. When we microdose bravery by letting go of measures of validation that are harmful, we make room to build a place of acceptance for ourselves and one another.

Brilliance Check: Reflect

What are my strengths, talents, and gifts?

In what areas am I most hard on myself?

During the stage of life I'm in, what resources can I draw on to keep cultivating self-acceptance?

How much time do I spend explaining myself?

To what extent do I expend energy to receive external validation?

Who or what do I compare myself to?

Which forms of healthy or unhealthy comparison do I see in my life?

What does blowing the whistle on perfectionism look like for me?

What aspects of myself am I most and least proud of?

What might people say about me that would make me know I'm microdosing bravery in inspirational ways?

Are there forms of risk I'm engaging with to numb or cope with insecurities?

What are some ways I can celebrate my genius and cultivate my multidimensional nature?

Action Steps: Move from External Validation to Self-Acceptance

Uncoupling from external validation can seem like a feat given our propensity for social comparison within our social media, perfectionism-driven world. Microdoses of bravery can include going against the grain, letting go of fear of judgment, trying new things that align with our desires and gifts, owning our brilliance by mining for strengths, and seeking opportunities to express ourselves even if outside forces are not providing validation.

1. **Be motivated by artists.** Listen to Anderson .Paak's "Celebrate" song. Reflect on the lyrics. What does this bring out in you?

2. **Choose to be inspired, not terrified.** Reflect on the words of Tracee Ellis Ross: "I am learning every day to allow the space

between where I am and where I want to be to inspire me and not terrify me." What are some tangible ways you can work toward maintaining inspiration and avoid being terrified? Who or what can help you stay motivated without constant comparison or worry you have to be anyone other than yourself?

3. **Strive for self-acceptance.** Reflect on this quote by Charlotte Eriksson: "You read and write and sing and experience, thinking that one day these things will build the character you admire to live as. You love and lose and bleed best you can, to the extreme, hoping that one day the world will read you like the poem you want to be." How can you use this at a source of help through times of being misunderstood? How might this influence your self-acceptance?

What if you woke up today and saw yourself as the gorgeous enigma you are? That you no longer have to explain, justify, or rationalize your essence and birthright to be the epic ball of energy that you are? That you are not on soul trial, defending your very being? What if this awareness enveloped you to the point of full liberation and creative expression? What if this sparks a contagion of revolutionary acts of truth telling and bravery? To the point that we stop caring what people think and more about dismantling secrets and shame and fear? In a way that allows you to fully emit and radiate your amazing tapestry of colors and textures in inexplicable ways. Ways that help you realize your true destiny and essence . . .

Session Twelve

You Are Not a Passive Bystander

When we drop fear, we can draw nearer to people, we can draw nearer to
the earth, we can draw nearer to all the heavenly creatures that surround us.
BELL HOOKS

Choose Values Over Passivity

I f you were invited to sit in a room alone and fill out a survey and smoke
started billowing out of the wall vent, you'd probably do something
about it. You'd probably get up and leave the room. At the very least, you
would let the people who invited you know what was going on. Or maybe not.

It's the late 1960s. Psychologists were on a mission to discover more
about "bystander effect," a fairly new term that emerged a few years pri-
or following the tragic death of Kitty Genovese in Queens, New York—
where it was reported that onlookers did nothing to intervene while she
was violently stabbed.[1]

Columbia University researchers John Darley and Bibb Latané decided to
take this on. Round one of their "smoke-filled room experiment" was staged
as follows: unsuspecting participants were shown to a room to sit alone and fill
out a survey. The researchers pumped smoke into the room, and right on cue,
the participants immediately left the room to alert them something was up.

Round two: Participants are accompanied to a room shared by secret confederates (actors) who were told to passively ignore the smoke. When the smoke poured in, the actors played it cool, and the participants followed suit. Even with clear signs of danger, only one participant got up and left. The remaining nine participants withstood six full minutes of smoke. They coughed, rubbed their eyes, and even opened a window, but because their peers were passive, they stayed in the room, despite the impending danger.[2]

It wasn't that the actors were brilliant or that the participants were lousy detectives. The experiment illustrates the human tendency to forego safety and common sense when aspects of our environments become normalized by those around us. It turns out that passivity has a contagion effect.

Another insight that emerged from the research of this era is that we are subject to something known as "diffusion of responsibility."[3] This means that within group situations, we are likely to forego our duty to act and instead rely on the actions of others. (Shout out to anyone who has ever had a pull-your-hair-out group project experience with teammates going MIA the whole time until they send over three gibberish slides a minute before deadline.)

The results of this experiment and discoveries about the human tendency to diffuse are concerning. It is scary to think that we could stay in the path of danger, even when warning signs are present because of the influence of bystander passivity. Given that we face the risk of behavior being influenced by the inaction of our environments, we must make agency our moral imperative.

We must courageously assert values, even within complex situations in which others might be underreacting and normalizing glaring issues. We cannot let such cues stunt our instincts. Honoring our microdosing bravery practice means we strategically attend to what is dangerous or disadvantageous to ourselves and one another, rather than falling prey to the passivity we rub elbows with . . .

Align Values to Behavior

Passivity's signature move is to diffuse responsibility. Microdosing bravery relies on us to 1) name our values and 2) align them to our behavior.

Luckily, we do not need years of psychotherapy, to go on an Amazonian ayahuasca expedition, or to sit through one of those ruthlessly boring team building meetings run by well-intended bosses where everyone gets *sticky note papercuts and a low-grade sharpie marker high* to identify our values and take the necessary risks that help move them forward. We can learn to live our true purpose and intentions and live them out through *values-aligned behavior.*

As Jeanette Winterson put it, "What you risk reveals what you value." If we value learning, we risk asking questions that may seem foolish to someone else. If we value social impact, we risk sticking our neck out to foster change. If we value relationships, we take the risk of being vulnerable to form and maintain connections.

> Clarity about what matters provides clarity about what does not.
> CAL NEWPORT

Identifying values is a critical step to living out our purpose. There are a wide range that we can draw upon to serve as guideposts for our lives. Values can include creativity, connection, honesty, bravery, social impact, adventure, compassion, reliability, and integrity. Values not only help us grow, but they can also help us to contribute.

Besides our own growth and well-being, values are needed EVERYWHERE WE LOOK in our social context. Moral bravery within our social world is especially vital. There's atrocious social injustice, inequities, and violence. We need it in our relationships, and to use our influence to help actively contribute toward a more humane, just, and peaceful world.

> Helped are those who risk themselves for others' sakes; to them will be given increasing opportunities for ever greater risks. Theirs will be a vision of the world in which no one's gift is despised or lost.
> ALICE WALKER

Even though it can be nerve-wracking, we are neurologically wired to take risks that help us to overcome these damning trends. By microdosing bravery, we can shift from *risk aversion* and instead increase our *risk affinity.* Even when things are delicate, and EVERYTHING is at stake. We can leverage our creativity and curious capacities so that we don't end up staying in the smoke-filled room, endangering ourselves and one another. We instead generate the moral bravery to refuse to be passive bystanders. This commitment positions us to be active contributions towards social change and improving the human condition, the ultimate offering to the world.

Cancel Behavior, Not Each Other

Moral bravery starts by calling out behavior. Cancel culture may well be the needed rebuttal to white, dominant, elitist group supremacy. The anger is palpable and justified. Especially for persons of color, women, the working class, LGBTQ persons, those who are not able-bodied, or "native." These social identity groups are those most apt to be marginalized, oppressed, discriminated against, aggressed, devalued, silenced, and violated. There are ENDLESS behaviors that need to be cancelled: racism, classism, misogyny, homophobia, xenophobia, hate crimes, aggressions, interpersonal and structural violence, and caste systems. Every one of these MUST. GO.YESTERDAY. Reparations must be made.

> In every community, there is work to be done. In every nation, there are wounds to heal. In every heart, there is the power to do it.
>
> MARIANNE WILLIAMSON

On a good day, cancel culture can expose inexcusable behavior, prompt teachable moments, and even provide a measure of entertainment. Still, these approaches are minimally effective, and on a bad day they can backfire. This is because they are built on the oversimplified premise that people are "good" or "bad."

> Fighting injustice can have a way of turning people against each other instead of being able to clap back at the origins of the problems. Tackling the deep and complex work of combating racial, social, economic, and environmental injustice and working for access, equity, equality, eradicating isms, peace, and ensuring human sustainability requires boldness, humility, hypervigilance, and relentless commitment to accountability . . .

In *Feminist Accountability: Disrupting Violence and Transforming Power*, Ann Russo explains that our traditional way of "punishing overt racist, sexist, homophobic, and xenophobic words and actions" positions us to think that some of us are "good" and some are "bad" when really anyone who is in the dominant group (i.e. white, male, middle/upper class, straight privilege) bears accountability. This helps us see the roots of oppression and violence as "operating on intimate, interpersonal, institutional and systemic levels, rather than beginning and ending with the individual." Behavior, then, can be seen as an "outcome of ongoing racial inequities, injustices, and abuses of power that are always/already operating in our lives." Focusing on behavior, where it originates from, and how systems of privilege operate is essential.[5]

Similarly, in *White Fragility: Why It's so Hard for White People to Talk About Racism,* Robin DiAngelo suggests that moving beyond the good/bad binary can prompt us to become "eager to identify our racist patterns because interrupting those patterns becomes more important than managing how we think we look to others."[6]

Cancel culture doesn't seem to be exactly cultivating an "eagerness to examine racist patterns." From a behavioral science standpoint, shaming techniques and eye-for-eye approaches are unlikely pathways to sustained behavior change. Rubbing noses in people's shit may feel like a justified punishment, but like with dogs, it rarely changes behavior, and instead can backfire and intensify undesirable behavior. For people to be inclined to see and smell their own shit, they have to take a step back. This doesn't mean they get a pass. Change relies upon accountability.

Fight for Accountability

Dominant group identities must be held relentlessly accountable. Those with privilege must not evade their responsibility to unlearn and relearn. In this, they must listen to and be led by nondominant voices, but not in a way that asks them to do all the heavy lifting. They've already done that. It's not only exhausting, but retraumatizing. As Robin DiAngelo puts it, "It is white people's responsibility to be less fragile; people of color don't need to twist themselves into knots trying to navigate us as painlessly as possible."[7] The onus is not on POCs to be the spokesperson for racism and to teach white people to be better. Or women to break down misogyny to mansplainers. It is not the job of LGBTQ persons to teach straight people to stop erasing and violating them. Dominant identities cannot be passive in this process.

Moral bravery in our fraught social context is asserted when we put our foot down against discriminatory behaviors and provide people the opportunities to microdose bravery to help us grow, unlearn, and relearn. This is not to say that we let anyone off the hook who engages in disparaging behavior.

The need for *values-aligned behavior* is everywhere we turn. We cannot navigate isms without a comprehensive accountability strategy. If we want real change, we also need to expose the conditions that perpetuate such behavior and to fight hard to change the underlying paradigms that support it. Clarity of values is essential to navigate these influential, deeply entrenched forces.

> Black and Third World people are expected to educate white people as to our humanity. Women are expected to educate men. Lesbians and gay men are expected to educate the heterosexual world. The oppressors maintain their position and evade their responsibility for their own actions. There is a constant drain of energy which might be better used in redefining ourselves and devising realistic scenarios for altering the present and constructing the future.
>
> AUDRE LORDE

When we are active contributors, we will be influential in the collective matrix. We work toward optimal individual and collective outcomes, and do not see them as mutually exclusive. Microdosing bravery means taking daily initiative to stand up and get everyone out of the smoke-filled room instead of falling into the dangerous trappings of passive bystandership and diffusion of responsibility. Instead, values must guide the relentless commitment to accountability.

PRACTICE REVERENCE

One way to foster change is to dislodge from the vices of what I call "selective neighboring." Selective neighboring involves only loving, caring for, and protecting neighbors that you agree with and that you directly engage in a system of tangible exchanges with. It involves only affiliating with people that share your precise ideology and ignoring and diminishing those who do not.

We need to shift from antiquated ways of seeing diversity. Throughout world history, diversity of the human spectrum has not been revered and nurtured. Widespread alignment with dangerous dominant group "norms" leads to "othering." People within "out" groups are marginalized and discriminated against according to race, class, sexual orientation, religion, country of origin, age, ability, and appearance.

To overcome this, some might suggest that we should learn to "tolerate" each other, rather than celebrate and revere the beauty of our simultaneous difference and sameness. Here are some steps to take so that we learn to relish in and leverage the amazing tapestry represented in the human spectrum:

> Washing one's hands of the conflict between the powerful and the powerless means to side with the powerful, not to be neutral.
> PAULO FREIRE

Architect Accountability: Know the Difference Between Tolerance, Acceptance, and Reverence

Tolerance. The word "tolerance" is often taught with regards to diversity. Tolerance isn't enough: it implies "putting up with." There are many things in life we have to tolerate—dentist visits, long lines, boring speeches, commercial interruptions, telemarketers, and flooded inboxes; but not each other.

Tolerating one another holds a connotation of being obligatory, but doesn't embody the spirit and will for genuine understanding, connection, solidarity, allyship, and genuine accountability.

Acceptance. This is a step forward, but still not enough. Acceptance seems like one group is assuming the position that they are right, and assuring the "less than" group that they are okay. This reinforces and perpetuates an "in" and "out" group dynamic. That those who are "accepting" are being generous to accept someone's "difference" (which signifies tacit beliefs that the nondominant is deviant or less than).

> Tyrants fear the poet.
> Now that we know it
> we can't blow it.
> We owe it
> to show it
> not slow it
> although it
> hurts to sew it
> when the world
> skirts below it.
> AMANDA GORMAN

Reverence. Is the most optimal and beneficial way that we can see one another. It embodies a complete sense of awe and wonder when we look at the human spectrum. It signifies deep respect and unconditional regard, especially for those who have endured marginalization, discrimination, and violence.

Reverence allows us to pay homage to the resilience and brilliance across our diverse spectrum of humanity. It allows us to marvel at the unique, distinctive attributes represented in every person and to honor their perspectives, perseverance, and possibilities.

Perhaps the greatest travesty of our modern world is the epidemic of loneliness, disconnect, and isolation. We must hold in the fore of our consciousness that there are no "strangers," no such thing as "other."

We must understand that the fundamental flaw with dominant group selective neighboring—the act of loving only those who look like, think like, love like, or agree with us—is inhumane and misguided. Accountability must be prioritized to move us away from the turmoil, terror, despair, and darkness perpetrated by systemic and interpersonal isms.

> Because love is an act of courage, not of fear, love is a commitment to others. No matter where the oppressed are found, the act of love is commitment to their cause—the cause of liberation.
>
> PAULO FREIRE

Dispelling such darkness is the most important risk worth taking, so that we can fully offer ourselves to the world in ways it desperately needs. The enormity can drive us to wonder whether our actions matter, but if each of us takes consistent approaches toward justice and love, rather than being a passive bystander, progress will be made.

You are not a passive bystander. You are an active contributor.

SESSION TWELVE WORKSHEET

Own Your Values

I am no longer accepting the things I cannot change. I
am changing the things I cannot accept.
ANGELA Y. DAVIS

Choose Values Over Passivity

Avoid Bystandership and Diffusion of Responsibility

Even when there are clear signs of danger, we can be lulled into inaction
when surrounded by passivity. Research has shown there is a human
tendency to diffuse responsibility. In today's
world, moral bravery is desperately needed, as we
contend with inequities, injustice, violence, and
hate. We can activate courage and align values
to behavior to resist passivity and bystandership.

When I dare to
be powerful, to
use my strength
in the service
of my vision,
then it becomes
less and less
important whether
I am afraid.
AUDRE LORDE

Values Check: Reflect

Are there areas of my life in which I am
passive?

Who or what do I diffuse responsibility to?

What are my core values?

What aspects of my life demonstrate accountability and values-
aligned behavior?

Who or what will help me become more aligned?

Action Steps: Align Values to Behavior

You don't have to stay within a smoke-filled room just because everyone else is. Determine your values and align them to behavior to help you ward off tendencies to diffuse responsibility. We can avoid the trappings of passivity and instead increase moral bravery. Small steps can make a big difference.

1. **Reject bystandership.** Reflect—are there any smoke-filled rooms I'm currently having a hard time exiting? What will it take to get up and leave?

2. **Map out a legacy statement.** What are my values? What do I want to be known for? How do I want to make people feel? What is my most desired contribution(s) within the world? How can I demonstrate accountability in being anti-racist, anti-sexist, anti-homophobic, anti-ableist, anti-ageist, and anti-xenophobic?

3. **Strive for accountability.** What forms of privilege exist in my life? Who or what holds me accountable? What can I do today to demonstrate accountability?

Session Thirteen

You Are Not a Prisoner

The function of freedom is to free someone else.
TONI MORRISON

Choose Liberation Over Imprisonment

When Paulo Coelho's family insisted he become a "proper" professional, like a doctor or lawyer, he balked. He knew he was destined to write his own story, not borrow tired pages from the commodity complex playbook. The one that promises a "nice," "normal," "stable," "noble" life, complete with family bragging rights.

His resistance came at a price: when he refused to conform, they called him delusional. They locked him up in an institution, labeling his lack of compliance as pathological.

While there, Coelho had a vision he was going to write the "book of the century." He was crystal clear that this was his destiny. The physical writing took Coelho only two weeks. He said it "was already written in my soul."[1]

The Alchemist tells the story of Santiago, a shepherd boy who leaves his home in Spain searching for purpose, love, and adventure. He learns to read the "omens" along the way—the "signs" that he's protected by the universe. The ones that affirm he is truly fulfilling his "Personal Legend": Coelho's term for one's calling in life.[2]

At first, *The Alchemist* sat on shelves, collecting dust. But since it was published in 1988, it has sold over 80 million copies. It holds the Guinness Book of World Records for the most translations (81 languages).[3]

> If you do not tell the truth about yourself you cannot tell it about other people.
> VIRGINIA WOOLF

Beyond the mega book sales, Coelho realized the ultimate meta feat. He achieved his own Personal Legend by writing a Personal Legend parable. Coelho is an artistic genius who has given us a new language to talk about the purpose we are destined to fulfill. We are alchemists of our destiny.

Finesse Your Fears

The path toward your Personal Legend is not always glamorous. It is generally fraught, exhausting, and tedious. We might not be locked up physically like Coelho was, but many of us can relate to the frustrations when people look at us like we have ten heads when we state our dreams, or when progress seems to be moving at turtle's pace when our hearts and livelihoods are on the line.

Our worst fear coming true is that we could become the very thing people accuse us of being. This is known as *stereotype threat*, the risk of conforming by force, of not wanting to be the stereotype that's been projected onto us based on our social identities.[4] Stereotype threat is often a root cause of fear. The risks of forced conformity to dominant standards are especially prevalent for those in nondominant groups. It has been identified as a serious contributing factor that influences racial and gender gaps.[5] Think women in math: STEM fields see disproportionate amounts of women making less and struggling with imposter syndrome.[6] Ask any Black woman how many times she's been told she's too loud, any Asian person who's been assumed to be excellent at math, or a transgender person who has suffered through internalized homophobia, thinking that they have some sort of perversion or pathology. The inner turmoil of stereotype threat and the resulting self-devaluation can force us to hide who we really are and do the standard thing everyone is doing, rather than to risk and do something greater, something that truly represents our Personal Legend.

Fear, whether driven by stereotype threat or otherwise, is what holds us back from claiming the dreams that have always belonged to us but can get hijacked if we're not hypervigilant. People try to talk us out of what we know instinctively, even when we have known it forever before we could even capture it with words.

If we're not attentive to this, we will relinquish our Personal Legend and miss out on the discoveries available when we answer the call to offer the world something truly distinctive.

> We know what the world wants from us. We know we must decide whether to stay small, quiet, and uncomplicated or allow ourselves to grow as big, loud, and complex as we were made to be.
> GLENNON DOYLE

Avoid Common Entrapments

There are many entrapments permeating our lives, hindering us from traveling the way we are supposed to. Naming them can be a powerful step in becoming truly free. Be on alert for:

Entrapments of relationships. Relationships are complicated. Many are held imprisoned by their partners and families, stuck with seemingly no choice for their own needs, wants, and ways to be validated and supported.

When people have a different blueprint for our life than what is meant to be, they may think they mean well, but are likely projecting their own insecurities, or living vicariously through us. Think socially awkward parent egging their kid on to be the next Ryan Seacrest; the overzealous parent whose kid MUST.GO.TO.IVY; the relationship partner who is intimidated by our growth, rather than supporting it; the heteronormative family insisting their LGBTQ child needs conversion therapy.

When we share our identities and dreams, those projecting at us might "encourage" us to "just think it through." They say we're living in la la land. That their views of reality, normality, success, stability, and marketable skills are more valuable than what they perceive as deviant, rebellious, intangible, whimsical dreams that aren't tied to precise outcomes or so-called norms. They would rather us pursue a simple, concrete, formulaic path that looks good to the outside world than one that is complicated, ambiguous, and difficult to explain.

Family roles can be intense and wear us down over time. Within romantic monogamous relationships, there can be tremendous pressure to be everything to that one person, which can lead to conflict, disappointment, resentment, and discontent. The relentless relationship propaganda flooding our feeds can disillusion us to choose a post-worthy person, versus seeking relationship and friendship structures that support our Personal Legends. People can spend their entire life pining for something idealized that doesn't exist, rather than taking the opportunity to creatively recognize love in all its forms.

> The way I see it, it's impossible to change things without encountering resistance.
> EVO MORALES

Entrapments of society. Be on guard against racism, sexism, classism, heterosexism, ageism, ableism, xenophobia, and religious bigotry. Social and economic injustice wreak havoc on basic needs and rights. They sabotage the opportunity for all to live out a Personal Legend and fully contribute to the matrix.

These conditions create a great deal of polarization and fighting, preventing us from seeing that we are all imprisoned by it and need to work together to form an effective revolt to break out of the jail collectively.

Those of us in lesser levels of imprisonment have a duty to help those who have had more shackles placed on them from the get-go because of race, class, gender, sexual orientation, and other "out" group social identity categories.

Entrapments of self. These do not appear out of thin air but are born out of society's entrapments. Watch out for perfectionism, imposter syndrome, isolation, self-loathing, the inner critic, unhealthy overachievement, fear of being found out, and tendencies to focus on status and earning, rather than community and Legend.

Do not waste energy on futile efforts to look good and be "perfect." Practice self-compassion and strive to liberate yourself from the vices of your overactive imagination when it's being too intense and critical. Resist stereotype threat and any form of internalized hatred that swells within.

Entrapments of energy. Social entrapments drain energy. Think of all the time wasted on social media, striving for things that don't make us happy, wishing for superficial pleasures and pursuits that do not bring us lasting happiness or move us closer to our Personal Legend.

We can get caught up trying to live up to expectations based on gender or other prescribed socially constructed expectations. Our capacity for liberation can be dangerously disrupted when we take on identities as a martyr, go-getter, sacrificial lamb, unhealthy overachiever, full package, superhero, tough guy, or fuck toy. These typecasts are hard to break out of, since they provide alluring aspects like the sense of feeling needed, wanted, powerful, admired, and hard to abandon. This can lead to an enormous waste of time, since it will never be enough—there will always be another level to attain, or someone who is "better" than us. Energy entrapments entice us to exert so much that we expect a big return, but instead can experience profound emptiness and mental health distress.

> We're all so small, and have such little time, unable to envision the majority of the world.
> MIEKO KAWAKAMI

Protect your energy from these traps at all costs. We need it preserved for the sake of the greater good. We cannot afford to throw it away, obsessing about how to get ahead for the sake of self or to build alleged immunity from rejection.

Break the Mold

The entrapments at hand can entangle some of us so severely it becomes impossible to discover or pursue our Personal Legend. Schools, companies, churches, and families are persuasive, promising to have our backs with their formula that guarantees a "meaningful life." The indoctrination comes early and stays late, trying to mold us into a set of beliefs and behaviors that are "acceptable," stifling creative expression and honoring the truest, deepest parts of our souls.

Microdosing bravery to get to liberation starts with paying homage to our true selves and celebrating our so-called differences rather than allowing them to be stamped as deviant. When we begin this process from within, through the support of a safe community, we clarify what's most sacred to us, building courage to relentlessly protect it and move freely, and offer the world our true, full spectrum selves, not the cookie cutter version.

> A normal person is the sort of person that might be designed by a committee. You know, 'each person puts in a pretty color, and it comes out gray.'
>
> ALLAN SHERMAN

This is something I personally experienced when I awakened to my capacity for love that wasn't limited to gender or heteronormative rules, something that was a big no-no growing up during the 1980s, pre-*Schitt's Creek* "I like the wine and not the label" era. There was no "pan" label except for actual Teflon, and "bi" people were seen as sinful, promiscuous, confused, and dirty choosers of an abominable lifestyle. It took years of processing and uncoupling from inner hate and fear to make the shift to disclosure starting when I awkwardly blurted out "I'm bi" after like three sips of wine at a cocktail party to Joan, who had just shared her own tumultuous path to liberation as a transgender woman. Joan didn't blink an eye: she'd been through it all, she could clearly read my angst like a book, and was like do your thinggg, you DON'T. HAVE. TO. EXPLAIN. YOURSELF. TO. ANYONE. Her words were like 1,000 Xanax for the soul. That little microdose of bravery, *aided by Chardonnay and brie cheese puffs with capers*, gave me the momentum to start telling my close LGBTQ friends, then eventually to people I felt safe with, then eventually to those I didn't. The sense of psychological safety and positive identity that built up helped me transition from a place of inner turmoil to love.

Embracing my Queerness has been one of the most liberating sources of joy in my life. Rather than stewing in shame and secrecy, I am proud of my capacity to love souls, not binary gender constructs. This has invited many wonderful people and experiences into my life, some salacious, but mostly just the opportunity to bask in The Great Gift of seeing and being seen. Being authentic and expressive in the ways I love has opened the path to liberation in every area of my life, personally and professionally. Clarifying our sexuality, rather than repressing it, is one of the most vital rites of passage in our development. It is a prime example that requires microdosing bravery so we maximize psychological safety and build community to mitigate unloving and hurtful reactions that will inevitably arise.

The hard pause of the COVID pandemic has called us all to carefully examine who we are and what's central to our lives; how we love, work, grow, and contribute best. Our new collective mandate is to better understand who we are so we can offer ourselves to the world, rather than conform to it at great cost.

To fully offer ourselves to the world, we need to protect ourselves from pressures to stay within the mold and uphold antiquated traditions. "Tradition" can often be code for continued dominant group control (white, male, straight, mid to high socioeconomic status, Christian, and middle-age social identities hold the greatest privilege). Longstanding cycles of racism, sexism, classism, heterosexism, ableism, ageism, xenophobia, and all forms of economic and social injustice are the traditions that need to be broken. We cannot stay locked up and punished for breaking rules that are inhumane.

> Go outside and let the sun spill into your heart. There. Can you feel it? It's the quiver of your soul. It makes you vulnerable, but it will never betray you.
>
> MARK NEPO

Imprisonment comes in many forms. Microdosing bravery begins when we reject the notion that we must check off boxes and live by rules that have no alignment to our souls. We cannot afford to allow our imaginations to become stunted. Imprisonment is when our creativity is snuffed out, interfering with the very journey we are destined and designed for. The one that helps us fully offer ourselves to the world.

Every one of us have been trapped into following the path of conformity and holding onto tradition. When disaster strikes, we soon realize that this is not our destiny. That we are not players in the board game of Life, rolling the dice and filling our little cars with plastic pink and blue family members and accepting the fate of which squares we land on. Life is short, there are no guarantees, and we cannot waste time chasing ideals that do not give us meaning.

We can do this hard work. When we take the action to release ourselves, we can free each other from the tyranny of conformity. We can be active contributors and stand against oppression, discrimination, and one group doing the defining and determining for all. This is the kind of liberator energy that needs to be spread.

This isn't as romantic as it sounds. Even when we dislodge from the grips of the mold, it doesn't mean that the difficult confrontations, upheaval, rejection, and moments of intense self-doubt won't get to us. This is why the microdosing approach to bravery is so essential. It takes time to detoxify from these ideals and to nourish ourselves for forward momentum so we can offer our full selves in service to the world.

> Responsibility to yourself means refusing to let others do your thinking, talking, and naming for you; it means learning to respect and use your own brains and instincts; hence, grappling with hard work.
> ADRIENNE RICH

It's scary to take the risk of following a Legend when there is resistance from people we look to for guidance. But holding on to fear blocks the space we need to live our truest life, one where we are completely ourselves and live the call—in full living color.

Fear of what people think, not having enough, and rejection from family and community of origin must be released in order to become liberated. Fear is deeply rooted in the commodity mindset which entrains us to self-protect and believe that we must check off certain boxes and land on certain squares to be legitimate. This is a dangerous entrapment. The global pandemic blew this wide open, inviting us to choose new pathways.

> In oneself lies the whole world and if you know how to look and learn, the door is there and the key is in your hand. Nobody on earth can give you either the key or the door to open, except yourself.
> JIDDU KRISHNAMURTI

Letting go of fears is provocative. It is not easy or without sacrifice. But when we let go of fear-based prescriptions for "happy" or "successful" living, that is when we find true contentment. We are not pieces of dough, subject to being cut into rigid shapes that do not represent our complexity and magic. We are here to break the mold.

Own Your Legend to Offer Yourself to the World

Discovering who we are is a vital piece of being able to offer ourselves fully to the world, in true *Alchemist* style. Here are some ways to start this complex process of taking responsibility and claiming your true identity:

Be true to your Legend. Take responsibility for who you are. Resist the pressure to stop on squares for the sake of the game people are pressuring you to play. This is your life, not a game. You cannot fake your destiny and be forced down roads that waste your precious energy and that squash your spirit. Microdose bravery by aligning your behavior to your soul.

Start by considering what you have always known to be true. What lights you up, and sparks your energy like nothing else? What is your purpose and calling? Who and what are you most drawn to? What matters most? If you struggle to find this, consider taking the Values in Action inventory developed by Drs Christopher Peterson and Martin Seligman or read Coelho's *The Alchemist* to better connect the dots between your values, Personal Legend, and the kind of behavior that can carry them forth. Give yourself permission to question what you've been taught and to reflect critically on what you know in your marrow.

> Fear keeps us focused on the past or worried about the future. If we can acknowledge our fear, we can realize that right now we are okay. Right now, today, we are still alive, and our bodies are working marvelously. Our eyes can still see the beautiful sky. Our ears can still hear the voices of our loved ones.
>
> THICH NHAT HANH

Be a reptile and a mammal. Breaking tradition can be both an exciting and scary space to operate within. Our brains are wired to enjoy novelty and variety, but they also crave the comforts of routine and consistency.

We all have different thresholds for microdosing bravery in this regard. Try allowing yourself to move about with the agility of a reptile but stay focused on creating spaces for nourishment and nurturing. Human beings are unique creatures. Allow yourself to embrace your multidimensionality and to find places and people that spark the varied sides of you that bring invigorating energy. Relentlessly hunt down spaces where people are curious about you, who see you, and are delighted when you arrive.

> I was never aware of any other option but to question everything.
>
> NOAM CHOMSKY

Without community, there is no liberation.

AUDRE LORDE

Love and be loved. Take a cue from Bob Marley's "Could You Be Loved" song: "Don't let them change ya, or even rearrange ya." Differentiating ourselves can put us at odds with people. We can experience loneliness, rejection, and scrutiny.

We cannot create, heal, grow, venture into the unknown, or shoulder our Personal Legend without any help along the way. Connection is everything. When we seek to spread love and light, we attract it. Letting go of fear can invite many forms of loving energy into our lives, including many surrogates and messengers who step in and bring just what we need at a particular moment.

If nothing saves us from death, at least love should save us from life.

PABLO NERUDA

Embrace your complexity. Resist the cookie cutter: you are not a piece of dough. You are not a plastic piece in a plastic car. Or a problem to be solved. You are not broken goods or weird or different or wrong when you don't conform. You are not too much. You do not have to play small and simple because it threatens someone else. Pull a Bonnie Raitt—give them something to talk about. Don't shy away from being you.

Know that safe is generally far from safe. What a waste it would be if we were to live a life where the majority of our energy is consumed by fear. Do not allow yourself to accumulate regrets because you stayed in a "safe" place. Avoiding risk is not as safe as it seems. There are a lot of comfortable uncomfortable people, those who are playing it "safe" but miserable under the surface. They have followed what they're "supposed" to do, yet experience great cognitive dissonance in the meantime. Don't let yourself become one of them.

The serious revolutionary, like the serious artist, can't afford to lead a sentimental or self-deceiving life.

ADRIENNE RICH

Resurrect your creativity. Break the mold. Honor yourself for the true gorgeous human rainbow you are. Listen to Pete Seeger's "Little Boxes" song to see beyond the so-called dream. Watch Sir Ken Robinson's famous TED Talk: "Do

Schools Kill Creativity?" Reflect on the song and the talk and consider that when we can become more present in the moment and attuned to the needs of our souls, we become liberated. We begin to express ourselves with full fervor and creativity. Do not let people, jobs, school, or anything squash your creative capacity. It is the spice of life.

So many institutions try to throw a wet blanket on our innate creative energies. Ironically, today's employers cite creativity among the top five most sought-after skills in the marketplace. Creativity is one of the most powerful offerings we can contribute to the world: we must nurture it, keep it alive and well, and inspire collective contagion.

> Instructions for living a life: Pay attention. Be astonished. Tell about it.
>
> MARY OLIVER

Tell your truths. Being true to who you really are is perhaps the greatest contribution you can make to the collective. Bleaching the messy parts of our stories isolates us from one another. Your truths are more universal than you think. Be proud of who you are. Watch Brené Brown's TED Talks and Netflix special on vulnerability. Listen to Sara Bareilles's "Brave" song. Consider ways you can let the words fall out, even when it's scary.

Shift your questions. Instead of asking: Am I too much? Are they right? Am I not enough? Am I weird? Ask yourself: Am I following my Legend? Am I living my life as art? Am I contributing to the matrix? Am I letting my light shine? Am I spreading love? Am I taking responsibility for my freedom? Am I helping inspire that in others? Am I offering myself to the world?

> He who robs us of our dreams robs us of our life.
>
> VIRGINIA WOOLF

Enjoy the journey. Stay on guard against romanticizing the future big win moments. Emancipate from anticipation. You are not your future big dopamine rushes. Embrace your now. Watch the Disney/Pixar movie *Up*. Notice the extreme focus on the fantasy of Paradise Falls and what it ends up being in reality. Watch or read *Charlie (Willy Wonka) and the Chocolate Factory* and notice the obsessiveness around the Golden Ticket and the unintended consequences it brings for the "lucky ones" who "win." Stop living for "one day" or putting off action steps towards your Personal Legend. We cannot wait for this or that to happen and think it's a shortcut to happiness. Live in the present moment. This is mindfulness. It's the rebuttal we need to end the mindlessness of being stuck in the past or future. All we have is this moment. As Annie Dillard puts it, "How we spend our days is, of course, how we spend our lives." Hold this sacred as you seek awe and gratitude in your own Personal Legend journey.

> The power for creating a better future is contained in the present moment: You create a good future by creating a good present.
> ECKHART TOLLE

Be an offering to the world. We are not here to be passive bystanders, but to actively contribute. When we actively pursue our own healing process through microdosing bravery, the cumulative effect is powerful. The resulting resilience helps us to become deeply connected to something beyond ourselves; we're then freed to truly serve the world with full fervor. The payoff of small risks is big. Resilience has a contagion effect.

> Service is the rent we pay for being. It is the very purpose of life, and not something you do in your spare time.
> MARIAN WRIGHT EDELMAN

Embrace Your Identity as a Liberator

If Paulo Coelho had listened to his family, maybe he would have been a lawyer with a comfortable uncomfortable life. If he had listened, he wouldn't have seen his book travel the world, much like Santiago, touching and inspiring people to live out their own Personal Legends. If he'd stayed in the prison of the linear and prescribed path, he wouldn't have become one of the greatest liberators of all time.

Who are you listening to? How is this affecting you? Are you creating space to live your Legend, or are you imprisoned by someone else's standards? These are questions that we must honestly ask and take action on if we find we're not on the path of our true calling.

All the microdoses of bravery you take can lead to you living your Legend and becoming a liberator who is a testament that intentional risks are worth taking. You are not your fear, keg stands, automations, or labels. Nor are you a snowflake, likes on your feed, your trauma, or accomplishments. You are not unguided, alone, or like anyone else. You are not a passive bystander or prisoner.

You are a brave microdoser, a strategic risk taker, the regulator of your emotions, and so much more. You are resilient, indomitable, secure, a whole being, aligned, connected, and inexplicable. You are an active contributor and a liberator, with so much to offer to this world.

> As we are liberated from our own fear, our presence automatically liberates others.
> MARIANNE WILLIAMSON

In her *Big Magic* book, Elizabeth Gilbert talks about how writers download from the Universe. She tells the story of a poet working out on the fields, who "received" a poem, and had to bolt home to get it on paper before she lost it. When she arrives, it's almost too late, but she manages to write it down. It comes out backward, and she has to read it back to front to decipher it. The poet said it was like catching the tail of a kite and pulling it into form.[7] The final insight of this session came in this fashion—all in one piece while I was meditating. Like your microdoses of bravery, my hope is that you can use this as nourishment and momentum to truly break free. You are not here to live a *what if* life. Now is your time for *what is*.

True freedom is telling your truths out loud in full living color. It is not letting anyone else tell it through their own distortions, assumptions, and projections. Freedom is not letting anyone try to define or misconstrue you. Between the eradication of privacy, and the metaphysical opportunities for truths to be revealed, we are being nudged in this age to choose the path of liberation. It is available to all. This doesn't happen in grand splendor—it is often far removed from the glamour of stages and red carpets, pomp and circumstance, and celebratory cheers. It happens on

cold bathroom floors and trips to the ER; on the darkest of
nights and at the most inconvenient times and places.
Answering the call to truth is not without consequence.
Exposure and expulsion are amongst the most frightening
propositions that we face as a sapient and sentient
species. Liberation does not come about without a knotted
stomach, dramatic sacrifice, and intense peril.

Thus, there is a new call to redefine "psychological safety."
We must stop limiting ourselves to language and constructs like
"mental health condition." We must start revealing and labeling
our honest experiences as the "human condition" . . . one that
is paradoxical, contradictory, raw, scary, and beautiful. One in
which we are all fighting for our lives, our sanity, dignity. One
where we are warding off existential crises on the daily.

Our fears of exposure cause us to gravitate to false securities—
those that cause us to bundle ourselves up within false identities
that ultimately lead to consequences that far surpass our deepest
angst of secrets being told. Now we have created a new lie.
One that starts as more palpable but morphs into something
fatally problematic. One that corrodes our very soul. The cover
ups, masks, and curated versions of ourselves ultimately rob
us of our lifeblood. They must be dislodged and denounced.

"Secrets" are illusions. Your "secret" is everyone's "secret."
The biggest lie your mind can tell is that you are the only
one who experiences the things you are afraid to tell.

Freedom from all of this should not be romanticized.
Liberation is confrontational, untimely, and fraught with
peril. Still, the alternatives are far more imprisoning. These
are the risks worth taking and ultimately, the very reason
we're all here for: to liberate ourselves and one another.

Offer Yourself to the World

Those who do not move, do not notice their chains.
ROSA LUXEMBURG

Choose Liberation Over Imprisonment

Own Your Path

We often wish for validation from family, community, and society. But often, they are fixated on narrow definitions of a "proper" life that do not encourage us to live fully and truly. We must name and relentlessly pursue our Personal Legend, the path we are destined for. We must not play safe for the sake of acceptance or validation. Tradition must be broken. We must learn to finesse our fears, albeit through a fraught, exhausting, and tedious process. We must avoid entrapments of relationships, society, self, and energy and take responsibility for nourishing ourselves through consistent microdoses of brave resistance. Fear must be let go of to make space for creative expression and honoring our truest selves. When we are true to our legend, embrace novelty, find spaces that nurture multidimensionality, love and are loved, resist the cookie cutter, realize that safe is generally far from safe, resurrect creativity, tell truths, shift questions, and enjoy the journey, we position ourselves to be an offering to the world.

Liberator Check: Reflect

What work have I already done to liberate myself from entrapments? What areas do I need to continue to work on?

What is my Personal Legend? In what ways am I being true to it? If unsure, what can I do to discover it?

What role do novelty and variety have in my life?

What types of spaces do I inhabit that nurture my multidimensionality? Where else might I find nourishment for it?

How is love showing up in my life? In what ways am I embodying and receiving it?

Where do I stand in relation to cookie cutter models of living? In what ways does my life represent a breakout from the mold?

To what extent do I play it "safe?" How does this serve me?

What forms of creativity are evident in my life? What brings me joy and flow? Am I giving myself permission to express my truest self in such ways?

In what ways am I actively questioning so-called norms, and resisting entrapments?

What is my offering to the world?

Action Steps: Offer Yourself to the World

The fight for liberation, both personally and socially, requires consistent microdoses of bravery to help us determine which risks are worth taking and to go about it in a way that's aligned with our values and Personal Legend. Our steadfast resistance to the mold can embolden us to liberate ourselves and one another: the very reason we are all here. Integrate these practices to help you grow your resilience, connect more, and offer yourself to the world:

1. **Give yourself permission to play.** We cannot expect to flourish if we squash our childhood spirit and dreams. Make an effort to "play" at least once a day. How does this affect you?

2. **Let your life be art.** Celebrate the wondrous creature you are. Do something artistic today, whether in how you wear your hair, in how you dress, in the words you use, in what you create. Let your zest be seen.

3. **Stay consistent in your change efforts.** As Ruth Bader Ginsburg put it, "Real change, enduring change, happens one step at a time."[8] Even when it feels tiring, stay the course. Consistency builds momentum that fosters real change. When weary, seek sources of replenishment. Over time, microdoses add up.

> There is always light, if only we're brave enough to see it, if only we are brave enough to be it.
>
> AMANDA GORMAN

4. **Own your liberator identity.** Listen to Jim Croce's "I Got a Name," focusing specifically on the lyric "they can change their minds, but they can't change me." Listen to Tracy Chapman's "Talkin' Bout a Revolution" song. Reflect on ways you can continue active contribution to fully own your liberator identity and offer the world your bravest, truest self.

ENDNOTES

Note to Reader

1. Patricia Williams, *Rabbit: The Autobiography of Ms. Pat* (New York: HarperCollins, 2017).
2. *APA Dictionary of Psychology*, s.v."Locus of Control," accessed June 16, 2021, dictionary.apa.org/locus-of-control.
3. Huiting Xie, "Strengths-Based Approach for Mental Health Recovery," *Iranian Journal of Psychiatry and Behavioral Sciences 7*, no. 2 (2013), 5–10.

Session One: You Are Not Your Fear

1. James E. Côté and Charles G. Levine, *Identity, Formation, Agency, and Culture: A Social Psychological Synthesis* (Mahwah, NJ: Lawrence Erlbaum Associates, 2002), 3-10.
2. Richard C. Schwartz and Martha Sweezy, *Internal Family Systems Therapy*, 2nd ed. (London: Guilford Press, 2019), 24–45.

Session Two: You Are Not Your Keg Stands

1. Max Klau, *Race and Social Change: A Quest, a Study, a Call to Action* (San Francisco: Jossey-Bass, 2017), 85–90.
2. Isabel Wilkerson, *Caste: The Origins of Our Discontent* (New York: Penguin Random House, 2020).

Session Three: You Are Not Your Automations

1. Lisa Feldman Barrett, "That Is Not How Your Brain Works: Forget These Scientific Myths to Better Understand Your Brain and Yourself," *Nautilus,* March 3, 2021, nautil.us/that-is-not-how-your-brain-works-9614/.
2. Lisa Feldman Barrett, *How Emotions Are Made: The Secret Life of the Brain* (New York: Houghton Mifflin Harcourt, 2017); Lisa Feldman Barrett, *7 ½ Lessons About the Brain* (New York: Houghton Mifflin Harcourt, 2020).

3. Daniel Kahneman, *Thinking, Fast and Slow* (New York: Farrar, Straus and Giroux, 2011).

4. Susan David, *Emotional Agility: Get Unstuck, Embrace Change, and Thrive in Work and Life* (New York: Penguin Random, 2016).

5. Norman Doidge, *The Brain That Changes Itself* (Harlow, England: Penguin Books, 2008).

6. Kateri McRae and James J. Gross, "Emotion Regulation," *Emotion* 20, no. 1 (2020): 1–9, doi: 10.1037/emo0000703.

7. Kristin Neff, *Self-Compassion: The Proven Power of Being Kind to Yourself* (New York: William Morrow, 2011).

8. Barrett, *How Emotions Are Made.*

9. James M. Rippe, *Lifestyle Medicine,* 3rd ed. (Boca Raton, FL: CRC Press, 2019).

Session Four: You Are Not a Snowflake

1. Robert M. Sapolsky, *Behave: The Biology of Humans at Our Best and Worst* (New York: Penguin Press, 2017).

2. Robert B. Brooks and Sam Goldstein, 2004. *The Power of Resilience: Achieving Balance, Confidence, and Personal Strength in Your Life* (Chicago: Contemporary Books, 2004); T. M. Yates, B. Egeland, and L. A. Sroufe, "Rethinking Resilience: A Developmental Process Perspective," in *Resilience and Vulnerability: Adaptation in the Context of Childhood Adversities,* S. S. Luthar, ed. (Cambridge: Cambridge University Press, 2003): 243–66, doi: 10.1017/CBO9780511615788.012.

3. Bruce J. Ellis et al., "Beyond Risk and Protective Factors: An Adaptation-Based Approach to Resilience," *Perspectives on Psychological Science* 12, no. 4 (July 2017): 561–87, doi: 10.1177/1745691617693054.

4. "Current Research on Developmental Assets," Search Institute, accessed May 3, 2021, search-institute.org/our-research/development-assets/current-research-developmental-assets/.

5. Claudia Harzer, "The Eudaimonics of Human Strengths: The Relations between Character Strengths and Well-Being," in *Handbook of Eudaimonic Well-Being,* J. Vitterso, ed. (Switzerland: Springer, 2016): 307–22, doi: 10.1007/978-3-319-42445-3_20.

6. Daniel J. Simons and Christopher F. Chabris, "Gorillas in Our Midst: Sustained Inattentional Blindness for Dynamic Events," *Journal of Perception* 28, no. 9 (September 1999): 1059–74, doi: 10.1068/p281059.

7. *APA Dictionary of Psychology*, s.v. "Confirmation bias," accessed June 16, 2021, dictionary.apa.org/confirmation-bias.

Session Five: You Are Not Your Trauma

1. Tara Westover, *Educated: A Memoir* (New York: Random House, 2018).

2. Bill Gates, "Tara Westover," *Time100*, accessed February 2, 2021, time.com/collection/100-most-influential-people-2019/5567699/tara-westover/.

3. Kleber, "Trauma and Public Mental Health."

4. "Trauma and Violence," U.S. Department of Health and Human Services, Substance Abuse and Mental Health Services Administration, accessed June 3, 2021, samhsa.gov/trauma-violence.

5. Grant et al., *Trauma-Informed Care in Behavioral Health Services*, for the U.S. Department of Health and Human Services, 2008.

6. Chelsea Church et al., "Childhood Trauma and Minimization/Denial in People with and without a Severe Mental Disorder," *Frontiers in Psychology* 8, no. 1276 (Aug. 24, 2017): doi: 10.3389/fpsyg.2017.01276.

7. Rena Romano, "Healing from Sexual Abuse Can Start With One Word," filmed November 2017 at TEDxOcala, Ocala, FL, video, 14:10, ted.com/talks/rena_romano_healing_from_sexual_abuse_can_start_with_one_word.

8. Bessel van der Kolk, *The Body Keeps the Score: Brain, Mind, and Body in the Healing of Trauma* (New York: Penguin Books, 2015).

9. Ilia N. Karatsoreos and Bruce S. McEwen, "Resilience and Vulnerability: A Neurobiological Perspective," *Public Medicine F1000 Prime Reports* 5, no. 13 (May 2013), doi: 10.12703/P5-13.

10. "Current Research on Developmental Assets," Search Institute, accessed May 7, 2021, search-institute.org/our-research/development-assets/current-research-developmental-assets/.

11. Meg Walkley and Tory L. Cox, "Building Trauma-Informed Schools and Communities," *Children & Schools* 35, no. 2 (April 24, 2013): 123–26, doi: 10.1093/cs/cdt007; Rolf J. Kleber, "Trauma and Public Mental Health: A Focused Review," *Frontiers in Psychiatry* 10, no. 451 (June 25, 2019): doi: 10.3389/fpsyt.2019.00451.

12. *V-A-R: Validate, Appreciate, Refer*®, Active Minds, accessed May 1, 2021, activeminds.org/about-mental-health/var/.

13. Karen Cusack et al., "Psychological Treatments for Adults with Posttraumatic Stress Disorder: A Systematic Review and Meta-analysis," *Clinical Psychology Review* 43 (February 2016): 128–41.

Session Six: You Are Not the Likes on Your Feed

1. Chris Smith, dir., *Fyre: The Greatest Party That Never Happened,* produced by Library Films, Vice Studios, and Jerry Media for Netflix, 2019.

2. "Revenue of Selected Social Media Companies from 2014 to 2019," Statista, accessed April 11, 2021, statista.com/statistics/271582/revenue-of-selected-social-media-companies/.

3. Jeff Orlowski, dir., *The Social Dilemma,* produced by Exposure Labs in association with Argent Pictures and The Space Program for Netflix, 2020.

4. Tal Ben-Shahar, *Happier: Learn the Secrets to Daily Joy and Lasting Fulfillment* (Boston: McGraw-Hill, 2007).

5. Jana Kasperkevic, "The Harsh Truth: US Colleges Are Businesses, and Student Loans Pay the Bills," *The Guardian,* October 7, 2014, theguardian.com/money/us-money-blog/2014/oct/07/colleges-ceos-cooper-union-ivory-tower-tuition-student-loan-debt.

6. Margery Williams, *The Velveteen Rabbit* (London: Egmont Books, 2004).

7. Sherry Turkle, *Alone Together: Why We Expect More from Technology and Less from Each Other,* 3rd ed., rev'd. and exp'd. (New York: Basic Books, 2017).

8. "The 'Loneliness Epidemic,'" Health Resources and Services Administration, January 2019, hrsa.gov/enews/past-issues/2019/january-17/loneliness-epidemic.

9. David C. Pollock and Ruth E. Van Reken, *Third Culture Kids: Growing Up among Worlds,* rev. ed. (Boston: Nicholas Brealey, 2009).

12. Ed Park, *The Telomere Miracle: Scientific Secrets to Fight Disease, Feel Great, and Turn Back the Clock on Aging* (Carlsbad, CA: Hay House, 2018).

11. Sonja Lyubomirsky, *The How of Happiness: A New Approach to Getting the Life You Want* (London: Piatkus Books, 2010).

Session Seven: You Are Not Your Accomplishments

1. Christina Maslach and Susan E. Jackson, "The Measurement of Experienced Burnout," *Journal of Organizational Behavior* 2, no. 2 (April 1981): 99–113, doi: 10.1002/job.4030020205.

2. Arianna Huffington, *Thrive: The Third Metric to Redefining Success and Creating a Life of Well-Being, Wisdom, and Wonder* (New York: Harmony, 2014).

3. "Burn-out an 'Occupational Phenomenon': International Classification of Diseases," World Health Organization, May 28, 2019, who.int/news/item/28-05-2019-burn-out-an-occupational-phenomenon-international-classification-of-diseases.

4. Tony Schwartz and Catherine McCarthy, "Manage Your Energy, Not Your Time," *Harvard Business Review* (October 2007), accessed August 2, 2020, hbr.org/2007/10/manage-your-energy-not-your-time.

5. I-Min Lee and David M. Buchner, "The Importance of Walking to Public Health," *Medicine & Science in Sports & Exercise* 40, no. 7 (2008), S512-18 , doi: 10.1249/MSS.0b013e31817c65d0.

6. Prabhjot Dhami, Sylvain Moreno, and Joseph F.X. DeSouza, "New Framework for Rehabilitation–Fusion of Cognitive and Physical Rehabilitation: The Hope for Dancing," *Frontiers in Psychology* 5 (2015): 1478, doi: 10.3389/fpsyg.2014.01478.

Session Eight: You Are Not Your Label

1. Jeffrey L. Geller and Mark R. Munetz, "Fred Frese: A Tribute to a Quintessential Prosumer," *Psychiatry Online,* 70, no. 3 (March 2019): 237–38, doi: 10.1176/appi.ps.70302.

2. Emmanuel Babalola, Pia Noel, and Ross White, "The Biopsychosocial Approach and Global Mental Health: Synergies and Opportunities," *Indian Journal of Social Psychiatry 33,* no. 4 (2017): 291–96.

3. Thomas P. Reith, "Burnout in United States Healthcare Professionals: A Narrative Review," *Cureus* 10, no. 12 (2018): e3681, doi: 10.7759/cureus.3681.

4. Frederick J. Frese, Edward L. Knight, and Elyn Saks, "Recovery from Schizophrenia: With Views of Psychiatrists, Psychologists, and Others

Diagnosed with This Disorder," *Schizophrenia Bulletin* 35, no. 2 (2009): 370–80, doi: 10.1093/schbul/sbn175.

5. Elyn R. Saks, *The Center Cannot Hold: My Journey through Madness* (New York: Hyperion, 2007).

6. Gilien Silsby, "When a Genius Takes on a Stigma," USC Gould School of Law website, March 5, 2018, gould.usc.edu/about/news/?id=4443.

7. "Mental Health by the Numbers," National Alliance on Mental Health, accessed June 15, 2021, nami.org/mhstats.

8. Arthur Kleinman, "Global Mental Health: A Failure of Humanity," *Lancet* 374, no. 9690 (2009): 603-4, doi: 10.1016/S0140-6736(09)61510-5.

9. Aaron Reuben and Jonathan Schaefer, "Mental Illness Is Far More Common Than We Knew," blog post, *Scientific American* (July 14, 2017), blogs.scientificamerican.com/ observations/mental-illness-is-far-more-common-than-we-knew/.

10. International Bipolar Foundation, "Five Positives of Living with Bipolar Disorder," accessed May 2, 2019, ibpf.org/articles/5-positives-of-living-with-bipolar-disorder-besides-creativity/.

11. Thom Hartmann, *Attention Deficit Disorder: New Ways to Work with ADD at Home, Work and School* (Grass Valley, CA: Underwood Books, 1997); Edward M. Hallowell and John J. Ratey, *Delivered from Distraction: Getting the Most Out of Life with Attention Deficit Disorder* (New York: Ballantine Books, 2017).

12. Aaron Lanou, Lauren Hough, and Elizabeth Powell, "Case Studies on Using Strengths and Interests to Address the Needs of Students with Autism Spectrum Disorders," *Sage Journals* 47, no. 3 (October 10, 2011), doi: 10.1177/1053451211423819.

13. Allen Frances, *Saving Normal: An Insider's Revolt against Out-of-Control Psychiatric Diagnosis, DSM-5, Big Pharma, and the Medicalization of Ordinary Life* (New York: William Morrow, 2013).

14. Colleen S. Conley, Joseph A. Durlak, and Alexandra C. Kirsch, "A Meta-analysis of Universal Mental Health Prevention Programs for Higher Education Students," *Prevention Science* 16, no. 4 (2015): 487–507, doi: 10.1007/s11121-015-0543-1.

15. Patricio V. Marquez and Shekhar Saxena, "Making Mental Health a Global Priority," *Cerebrum* (July–August 2016), published online July 1, 2016, National Center for Biotechnology Information, cer-10;

"Substantial Investment Needed to Avert Mental Health Crisis," World Health Organization, May 14, 2020, who.int/news/item/14-05-2020-substantial-investment-needed-to-avert-mental-health-crisis.

16. Lori DeMilto and Mary Nakashian, *Using Social Determinants of Health Data to Improve Health Care and Health: A Learning Report* (May 2, 2016), for the Robert Wood Johnson Foundation, rwjf.org/en/library/research/2016/04/using-social-determinants-of-health-data-to-improve-health-care-.html.

17. Richard Horton, "Launching a New Movement for Mental Health," *Lancet* 370, no. 9590 (2007): 806, , doi: 10.1016/S0140-6736(07)61243-4.

Session Nine: You Are Not Unguided

1. Ruud G. J. Meulenbroek and Arend W. A. Van Gemmert, "Advances in the Study of Drawing and Handwriting," *Human Movement Science* 22, no. 2 (2003): 131-35, , doi: 10.1016/S0167-9457(02)00155-0.

2. Nicole Spector, "This Is Your Brain on Prayer and Meditation," NBC News, October 20, 2017, nbcnews.com/better/health/your-brain-prayer-meditation-ncna812376.

3. Bhagwan Shree Rajneesh, *Tantra: The Supreme Understanding* (Rajneeshpuram, Waco County, OR: Rajneesh Foundation International, 1984).

4. Leonard Wisneski, *The Scientific Basis of Integrative Health* (Boca Raton, FL: Routledge, 2017).

5. Oliver Sacks, *Musicophilia: Tales of Music and the Brain* (New York: Alfred A. Knopf, 2007).

6. Roxana Robinson, *Georgia O'Keeffe: A Life* (Hanover: University Press of New England, 1999).

Session Ten: You Are Not Alone

1. Nancy Privett, *Stepping into the Aquarian Age: A Guidebook for the New Evolutionary Cycle* (Lviv, Ukraine: Old Lion Publishing, 2001).

2. Linda M. Hartling, "Strengthening Resilience in a Risky World: It's All About Relationships," *Women & Therapy* 31, nos. 2-4 (2008): 51-70, doi: 10.1080/ 02703140802145870; Gill Windle and Kate M. Bennett,

"Caring Relationships: How to Promote Resilience in Challenging Times," in *The Social Ecology of Resilience,* Michael Ungar, ed. (New York: Springer, 2012), doi: 10.1007/978-1-4614-0586-3_18; Christian T. Gloria and Mary A. Steinhardt, "Relationships Among Positive Emotions, Coping, Resilience and Mental Health," *Stress Health* 32, no. 2 (2016): 145–56, doi: 10.1002/smi.2589.

3. J. S. Gore, D. P. Griffin, and D. McNierney, "Does Internal or External Locus of Control Have a Stronger Link to Mental and Physical Health?" *Psychological Studies* 61, no. 3 (2016): 181–96, doi: 10.1007/s12646-016-0361-y.

4. H. M. Lefcourt, "Locus of Control," in *Measures of Personality and Social Psychological Attitudes,* J. P. Robinson, P. R. Shaver, and L. S. Wrightsman, eds., (Cambridge, MA: Academic Press, 1991), 413–99, doi: 10.1016/B978-0-12-590241-0.50013-7.

Session Eleven: You Are Not Like Anyone Else

1. L. Wheeler, "A Brief History of Social Comparison Theory," in *Social Comparison: Contemporary Theory and Research,* J. Suls and T. A. Wills, eds., (Mahwah, NJ: Lawrence Erlbaum Associates, 1991), 3–21.

2. L. Wheeler and K. Miyake, "Social Comparison in Everyday Life," *Journal of Personality and Social Psychology* 62, no. 5 (1992): 760–73, doi: 10.1037/0022-3514.62.5.760; Jerry Suls, René Martin, and Ladd Wheeler, "Social Comparison: Why, With Whom, and With What Effect?" *Current Directions in Psychological Science* 11, no. 5 (October 2002): 159–63, doi: 10.1111/1467-8721.00191.

3. Jean M. Twenge et al., "Age, Period, and Cohort Trends in Mood Disorder Indicators and Suicide-Related Outcomes in a Nationally Representative Dataset, 2005–2017, *Journal of Abnormal Psychology* 128, no. 3 (2019): 185–99, doi: 10.1037/abn0000410; Lancet Global Mental Health Group, "Scale up services for mental disorders: a call for action," *Lancet* 370, no. 9594 (2007): 1241–52, doi: 10.1016/S0140-6736(07)61242-2.

4. Gordon L. Flett and Paul L. Hewitt, "Reflections on Three Decades of Research on Multidimensional Perfectionism: An Introduction to the Special Issue on Further Advances in the Assessment of Perfectionism," *Journal of Psychoeducational Assessment* 38, no. 1 (February 2020):

3–14, doi: 10.1177/ 0734282919881928; T. Curran and A. P. Hill, "Perfectionism Is Increasing over Time: A Meta-Analysis of Birth Cohort Differences from 1989 to 2016," *Psychological Bulletin* 145, no. 4 (2019): 410–29, doi: 10.1037/bul0000138;

5. P. Jefferies and M. Ungar, "Social Anxiety in Young People: A Prevalence Study in Seven Countries," *PLOS ONE* 15, no. 9 (2020): e0239133, doi: 10.1371/journal.pone.0239133.

6. Miriam-Webster Unabridged Dictionary, s.v. "Enigma," accessed May 1, 2021, merriam-webster.com/dictionary/enigma.

7. S. Lyubomirsky and H. S. Lepper, "A Measure of Subjective Happiness: Preliminary Reliability and Construct Validation," *Social Indicators Research* 46 (1999): 137–55, doi: 10.1023/A:1006824100041; Fredrik Ullén et al., "Proneness for Psychological Flow in Everyday Life: Associations with Personality and Intelligence," *Personality and Individual Differences* 52, no. 2 (January 2012): 167–72, doi: 10.1016/j.paid.2011.10.003.

Session Twelve: You Are Not a Passive Bystander

1. Jack Cieciura, "A Summary of the Bystander Effect: Historical Development and Relevance in the Digital Age," *Inquiries Journal* 8, no. 11 (2016), inquiriesjournal.com/a?id=1493.

2. B. Latane and J. M. Darley, "Group Inhibition of Bystander Intervention in Emergencies," *Journal of Personality and Social Psychology* 10, no. 3 (1968): 215–21, doi: 10.1037/h0026570.

3. J. M. Darley and B. Latane, "Bystander Intervention in Emergencies: Diffusion of Responsibility," *Journal of Personality and Social Psychology* 8, no. 4, Pt.1 (1968): 377–83, doi: 10.1037/h0025589.

4. Lobna Chérif, Valerie M. Wood, and Christian Watier, "Testing the Effectiveness of a Strengths-Based Intervention Targeting All 24 Strengths: Results from a Randomized Controlled Trial," *Psychological Reports* 124, no. 3 (2021): 1174–83, doi: 10.1177/0033294120937441.

5. Ann Russo, *Feminist Accountability: Disrupting Violence and Transforming Power* (New York: NYU Press, 2018).

6. Robin DiAngelo, *White Fragility: Why It's So Hard for White People to Talk About Racism* (Boston: Beacon Press Books, 2018).

7. DiAngelo, *White Fragility.*

Session Thirteen: You Are Not a Prisoner

1. Hannah Pool, "Question Time: Paulo Coelho," Guardian, March 18, 2009, theguardian.com/books/2009/mar/19/paulo-coelho-interview.

2. Paulo Coelho, *The Alchemist* (New York: HarperCollins, 1998).

3. Bernadine Racoma, "*The Alchemist* in 56 Languages: Most Translated Book by a Living Author," DayTranslations blog, December 2, 2013, daytranslations.com/blog/alchemist-most-translated-book/.

4. Steven J. Spencer, Christine Logel, and Paul G. Davies, "Stereotype Threat," *Annual Review of Psychology* 67, no. 1 (2016): 415-37, doi: 10.1146/annurev-psych-073115-103235.

5. Claude M. Steele, *Whistling Vivaldi: How Stereotypes Affect Us and What We Can Do* (New York: W. W. Norton, 2010).

6. S. Mullangi and R. Jagsi, "Imposter Syndrome: Treat the Cause, Not the Symptom," *JAMA* 322, no. 5 (2019): 403–4, doi: 10.1001/jama.2019.9788.

7. Elizabeth Gilbert, *Big Magic: Creative Living Beyond Fear* (New York: Riverhead Books, 2015).

8. Ruth Bader Ginsburg, *My Own Words* (New York: Simon & Schuster, 2016).

ACKNOWLEDGMENTS

Everywhere I go, people tell me that they want to write a book, but they're afraid it's too much of a risk. It might upset people. It feels vulnerable. Seems like a lot of work. It's probably not as glamorous as it looks.

I flash a knowing smile: this is all true.

Writing is the most frustrating, exhausting head game. It always wins the staring contest.

It's also a therapeutic, sacred act: my longest-term love affair.

Bringing your work to the public is terribly humbling. The minute you publish, your theories have already been overturned. This is frightening and exhilarating. Still, the benefits outweigh the risks.

Microdosing bravery, risks, healing, growth, resilience, and liberation do not happen in isolation. It happens in community. The same is true for writing.

Thank you, Marilyn Allen, for not running away, despite my social awkwardness, and to Haven Iverson, Mike Onorato, Christine Day, Laurel Szmyd, and the incredible team at Sounds True for your commitment to this work. Bob Brooks and Agapi Stassinopoulos: you are my hero legacy influencers. Thank you, Rob DeVirgilio, for generously reading through my manuscript before I had my juice shots. I owe you all the Ben and Jerry's.

Deepest reverence and gratitude to my Active Minds and NAMI fam, and to the extraordinary cast of characters in my story: all my sibs and fam, Heidi Eastman Maxwell, Scott Costa, Karen Hayes McNary, Karen Porter, Nancy Roy, Ying Cao, Robert Kwong, Sharon Cruz, Barbara Ohrstrom, Evangeline Harris-Stefanakis, Byron Morgan, Tyler, Joanna, Cameron, and Rachel Mansfield, Vito Rubini, Paul Shumway, Gary Gomes, Elizabeth Shaw O'Kane, Karyne Martins, Liz Zulick, Earlene Avalon, Jacques Alexis, Patti Goodman, Stephen Rando,

Daniela Winston, Mely Wu, Jacob Theodoris, Nicollette Aduama, David Fields, Shan Mohammed, David O'Malley, Jamu White, Sunny Rodrigues, Thor Blanco-Reynoso, Rebecca Bai, Fredy Muks, Jay Q, J. Smitty, Priyantha Herath, Steven Soares, Shelby Elsbree, David Van Nuys, Beth Kurland, Alfiee Breland-Brown, Cynde Strand, Megan McDonough, and my performing arts teachers and community: Annie Lanzillotto, Kelly Dooley, Frances Callier, Katie Goodman, and to Matt Chapuran and the Lyric Stage Company of Boston for taking a risk to host my show.

To my students, patients, and colleagues: you inspire me. Thank you Carol Pelletier Radford for Shirley Valentine retreats, and Mary Ludden for Hogfish interventions and the best co-inspiration.

Mom and Dad, I love you. Kathleen Mackenzie, you are my soul sister in all the universes and lifetimes. My beautiful cubs, Tori Jae and Ryan John, I hold you unequivocally sacred in my heart, e.e. cummings style.

xo,

kris

(kris(ten) lee, 2022)

RECOMMENDATIONS FOR IDENTIFYING RISKS WORK TAKING AND GROWING RESILIENCE

Session One

Clarify your values. Consider taking the Values in Action inventory via viacharacter.org.

Don't go along to get along. Read Glennon Doyle's *Untamed*. Watch Justin Baldoni's TED Talk, "Why I'm Done Trying to be Man Enough." Read Jared Yates Sexton's book, *The Man They Wanted Me to Be: Toxic Masculinity and a Crisis of Our Own Making*. Read William Pollack's *Real Boys: Rescuing Our Sons from the Myths of Boyhood*, and Mary Pipher's *Reviving Ophelia: Saving the Selves of Adolescent Girls* to consider how gender constructs influence development. Read Cordelia Fine's *Delusions of Gender: How Our Minds, Society, and Neurosexism Create Difference*.

Operate from an empathic, not a blaming lens. Watch Brené Brown's RSA short clip "The Power of Empathy" as a potential conversation tool for tense relationships where you might not feel heard. Check out the work of Susan David's *Emotional Agility* and Harriet Lerner's Dance book series to bolster your empathy and communication efficacy. Take Gary Chapman's 5 Love Languages Quiz to better understand conflict and identify ways to grow and connect with those you love.

Keep your sense of humor. The movie *Parental Guidance* offers seriously funny relief on today's generational parenting differences. Writers Erma Bombeck and Anne Lamott are timeless sources of wit and wisdom. As Lamott puts it: "You can get the monkey off your back, but the circus never leaves town." Comedians and entertainers like Ms. Pat, Aida Rodriguez, Sebastian Maniscalco, Chris DiStefano, and The Portuguese Kids hit funny bones close to home. Watch *The Marvelous Mrs. Maisel* and *Life in Pieces* to know your family dynamics are not the only ones that are complex.

Learn more about family and interpersonal dynamics. Consider taking a Riso-Hudson Enneagram Type Indicator to better understand how personalities intersect. Learn about healing through family constellations through the work of Peter Faust and Bert Hellinger. Read Frank J. Sulloway's *Born to Rebel: Birth Order, Family Dynamics, and Creative Lives* to understand influences on risk taking and factors that provide us with the impetus to carve out a meaningful path.

Session Two

Examine the context of fear. Take a Harvard Implicit Association Test online, read the work of Isabel Wilkerson and Ibram X. Kendi. Watch Bryan Stevenson's "We Need to Talk About an Injustice" TED Talk.

Use light to dispel darkness. Check out Trevor Noah's *The Daily Show*, Sarah Silverman's *I Love You, America*, and John Oliver's *Last Week Tonight* to use lightness as a tool toward facing dark sides of life that need reform.

Session Three

Work on emotional granularity. Watch Lisa Feldman Barrett's TED talk and read her books and articles to help you build granularity.

Be a generous, consistent investor in your body reserves. Check out the work of BJ Fogg including his TEDx talk, "Forget Big Change, Start with a Tiny Habit," for ideas on how to operationalize your own unique plan.

Give yourself room to grow. Consider listening to the *Hidden Brain* and *The Infinite Monkey Cage* podcasts for fun lessons about science and the brain. Check out the mindset work of Carol Dweck.

Session Four

Seek community. Consider listening to Glennon Doyle's *We Can Do Hard Things* or Brené Brown's *Unlocking Us* podcasts.

Immerse yourself in well-being resources. Check out the work of the Positive Psychology Center at University of Pennsylvania: ppc.sas.upenn. edu/; Sonja Lyubomirsky: sonjalyubomirsky.com/positive-psycholo-gy-laboratory/; and the Whole Being Institute: wholebeinginstitute.com/.

Session Five

Seek professional help. Primary care physicians, insurance companies, human resource departments, and school and university resource centers, along with referrals from places like *Psychology Today*, National Alliance on Mental Illness, American Psychological Association, and National Association of Social Workers can all be sources to identify solid match therapists and interventions.

Identify right fit healing activities. Modalities like EMDR and neurofeedback, amongst many integrative health practices, are demonstrating promise in helping heal trauma.

Increase your trauma literacy. Read the work of Gabor Maté. Watch films like *Strong at the Broken Places* and read stories of people who have overcome such as Patricia Williams (Ms. Pat), Tara Westover, and Demi Moore. Read Judith Herman's *Trauma and Recovery: The Aftermath of Violence—from Domestic Abuse to Political Terror*. Read *The Body Keeps the Score: Brain, Mind, and Body in the Healing of Trauma* and listen to the *Huberman Lab Podcast* for deeper learning and strategies.

Develop communication efficacy. Check out the V-A-R tool at ActiveMinds.org.

Session Six

Rethink social "norms." Watch Cameron Russell's TED Talk, "Looks Aren't Everything—Believe Me, I'm a Model." Watch Jennifer Siebel Newsom's *Miss Representation* and *The Mask You Live In* to understand the impact of today's pressures on our well-being.

Session Seven

Calibrate your own treadmill. Read Tim Ferriss' *The 4-Hour Workweek*, and listen to his podcast for innovative approaches to working. Listen to *Impact Theory* with Tom Bilyeu.

Enact your self-care plan. Visit the Thrive Global website led by Arianna Huffington for a host of resources on preventing burnout. Read Brigid Schulte's *Overwhelmed: Work, Love, and Play When No One Has the Time*. Consider your views of leisure and how you spend your time. Be sure to add play to your list of daily activities.

Move from me to we. Read Claude Steele's *Whistling Vivaldi* to identify the role of stereotype threat on behavior.

Session Eight

Redefine normal. Check out Allen Frances' work, including his book and his *Psychology Today* column. Read the stories of those in the Active Minds Speakers Bureau on their journey of mental health. Watch Temple Grandin's *Spectrum: A Story of the Mind*. Read Kay Redfield Jamison's *An Unquiet Mind: A Memoir of Moods and Madness*. Watch singer-songwriter Meg Hutchinson's *Pack Up Your Sorrows: A Story of Illness, Hope, and Transformation*.

Seek community and solidarity. Watch stories on mental health recovery from This Is My Brave. Take a look at the resources of the National Alliance on Mental Illness, along with groups like African American Knowledge Optimized for Mindfully Healthy Adolescents (AAKOMA) Project, and Born This Way Foundation. Keep crisis resources handy such as the Trevor Project via 1-866-488-7386, Trans Lifeline 1-877-565-8860, The National Suicide Prevention Lifeline 1-800-273-8255, Crisis Text Line US: Text HOME to 741741 Canada text [1]: 686868l.

Session Nine
See session worksheet.

Session Ten
See session worksheet.

Session Eleven
See session worksheet.

Session Twelve

Strive for accountability. Read *Feminist Accountability* by Ann Russo. Listen to Dr. Scott Barry Kaufman, "On Human Nature and Human Progress" (the Noam Chomsky interview is powerful). Learn about the work of Progressive International: progressive.international/, a global organization focused on uniting, organizing, and mobilizing progressive forces. Check out the Peace Institute: ipinst.org/, and the Stanford Center for Racial Justice: law.stanford.edu/stanford-center-for-racial-justice/. Learn about the Good Project: thegoodproject.org/, founded by psychologists Mihaly Csikszentmihalyi, William Damon, and Howard Gardner. Visit blacklivesmatter.com/ and stopaapihate. org/. Watch programs like *13th* and *When They See Us*.

Session Thirteen

Let your life be your art. Listen to Lady Gaga's "Born this Way," Kelly Clarkson's "Breakaway," and Indigo Girls' "Closer to Fine." Visit your local art museums and galleries. Notice the art in nature, in typography within storefronts, in the lines etched on faces. Visit Harvard's education portal for various virtual opportunities: edportal.harvard.edu/. Consider joining artist groups and communities for co-inspiration. Art comes in endless forms: the way we think, talk, dress, emote, sing, dance, write, paint, draw, find humor in things, and beyond. Identify your favorite modes of expression and ritualize them on the daily.

Take a cue from Jeanette Winterson's book, *Why Be Happy When You Could Be Normal*, and her show and book, *Oranges Are Not the Only Fruit*, that brilliantly chronicle her strict upbringing and relentless journey to live her truths. Visit iO Tillett Wright's Self-Evident Truths project online. Visit Glaad.org and the Born This Way Foundation for a host of vital resources honoring the spirit and stories of the LGBTQ community. Seek local pride organizations and offerings.

Own your liberator identity. Read the stories of Nelson Mandela, and Martin Luther King, Jr. Reflect on these quotes from Dorothy Day: "Don't worry about being effective. Just concentrate on being faithful to the truth," and "The greatest challenge of the day is: how to bring about a revolution of the heart, a revolution which has to start with each one of us." Read *Freedom Is a Constant Struggle* by Angela Y. Davis. Watch Amanda Gorman's 2021 Inauguration poem, "The Hill We Climb." Watch Gorman's The Moth GrandSLAM "Roar" story to see her bravery exemplified over time.

ABOUT THE AUTHOR

D r. Kris(ten) Lee, EdD, LICSW (she/her/they), known as "Dr. Kris," is an internationally recognized, award-winning Behavioral Science and Leadership professor, clinician, researcher, activist, comedian, and artist. She is the author of award-winning *Reset: Make the Most of Your Stress* and bestselling *Mentallilgence: A New Psychology of Thinking* and host of Crackin' Up: Where Comedy Meets Therapy. Her research and teaching interests include individual and organizational resilience, particularly for marginalized and underrepresented populations. In her spare time, she can be found attempting tricky yoga poses, telling stories, doing juice shots, and eating peanut butter cups, but not all at once. She lives in Boston, Massachusetts and Providence, Rhode Island.

ABOUT SOUNDS TRUE

Sounds True is a multimedia publisher whose mission is to inspire and support personal transformation and spiritual awakening. Founded in 1985 and located in Boulder, Colorado, we work with many of the leading spiritual teachers, thinkers, healers, and visionary artists of our time. We strive with every title to preserve the essential "living wisdom" of the author or artist. It is our goal to create products that not only provide information to a reader or listener but also embody the quality of a wisdom transmission.

For those seeking genuine transformation, Sounds True is your trusted partner. At SoundsTrue.com you will find a wealth of free resources to support your journey, including exclusive weekly audio interviews, free downloads, interactive learning tools, and other special savings on all our titles.

To learn more, please visit SoundsTrue.com/freegifts or call us toll-free at 800.333.9185.

BOULDER, COLORADO